TEEN LEGAL RIGHTS

TEEN LEGAL RIGHTS

FOURTH EDITION

David L. Hudson Jr.

Belmont University, USA

BLOOMSBURY ACADEMIC
NEW YORK • LONDON • OXFORD • NEW DELHI • SYDNEY

BLOOMSBURY ACADEMIC
Bloomsbury Publishing Inc
1385 Broadway, New York, NY 10018, USA
50 Bedford Square, London, WC1B 3DP, UK
29 Earlsfort Terrace, Dublin 2, Ireland

BLOOMSBURY, BLOOMSBURY ACADEMIC and the Diana logo are trademarks of
Bloomsbury Publishing Plc

First published by Greenwood in the United States of America 2015
This fourth edition first published by Bloomsbury Academic 2024

Cover design: Matt Beard
Cover image © gaellemarcel via Unsplash

Library of Congress Cataloging-in-Publication Data

Names: Hudson, David L., 1969- author.
Title: Teen legal rights / David L. Hudson, Jr., Belmont University, USA.
Description: Fourth Edition. | New York: Bloomsbury Academic, 2024. | Audience: Grades 10-12
Identifiers: LCCN 2024014212 (print) | LCCN 2024014213 (ebook) |
ISBN 9781440880292 (hardback) | ISBN 9798765118740 (paperback) |
ISBN 9798216184386 (epub) | ISBN 9781440880308 (ebook)
Subjects: LCSH: Minors–United States–Juvenile literature. |
Teenagers–Legal status, laws, etc.–United States–Juvenile literature.
Classification: LCC KF479 .H46 2024 (print) | LCC KF479 (ebook) |
DDC 346.7301/35–dc23
LC record available at https://lccn.loc.gov/2024014212
LC ebook record available at https://lccn.loc.gov/2024014213

ISBN: HB: 978-1-4408-8029-2
ePDF: 978-1-4408-8030-8
eBook: 979-8-2161-8438-6

Typeset by Deanta Global Publishing Services, Chennai, India

CONTENTS

TABLES

INTRODUCTION TO THE FOURTH EDITION

The purpose of *Teen Legal Rights*, fourth edition, is to educate teens, parents, teachers, and counselors about the legal rights of young people and to explain the many aspects of American law that teens want to know more about. Like its 1994, 2000, and 2015 predecessors, this revised, updated, and expanded edition is in question-and-answer format. The legal landscape for teens has shifted dramatically since 2015, with the emergence of new laws impacting teens on a broad range of issues, including education, abortion, LGBTQ and trans rights, immigration, social media use, and privacy.

As a practical matter, minors in America had no legal rights at the beginning of the twentieth century. In courts of law, they were regarded as little more than "property." Children in the upper and middle classes were usually healthy and safe. But if a child's parents were poor, the child might be a wage earner, grossly overworked and grossly underpaid, by the age of eight. If a youngster's parents were cruel and abusive, whatever their socioeconomic station, the child undoubtedly suffered both emotionally and physically. In the early 1900s countless immigrant children worked in mills and mines. Orphanages and care homes warehoused abandoned, abused, and needy youths, and often these institutions treated these young people with great cruelty.

As America began to discuss and document these injustices, and as the rights of both workers and women expanded, young people came to be perceived as more than a property interest. By 1910, this perception gave rise to the idea that children should be protected and that governments should play a role in child protection efforts. As a result, Americans began to regard even the poorest children differently. Settlement houses appeared in most US cities. However, the idea of "children's rights" did not yet exist. It would not take hold until the 1950s and would not truly flourish until after 1970.

Today America's young people are protected as never before. Some believe they are a privileged class. Their legal rights are fully established, and indeed, many an American law practice thrives on matters pertaining to youth. Even so, the rights of young people will always exist in relation to, and usually in a tug-of-war with, the idea of the primacy of the family. What this means in modern America is that as families continue to change—as single-parent families and two-worker families become as familiar as the traditional model of a working father and stay-at-home mother, as LGBTQ families become more common, and as minors become independent in new ways—their rights will change as well.

Teen Legal Rights, fourth edition, addresses young persons' rights at home, at school, on the job, in civil and criminal courts, and in their private relationships. It also discusses the rights of racial and ethnic minorities, the rights of minors online, gay and lesbian rights, trans youth, immigration law, and minors' rights and restrictions in the area of birth control. The reader will find that the tables, bibliographical material, and glossary in this edition are more comprehensive, and accordingly, more informative.

Although the rights and responsibilities discussed in *Teen Legal Rights* apply to "minors"—the legal term for young people under age eighteen—the terms "teen" and "teenager" are also used in a general sense to apply to minors. The terms "child" and "children" are used when the issue relates to the relationship of parent and child.

CHAPTER 1

Behind the Wheel

OBTAINING A DRIVER'S LICENSE

At what age can a young person obtain a driver's license?

In most states the age is sixteen. Most states require teens to drive on a learner's permit before they can take the test for a regular driver's license. With a learner's permit, a young person may operate a vehicle only if a licensed adult driver is also in the front seat. Once the permit holder has driven on a learner's permit for a specified number of weeks or months, he or she may apply for a regular license.

Some states require young people to pass a driver's education course before applying for a driver's license. Whether or not a driving course is required, a teen who passes a driving course is usually able to obtain car insurance at lower rates.

See Table 1.1 for a summary of state licensing laws for driving.

Is driving without a license illegal?

Yes, driving without a license is illegal. Both adults and minors must have a current driver's license to drive a vehicle, and the license must be in the driver's possession while driving. However, in Mississippi and a few other states, a license or permit isn't required to operate farm equipment.

What are the age requirements for minors to obtain a learner's permit and/or a regular driver's license?

TABLE 1.1: Driver's License Laws by State

State	*Minimum Age for Learner's Permit*	*Minimum Age for Intermediate License with Nighttime Driving and Passenger Restrictions*	*Minimum Age for License with Full Privileges*
Alabama	15	16	17
Alaska	14	16	16 and 6 months
Arizona	15 and 6 months	16	16 and 6 months
Arkansas	14	16	18
California	15 and 6 months	16	17
Colorado	15 (w/driver's ed.) 15 and 6 months (w/ driver awareness program) 16 (w/out driver's ed. or program)	16	17
Connecticut	16	16 and 4 months	Night: 18 Passenger: 17 and 4 months
Delaware	16[a]	16 and 6 months[a]	17[a]
District of Columbia	16	16 and 6 months	18
Florida	15	16[b]	18
Georgia	15	16	18
Hawaii	15 and 6 months	16	17
Idaho	14 and 6 months	15	Night: 16 Passenger: 15 and 6 months
Illinois	15	16	Night: 18 Passenger: 17
Indiana	15 (w/ driver's ed.) 16 (w/out driver's ed.)	16 and 3 months (w/ driver's ed.) 16 and 9 months (w/out driver's ed.)	Night: 18 Passenger: 16 and 9 months (w/ driver's ed.) 17 and 3 months (w/ out driver's ed.)
Iowa	14	16	17

TABLE 1.1: (Continued)

State	*Minimum Age for Learner's Permit*	*Minimum Age for Intermediate License with Nighttime Driving and Passenger Restrictions*	*Minimum Age for License with Full Privileges*
Kansas[c]	14	16	16 and 6 months
Kentucky	16	16 and 6 months	17
Louisiana	15	16	17
Maine	15	16	16
Maryland	15 and 9 months	16 and 6 months	Night: 18
			Passenger: 16 and 11 months
Massachusetts	16	16 and 6 months	Night: 18
			Passenger: 17
Michigan	14 and 9 months	16	17
Minnesota	15	16	Night: 16 and 6 months
			Passenger: 17
Mississippi	15	16[b]	18
Missouri	15	16	18
Montana	14 and 6 months	15	16
Nebraska	15	16	Night: 17
			Passenger: 16 and 6 months
Nevada	15 and 6 months	16	Night: 18
			Passenger: 16 and 6 months
New Hampshire	15 and 6 months	16	Night: 17 and 1 month
			Passenger: 16 and 6 months
New Jersey	16	17	18
New Mexico	15	15 and 6 months	16 and 6 months
New York	16	16 and 6 months	17 (w/ driver's ed.)
			18 (w/out driver's ed.)
North Carolina	15	16	16 and 6 months

(Continued)

TABLE 1.1: (Continued)

State	*Minimum Age for Learner's Permit*	*Minimum Age for Intermediate License with Nighttime Driving and Passenger Restrictions*	*Minimum Age for License with Full Privileges*
North Dakota	14	16; 15 for parent-restricted license[b]	16
Ohio	15 and 6 months	16	Night: 18
			Passenger: 17
Oklahoma	15 and 6 months	16	16 and 6 months (w/ driver's ed.)
			17 (w/out driver's ed.)
Oregon	15	16	17
Pennsylvania	16	16 and 6 months	17 (w/ driver's ed. and 12 mo. free of crash or conviction)
			18 (w/out driver's ed.)
Rhode Island	16	16 and 6 months	17 and 6 months
South Carolina	15	15 and 6 months	16 and 6 months
South Dakota	14	14 + 180 days (less 90 days w/ driver's ed.)[b]	16
Tennessee	15	16	17
Texas	15	16	18
Utah	15	16	Night: 17
			Passenger: 16 and 6 months
Vermont	15	16	16 and 6 months
Virginia	15 and 6 months	16 and 3 months	18
Washington	15	16	18
	15 and 6 months (w/out driver's ed.)		
West Virginia	15	16	17
Wisconsin	15 and 6 months	16	16 and 9 months
Wyoming	15	16	16 and 6 months

[a]If a teen driver or their passenger under age eighteen is found not to be wearing a seat belt, the permit holder will have his or her license suspended for two months.

[b]No passenger restrictions on intermediate license.

[c]At age fifteen, novice drivers can drive without supervision to and from work or school.

Source: Adapted from the Governors Highway Safety Association, "Teen and Novice Drivers," https://www.ghsa.org/state-laws/issues/teen%20and%20novice%20drivers (accessed August 15, 2023).

States have different driver's license laws. The age requirements for young people to obtain a learner's permit and a regular license and the costs vary state by state.

Must a teenager have a parent's or legal guardian's permission to obtain a learner's permit or driver's license?

Yes. In most states a parent must sign the minor's license or permit application. If the parent refuses, the minor can't obtain a driver's license and therefore can't legally drive.

If someone other than a parent, such as a legal guardian or foster parent, is in charge of the minor's care and upbringing, he or she is the one who must sign (and may refuse to sign) the application. For more about guardians, see Chapter 3, "At Home," and for more about foster parents, see Chapter 10, "Your Right to Be Healthy and Safe from Abuse."

If state law requires parental consent for a young person to obtain a driver's license, at what age is consent no longer needed?

The age of consent is usually age eighteen, which is the age of majority in most states. For more about the age of majority, see Chapter 3, "At Home."

Can a parent revoke a minor's license or learner's permit?

It depends on the state's driving laws, but whether or not a state allows this, it is clearly within the authority of parents to forbid a minor to drive.

RESPONSIBILITY FOR ACCIDENTS

What should a teen do if involved in a traffic accident?

The first rule is *stay at the scene of the accident.* In most states it is at least a misdemeanor to leave the scene of an accident before the police arrive and all the required paperwork is completed.

The second rule is *keep a clear head.* As soon as possible, take the following measures:

1. Write down the license plate number and a description of every other car involved in the accident.
2. Check to see whether anyone in any car has sustained an injury.
3. Check to see the extent of property damage to all cars and any other property.
4. Call the police and also a parent, or ask another person to do so, particularly if an injury or property damage has occurred.
5. Exchange names, addresses, and telephone numbers with all other drivers and obtain the names of their auto insurance companies and auto policy numbers.
6. Ask any witnesses to the accident, including passengers, for their addresses and telephone numbers.

7. Check the licenses of other drivers to determine whether they are carrying their own licenses and whether the licenses are subject to any restrictions.

The third rule is *cooperate with the arriving police officer*. Answer his or her questions accurately and courteously. The police officer will undoubtedly ask to see driver's licenses or other identification from all drivers. For more about police questioning, see Chapter 12, "Teens and Crime."

If a minor injures someone or damages property through his or her own fault while driving, who is financially responsible?

Usually the minor's parents are financially responsible. In every state, one of the conditions for obtaining a driver's license or learner's permit is that the applicant agrees to be financially responsible for injuries or property damage he or she causes as a result of negligent or reckless driving. If a parent is required to sign a teenage child's application for a license or permit, most states hold *both* parents responsible for injuries or property damage caused by the minor's negligent or reckless driving, even if only one parent signed.

Parents can be held liable for injuries or property damage caused by a minor child while driving for either personal enjoyment or a family purpose, such as running an errand. They also can be held liable for permitting a minor child to drive without a driver's license or a learner's permit.

Does this mean a teenage driver can't be held liable for injuries or property damage caused by his or her acts behind the wheel?

No. Almost anyone, including minors, can be taken to court for negligently or recklessly causing injuries or property damage. However, minors usually are "judgment proof," which means they normally don't have the money to satisfy court-ordered judgments for damages. This is why state driving laws hold parents financially responsible for injuries or property damage caused by the careless acts of their minor children. For more about court actions to recover money, see Chapter 17, "Taking Matters to Court."

If a teen's parents are divorced, who is held liable for injuries caused by the teen while driving?

Usually both of the parents, regardless of who has been awarded custody. If a minor's parents divorce *before* the minor is granted a license, in many states parental liability depends on which parent has custody on the date of the application. In joint custody situations, both parents continue to be liable. For more about custody in divorce matters, see Chapter 7, "If Your Parents Divorce."

Can parents avoid being held liable for a minor child's careless acts while driving?

Sometimes. In many states if a minor has a decent income and owns property, the parents may file a statement with the state department of motor vehicles attesting to the minor's separate financial responsibility. Once they do, they can't be held liable for injuries or property damage caused by the minor's negligence or recklessness while driving, except when their actions contribute to the cause of the accident.

In certain states parents can't be held responsible for a minor child's negligence or recklessness if the minor buys a car with his or her own money and also holds title to it.

If a teen lends the family car to a friend, can the teen's parents be held responsible for injuries or property damage caused by the driver?

Yes. Similarly, if a teen is driving a friend's car with permission, the teen is usually covered under the car owner's policy.

AUTO INSURANCE

How does auto insurance work?

When a person has auto insurance, an insurance company has agreed to pay for property damage and medical care in connection with the ownership and operation of a particular vehicle. The company's agreement to pay under the terms of its insurance policy is conditioned on the payment of a "premium," which is the cost of the insurance coverage.

An insurance company will only pay for medical care or property damage up to its policy limits. These limits are shown on the "declarations" page of the insurance policy, which describes the type and amount of coverage.

Insurance companies will usually pay for their own insured's medical care upfront, regardless of who caused the accident. But if the other driver was at fault, the insurer may "subrogate," or attempt to recover its costs from the other driver or the other driver's insurer.

If an insured is at fault for an accident, or if his or her insurance company decides to settle out of court in a disputed case, the insurance company will pay for the other party's property damage up to its policy limits. Also, the insurance company will pay for its own insured's property damage.

Sometimes insurance will also cover towing costs, and it may also provide reimbursement for the cost to rent a car while the damaged car is repaired.

When it comes to families, the auto insurance buyer—the "policyholder"—usually is an adult driver of the family car. A spouse and any children under age twenty-one may be insured under the same policy.

What is a "deductible"?

A deductible is the amount an insured pays for vehicle repairs out of pocket. After the deductible is satisfied, the insurance company then pays, but only up to its policy limits. Usually, if the deductible is higher, the insurance premium is lower. If someone other than the insured was at fault, the insured may ultimately be reimbursed his or her deductible.

What "risks" does auto insurance cover?

Quite a variety. These are the types of coverage included in a standard auto insurance policy:

1. "Collision" coverage, which pays for damage to the insured car when an insured driver isn't at fault.
2. "Comprehensive" coverage, which pays for damage to the insured car resulting from fire, theft, vandalism, hail, falling objects, windshield breaks, and collisions with animals.
3. "Medical payments" coverage, which pays for medical expenses that an insured driver and any passengers incur as a result of a traffic accident. It also covers injuries suffered by an insured person while riding in another car or walking.
4. "Bodily injury liability" coverage, which pays for claims against an insured resulting from injuries to passengers, pedestrians, and persons in other vehicles, up to the policy limits. Bodily injury liability insurance also pays for legal expenses incurred to defend the insured in a lawsuit. If an injury is serious or fatal, liability claims for bodily injury can add up to many thousands of dollars.
5. "Property damage liability" coverage, which pays for claims against an insured when the insured's car causes damage to someone else's property. Usually the damaged property is another driver's car, but it also might be a building, telephone pole, or lamppost.
6. "Uninsured motorist" coverage, which pays medical costs for an insured's bodily injuries and car damage when another person is at fault, but that person either doesn't have liability coverage or flees the scene. Uninsured motorist coverage often pays for auto damage and bodily injuries in hit-and-run situations.

Is a minor required to have auto insurance?

In most states, all drivers must have a minimum amount of auto *liability* insurance. Proof of auto liability insurance in the legally required amount is the standard way for a person to establish financial responsibility. In many states it is the *only* way.

Can minors buy their own auto insurance?

Usually they are unable to buy their own auto insurance. Insurance companies have calculated that teen drivers are very poor insurance risks. They can't profit by insuring teen drivers separately unless exorbitant premiums are charged, because teens as a group have a high accident rate and many insurance claims. (Teenage women are a safer risk than teenage men, but only slightly.)

But, as stated previously, insurance companies will cover teen drivers under their parents' policy. The additional premium to cover a minor under an adult policy is high, but at least it is affordable. This is the way most teen drivers are insured and, again, the way their financial responsibility is established.

If a claim is made on an insurance policy following an accident, will the premium increase?

Usually the premium will increase if the insured was at fault in the accident and the insured files a claim. The rates of increase vary from insurance company to company. Some common estimates are that the rates will rise anywhere from 10 percent to 40 percent.

Multiple moving violations can also cause the cost of insurance to increase—particularly the cost to cover teens. Again, this varies based on an insured's driving record and the different factors that insurance companies use to assess risk.

Is there anything a teen can do to reduce the premium charged for his or her part of the car insurance?

Yes. Many insurance companies reduce the premium for teen drivers if the teen doesn't smoke. Some companies also reduce the premium if the teen maintains good grades.

If a minor's parents are divorced, which parent's policy is he or she covered under?

Usually the custodial parent's policy, although if the minor is permitted to drive both parents' cars, each must cover the minor.

What is "no-fault" insurance?

It is a type of auto insurance in which each party looks to his or her own insurer for payment, regardless of who caused the accident. Under state no-fault insurance laws, negligence doesn't have to be established before an insurance company agrees to pay. The insured receives prompt payment from his or her insurer, and no subrogation follows.

Usually no-fault insurance only applies to injuries and not to property damage. The trade-off for the insurance companies in states with no-fault insurance is that the insured's right to go to court for additional damages is restricted.

How does no-fault insurance differ from traditional car insurance?

It differs in the manner in which the innocent party collects. With regular auto insurance, an accident victim makes a claim against the other driver's insurance company. Before that insurer will pay, the accident victim must establish that the other driver was negligent or reckless. This may be difficult if the cause of the accident is tough to determine.

If the other driver was at fault, the amount payable to the accident victim must be calculated. The figure depends on such factors as the victim's medical expenses, property damage, lost wages, and pain and suffering. Sometimes added are the lawyer's fees for proving who was at fault.

For more about lawsuits, including how to calculate damages in personal injury cases, see Chapter 17, "Taking Matters to Court."

TRAFFIC OFFENSES

If a person commits a minor traffic offense, is he or she placed under arrest?

No. The person is simply cited for violating a traffic law.

If a minor commits a traffic offense, does the case go to juvenile court?

Not usually. In most states, all minor traffic offenses go to the state's adult traffic court. But juvenile courts have the power to suspend a minor's driver's license if the minor commits a delinquent act involving a car. For more about juvenile courts, see Chapter 12, "Teens and Crime."

What kinds of punishment can a teenage driver receive for a traffic offense?

It depends on the nature and severity of the offense and also the state in which the offense was committed. In any traffic court, fines can be swiftly imposed, and licenses can be suspended or revoked.

Can a minor's license be revoked because of too many traffic tickets?

Yes. In every state both teen and adult drivers may lose their licenses if they are "habitual violators." This happens most often when the offense is DUI (driving under the influence).

What is the punishment for DUI?

It varies from state to state, but for a first offense the license of the drunk driver is usually suspended or revoked. Sometimes the offender will receive a restricted license, allowing him or her to drive to work but nowhere else. Weekend detention is often given, as the minimum punishment for a DUI conviction is 48 hours in jail. Repeat offenders are always punished more severely. Most DUI convictions almost always carry fines.

If an individual has been drinking or using drugs, that individual should have a "designated driver" take the wheel. Another option is to use a third-party driver app on their phone to call an "Uber" or a "Lyft" instead of operating their own vehicle.

These rules of thumb apply to adults as well as teens.

Can't my lawyer plead the case down to "reckless driving"?

It depends. Prosecutors have control over whether to offer plea bargains that allow a driver to plead to a lesser offense such as "reckless driving." That is something that you need to talk about with your lawyer.

See Chapter 11, "Alcohol and Drugs," for more about the legal aspects of drinking and driving.

Does a police officer need a search warrant to search a car?

Generally, the police do not need a search warrant to search a car. This is because the US Supreme Court established the "automobile exception" to the Fourth Amendment in *Carroll v. United States* (1925). The automobile exception recognizes that the police should be granted more leeway with respect to searching an automobile, which is inherently mobile, than a house. If a person is arrested for an offense involving a car, both the car and the arrested person may be searched. This is called a "search incident to an arrest." No warrant is required, but the police must limit their search to areas within the arrested person's reach just prior to the arrest and to items in plain view (such as items in the back seat).

In addition, police officers can search a car if they have "probable cause" to believe that evidence of a crime is in the car, and it may vanish if not seized right away. And if the car is "impounded" by the police to preserve evidence, police personnel may inventory its contents, but may only search the trunk and glove box after obtaining a warrant.

All this being said, the police still must have a lawful justification for pulling over your vehicle in the first place. However, any traffic infraction gives the police the authority to pull over your vehicle.

For more about police searches and search warrants, see Chapter 12, "Teens and Crime."

Can a minor be arrested for having a weapon in the car?

A minor needs written permission from a parent to possess a weapon or ammunition. If a minor can't produce this upon request, a police officer may place the minor under arrest for possessing a weapon, regardless of the time or place.

Firearms may not be sold to minors.

If you are in possession of a gun or other weapon at the time of a car stop, don't try to hide the gun or even touch it. Immediately put both hands on the steering wheel. The police officer will see the weapon if it is in plain view. If the officer asks whether you have a gun or other weapon in the car, tell the truth.

Is hitchhiking illegal?

It depends on state or local law. Some states and cities prohibit hitchhiking altogether, some don't regulate it at all, and others permit it only when the hitchhiker is standing at a certain location near the roadway. For example, some states prohibit hitchhiking on freeways, urban roadways, bridges, and highway on-ramps and off-ramps, but permit it on other roads and streets. Some state laws specifically prohibit hitchhiking on a public way during nighttime hours.

Can a minor ride on a motorcycle without wearing a helmet?

Again, it depends on state or local law. Some states require anyone—a minor or an adult—to wear a helmet if he or she operates a motorcycle or rides on a motorcycle as a passenger. Alabama, for example, mandates a helmet for anyone on a motorcycle.

TABLE 1.2: State Laws Regarding Driving with Cell Phones

State	*Handheld Ban*	*All Cell Phone Ban, Novice Drivers*	*Text Messaging Ban, All Drivers*	*Text Messaging Ban, Novice Drivers*
Alabama	Yes	16, or 17 w/ Intermediate License < 6 months	Yes	Covered under all-driver ban
Alaska			Yes	Covered under all-driver ban
Arizona	Yes	Intermediate Permit Holders < 18	Yes	Covered under all-driver ban
Arkansas	School and work zone only	< 18	Yes	Covered under all-driver ban
California	Yes	< 18	Yes	Covered under all-driver ban
Colorado		< 18	Yes	Covered under all-driver ban
Connecticut	Yes	< 18	Yes	Covered under all-driver ban
Delaware	Yes	Learner's or Intermediate License	Yes	Covered under all-driver ban
District of Columbia	Yes	Learner's Permit	Yes	Covered under all-driver ban
Florida	School and work zones only		Yes	Covered under all-driver ban
Georgia	Yes		Yes	Covered under all-driver ban
Hawaii	Yes	< 18	Yes	Covered under all-driver ban
Idaho	Yes		Yes	Covered under all-driver ban
Illinois	Yes	<19	Yes	Covered under all-driver ban
Indiana	Yes	< 21	Yes	Covered under all-driver ban
Iowa		Restricted or Intermediate License	Yes	Covered under all-driver ban
Kansas		Learner's or Intermediate License	Yes	Covered under all-driver ban
Kentucky		< 18	Yes	Covered under all-driver ban

TABLE 1.2: (Continued)

State	*Handheld Ban*	*All Cell Phone Ban, Novice Drivers*	*Text Messaging Ban, All Drivers*	*Text Messaging Ban, Novice Drivers*
Louisiana	Learner or Intermediate License (regardless of age)	1st year of License (Primary for < 18)	Yes	Covered under all-driver ban
Maine	Yes	Learner's or Intermediate License	Yes	Covered under all-driver ban
Maryland	Yes	< 18	Yes	Covered under all-driver ban
Massachusetts	Yes	< 18	Yes	Covered under all-driver ban
Michigan	Yes		Yes	Covered under all-driver ban
Minnesota	Yes	< 18 w/ Learner's or Provisional License	Yes	Covered under all-driver ban
Mississippi			Yes	Covered under all-driver ban
Missouri	Yes		Yes	Covered under all-driver ban
Montana				
Nebraska		< 18 w/ Learner's or Intermediate License	Yes	Covered under all-driver ban
Nevada	Yes		Yes	Covered under all-driver ban
New Hampshire	Yes	< 18	Yes	Covered under all-driver ban
New Jersey	Yes	Permit or Provisional License	Yes	Covered under all-driver ban
New Mexico		Learner's or Provisional License	Yes	Covered under all-driver ban
New York	Yes		Yes	Covered under all-driver ban
North Carolina		< 18	Yes	Covered under all-driver ban
North Dakota		< 18	Yes	Covered under all-driver ban
Ohio	Yes	< 18	Yes	Covered under all-driver ban

(*Continued*)

TABLE 1.2: (Continued)

State	*Handheld Ban*	*All Cell Phone Ban, Novice Drivers*	*Text Messaging Ban, All Drivers*	*Text Messaging Ban, Novice Drivers*
Oklahoma	Learner's or Intermediate License		Yes	Covered under all-driver ban
Oregon	Yes	< 18	Yes	Covered under all-driver ban
Pennsylvania			Yes	Covered under all-driver ban
Rhode Island	Yes	< 18	Yes	Covered under all-driver ban
South Carolina			Yes	Covered under all-driver ban
South Dakota		Learner's or Intermediate License	Yes	Covered under all-driver ban
Tennessee	Yes	Learner's or Intermediate License	Yes	Covered under all-driver ban
Texas	School crossing zones on public school property only	< 18	Yes	Covered under all-driver ban
Utah		< 18	Yes	Covered under all-driver ban
Vermont	Yes	< 18	Yes	Covered under all-driver ban
Virginia	Yes		Yes	Covered under all-driver ban
Washington	Yes	Learner's or Intermediate License	Yes	Covered under all-driver ban
West Virginia	Yes	< 18 w/ Learner's or Intermediate License	Yes	Covered under all-driver ban
Wisconsin	Work zones only	Learner's or Intermediate License	Yes	Covered under all-driver ban
Wyoming			Yes	Covered under all-driver ban

Source: Adapted from Governors Highway Safety Association, "Distracted Driving," https://www.ghsa.org/state-laws/issues/distracted%20driving (accessed August 15, 2023).

Alabama's law provides that "[n]o person shall operate or ride upon a motorcycle or motor-driven cycle unless he is wearing protective headgear." Some states, such as California, go into greater detail on the safety requirements for helmets. California law provides that the helmet must fit the "wearing person's head securely without excessive lateral or vertical movement."

In other states the helmet requirement applies only to minors. For example, Alaska law provides: "A person who is 18 years of age or older may not be required to wear a helmet while operating a motorcycle if the person is the holder of a license or endorsement to operate a motorcycle."

Some states also require individuals—adults or minors—to wear shoes if they operate or ride on a motorcycle.

Do any laws regulate the use of cell phones in vehicles?

Yes, many states regulate the use of cell phones in vehicles. This is because so-called distracted driving has become an epidemic. Texting while driving is dangerous and illegal. Many states prohibit the use of handheld cell phones by drivers in moving automobiles.

For example, the state of Arkansas prohibits the use of cell phones by motorists traveling through highway work zones and school zones. Other states only allow the use of cell phones in vehicles if the cell phones are equipped so that the driver can use the phone without holding it in his or her hands. For example, California's law provides: "A person shall not drive a motor vehicle while using a wireless telephone unless that telephone is specifically designed and configured to allow hands-free listening and talking, and is used in that manner while driving." In 2023, a state law went into effect in Michigan limiting drivers to "hands free" use of cell phones and other electronic devices. Anyone caught using cell phones for *any* purpose while driving is subject to being pulled over and ticketed. According to the Governors Highway Safety Association, thirty-seven (37) states and the District of Columbia have laws that prohibit the use of cell phones by novice drivers; forty-eight (48) states and the District of Columbia have laws specifically prohibiting "texting" while driving. Washington was the first state to pass such a law, in 2007.

If you are driving carelessly because you are arguing on a cell phone, a police officer can pull you over and ticket you.

Most states have an "emergency" number for cell phone users. In addition, the emergency number (800) 525-5555 will direct your phone call to the state police.

See Table 1.2 for state laws regarding cell phone use.

CURFEWS

What is a curfew?

It is a state or local law that prohibits individuals from being on the street between specific hours after dark. Many states have laws that empower cities or municipalities to pass curfews for minors. While curfews usually apply to young people, they have also been applied to adults.

Under curfew laws, being on the street includes riding or sitting in a car. For example, Connecticut has a law providing that sixteen- and seventeen-year-old drivers may not operate vehicles between the hours of 11:00 p.m. and 5:00 a.m. But a minor usually isn't in violation of a curfew law, whether on the street or in a car, if he or she is with an adult.

Young people need to be aware of curfew regulations, because a minor who repeatedly violates curfew laws could be considered delinquent and be made a ward of the state.

When are curfews illegal or unconstitutional?

Curfew laws are unconstitutional if they are considered too broad or too vague. A curfew law might also infringe upon the fundamental right of a parent to rear his or her children as he or she sees fit. As explained in Chapter 12, a law must be written clearly and specifically, so that citizens have fair notice of exactly what actions the law prohibits. Many courts have ruled that curfew laws that simply prohibit "loitering" or "vagrancy" are unenforceable because they forbid perfectly legal acts such as having a smoke outside a restaurant.

In a 1971 case from the state of Washington, a city ordinance that simply declared "loitering" and "wandering" illegal was declared unconstitutional after a high school senior was pulled over at 4:30 a.m. by the police. The young man was returning from a party and wanted to take a drive along the beach near downtown Seattle. The statute was declared unconstitutional because its wording made his perfectly innocent behavior illegal.

On the one hand, many state courts, and even the US Supreme Court, have let stand well-drafted curfew laws as a way to reduce juvenile crime at night. The justification for these laws is the vulnerability of minors, their relative lack of maturity when it comes to decision making, and the importance of parental discipline.

On the other hand, a federal district court in Indiana invalidated that state's curfew law, finding that it infringed on parental rights to direct the care, custody, and control of their children.

What happens if a minor violates a curfew?

The police have a number of options. If the minor has a legitimate reason for being out, the police officer might send the minor home with a stern warning. In other cases the minor might be taken home, cited for a minor traffic violation, or transported to the police station and "booked," for committing another, more serious act.

The best way to find out if a city or state has a curfew is to ask a police officer, call the police station and inquire, or go to the public library and read up on local curfew laws. A reference librarian can provide assistance in finding the law.

OWNING AND RENTING A CAR

Can a teen buy a car?

Nothing in the law prevents a minor from buying a car or other expensive item. But some car dealers refuse to sell to minors for one basic reason. As discussed in Chapter 16, minors are permitted to walk away from or "disaffirm" most contracts, provided they do so soon after the purchase. This rule of law, which strikes many as out-of-date and even unfair, is supposed to protect minors from unscrupulous salespeople.

This means, for example, that if a minor buys a car but then decides the purchase was a bad idea, the dealer can't refuse to take the car back even if the minor paid full price. (However, the dealer may reduce the refund to reflect any damage or wear and tear to the car while it was in the minor's possession.) Basically, the law places the risk of financial loss on the dealer and not the minor.

In some states, minors may only disaffirm contracts until age sixteen.

If a teen does buy a car, it must be titled, registered, and licensed, and the teen driver must have auto insurance.

Can a teen take out a car loan?

That would be difficult. In order for a teen to obtain a car loan, he or she would have to be earning enough money to make monthly loan payments without a lot of effort. Most teens don't earn this much. Besides, most lenders have a basic policy of rejecting all loan applications from minors.

Can a teen rent a car?

Whether a minor can rent a car depends on whether the car rental agency is willing to rent cars to minors. Few will rent to persons under age twenty-five.

FOR FURTHER READING

Federal Communications Commission. "The Dangers of Texting While Driving." http://www.fcc.gov/guides/texting-while-driving.

Ferguson, Susan A. *Speeding-Related Fatal Crashes among Teen Drivers and Opportunities for Reducing the Risks*. Washington, DC: Governors Highway Safety Association, June 2013. http://www.ghsa.org/html/publications/pdf/sfteens_speed.pdf.

Hollister, Tim and Sandy Spavone. *Not So Fast: Parenting Your Teen through the Dangers of Driving*. Chicago, IL: University of Chicago Press, 2013.

Kiesbye, Stefan. *Cell Phones and Driving*. Farmington Hills, MI: Greenhaven Press, 2010.

OTHER INFORMATION SOURCES

Organizations

American Automobile Association Foundation for Traffic Safety, 607 14th Street, NW, Suite 201, Washington, DC 20005. (202) 638–5944. E-mail: aaafts@aaafts.org. Home page: www.aaafoundation.org.

Governors' Highway Safety Association, 444 N. Capitol St. NW, Suite 722, Washington, DC 20001. (202) 789–0942. E-mail: headquarters@ghsa.org. Home page: www.ghsa.org.

Mothers Against Drunk Driving (MADD), 511 E. John Carpenter Freeway, Suite 700, Irvings, TX 75062. (800) GET-MADD. E-mail: http://www.madd.org/about-us/contact-us/send-to-friend.jsp?pid=133304623&itemID=133770664. Home page: www.madd.org.

National Motorists Association, 1001 Arboretum Dr, Ste 120 Waunakee, WI 53597. (608) 849–8697. E-mail: nma@motorists.org. Home page: www.motorists.com.
Students Against Destructive Decisions, Inc. (SADD), 655 15th St. NW, Suite #800 Washington, DC 20005, 1-877-SADD-INC. Home page: www.sadd.org.

Online Sources

Curfew.org: http://www.curfew.org
Distracted Driving Distracted Driving Dangers and Statistics | NHTSA
TeenDriving.com: http://teendriving.com

CHAPTER 2

At School

ATTENDANCE AND GRADES

Does everyone in the United States have the right to an education?

Every young person in the United States has the right to a free public education, and every young person in the United States has an obligation to attend school. State laws, called compulsory education laws, guarantee this. Minors in most states must attend school between the ages of seven and sixteen, and in some states they are required to attend longer. For example, in Oregon, the age range is between seven and eighteen. A student can only quit school if the applicable state law no longer requires attendance. Several states have provisions in their state constitutions that mandate compulsory education. New Mexico's Constitution provides: "Every child of school age and of sufficient physical and mental ability shall be required to attend a public or other school during such period and for such time as may be prescribed by law." Idaho's Constitution has a similar provision: "The legislature may require by law that every child shall attend the public schools of the state, throughout the period between the ages of six and eighteen years, unless educated by other means, as provided by law."

In many states a student who misses too much school may be brought under court supervision so that his or her attendance can be monitored by a probation officer. Parents can be prosecuted for "education neglect" for failing to keep a child in school.

See Table 2.1 for age requirements for school attendance in the fifty states and the District of Columbia.

TABLE 2.1: Age Requirements for School Attendance by State

State	*Ages of Required School Attendance*	*Minimum Age from Which Free Education Must Be Offered*	*Maximum Age to Which Free Education Must Be Offered*
Alabama	6–17	5	17[a]
Alaska	7–16	5	20
Arizona	6–16	6	21
Arkansas	5–18	5	21
California	6–18	5	21
Colorado	6–17	5	21
Connecticut	5–18	5	21
Delaware	5–16	5	21
District of Columbia	5–18	5	†
Florida	6–16	4	–
Georgia	6–16	5	19
Hawaii	5–18	5	20
Idaho	7–16	5	21
Illinois	6–17	4	21
Indiana	7–18	5	22
Iowa	6–16	5	21
Kansas	7–18	5	†
Kentucky	6–18	5	21
Louisiana	7–18	5	21
Maine	7–17	5[b]	20
Maryland	5–18	5	21
Massachusetts	6–16	3	22
Michigan	6–18	5	20
Minnesota	7–17	5	21
Mississippi	6–17	5	21
Missouri	7–17	5	21
Montana	7–16	5	19
Nebraska	6–18	5	21
Nevada	6–18	5	21
New Hampshire	6–16	–	21

TABLE 2.1: (Continued)

State	*Ages of Required School Attendance*	*Minimum Age from Which Free Education Must Be Offered*	*Maximum Age to Which Free Education Must Be Offered*
New Jersey	6–16	5	20
New Mexico	5–18	5	–
New York	6–16	5	21
North Carolina	7–16	5	21
North Dakota	7–16	5	21
Ohio	6–18	5	22
Oklahoma	5–18	5	21
Oregon	6–18	5	19
Pennsylvania	8–17	6	21
Rhode Island	5–18[c]	5	21
South Carolina	5–17	5	22
South Dakota	6–18[d]	5	21
Tennessee	6–18	5	–
Texas	6–19	5	26
Utah	6–18	5	–
Vermont	6–16	5	†
Virginia	5–18	5	20
Washington	8–18	5	21
West Virginia	6–17	5	22
Wisconsin	6–18	4	20
Wyoming	7–16	5	21

– Not available. In this state, local education agencies determine the maximum age.

† Not applicable. State has not set a maximum age limit.

[a] In Alabama's city school systems, students are entitled to admission until age nineteen.

[b] In Maine, students must be at least five years old before October 15, or four years old by October 15, if they are enrolled in a public preschool program prior to kindergarten (where offered).

[c] In Rhode Island, the compulsory age is sixteen if a student has an alternative learning plan for obtaining a high school diploma or its equivalent.

[d] In South Dakota, the compulsory age limit is sixteen if a child enrolls in a general education development test preparation program that is school based or for which a school contracts, and the child successfully completes the test or reaches the age of eighteen.

Source: National Center for Education Statistics, US Department of Education, https://nces.ed.gov/programs/statereform/tab1_2-2020.asphttp:// http://nces.ed.gov/programs/statereform/tab5_1.asp (accessed August 15, 2023).

Are teens allowed to remain in high school longer than it normally takes to finish?

Yes, although most states have a maximum age limit. It varies from state to state, but most set it at age twenty-one. Some states have adult high school completion programs. Often there are age restrictions on these programs.

Can a student's grades be lowered for poor attendance?

This practice has been tested in courts across the country, with varying results. Some have ruled it isn't improper to grade "truants" or "tardies" more harshly, because learning to be responsible is consistent with the overall goals of a school curriculum. Others say that lowering grades for poor attendance misses the point of what grades are really for.

In one case, a Kentucky public high school was forbidden to lower a student's grades for absences due to a suspension. Since the student was denied credit for work he missed during his suspension, additional grade reductions for his absences were said to be "overkill."

If a school has a policy of lowering grades for truancy, the school should tell the students at the beginning of the year how many absences will result in reduced grades and whether the rule applies to both excused and unexcused absences. If grades can also be lowered for misconduct, students should be told what kinds of behavior might actually result in lowered grades.

Can a student flunk out of public high school?

"Flunking out" is a phrase usually associated with college, but it does have an equivalent in the high school setting.

If a student doesn't attend school for a specified number of days in a school year, he or she can be expelled and will usually lose school credit for that year. Furthermore, if a student doesn't fulfill the requirements of a particular course of study, he or she won't graduate. The student may repeat courses until reaching the maximum age for attending high school, but has to leave upon reaching that age if he or she doesn't graduate first. After that the student can obtain a graduate equivalency degree, or GED, but generally would be unable to receive a high school diploma in the absence of a special state law or program.

Are married students required to stay in school? Can married students be kept out of school?

In answer to the first question, married students usually are "emancipated" from the obligation of having to attend high school, even if they are otherwise too young to quit. As to the second question, the Constitution requires that all students be permitted to attend classes and participate in their high school graduation ceremonies regardless of marital status.

For more about emancipation, see Chapter 5, "On Your Own," and for more about teen marriages, see Chapter 9, "Marrying and Having Children."

Can a pregnant teen be prevented from attending high school? Can students with children be prevented from attending high school?

The answer to both questions is no. In times past, pregnant students either dropped out of high school or were told to leave, and of course many never went back. But these days, pregnancy and parenthood can't be used as a justification for keeping a student from completing high school. Puerto Rico even has a law known as the Pregnant Students' Bill of Rights, passed in 2004.

Federal ed guidelines require that public school officials provide pregnant students with educational opportunities and they cannot force them to attend alternative educational opportunities. Instead, they have an affirmative obligation to protect pregnant students. These obligations are important, because of the historic discrimination against such pregnant students.

Most school districts have special programs for teen mothers, either on or off campus. Florida law provides: "Pregnant students may attend alternative education programs or adult education programs, provided that the curriculum allows the student to continue to work toward a high school diploma." But, again federal ed requirements state that state officials cannot force pregnant students off-campus to another location. They have to provide them with the same educational opportunities as other students. Otherwise, the school drifts into the unwanted realm of pregnancy discrimination.

A school counselor can provide information on opportunities for pregnant and married students.

Can students who have HIV/AIDS (human immunodeficiency virus/acquired immunodeficiency syndrome) be prevented from attending high school?

No, students with HIV cannot be prevented from attending high school. In the 1980s, some school boards tried to bar students with HIV/AIDS from attending classes, but courts ordered the students enrolled once health officials certified that they weren't likely to infect others.

HIV is the virus that causes AIDS. It can be transmitted during sexual intercourse. Although HIV/AIDS is a very serious disease, there are now drugs that can treat HIV and provide health care options that were not imaginable even a decade earlier.

FREEDOM OF EXPRESSION

Congress shall make no law . . . abridging the freedom of speech, or of the press.

—First Amendment, US Constitution

Does the First Amendment protect all high school students?

No. The First Amendment, the first freedom in the Bill of Rights of the US Constitution, only protects public school students. It does not protect private school students. The reason is that the First Amendment is part of the Bill of Rights, which only protects us from actions by governmental or state officials. This concept is called "the state action doctrine." Its protections do not apply to private individuals or institutions.

Public school principals and teachers are state actors or government officials. Thus, they are subject to First Amendment principles. But private school officials are not part of the government and thus are not state actors. This means that they are not bound by the First Amendment in how they run their schools.

Do public school students have free speech rights at school?

Yes. The constitutional guarantee of free expression extends to public high school students. However, these rights can be limited in certain situations, as this section explains.

The right of students in public schools to express their opinions freely is guided by an important US Supreme Court case, *Tinker v. Des Moines Independent School District*. This 1969 decision established that students in public high schools do not forfeit their constitutional right of free expression when they step onto school property. It is still regarded today as a watershed ruling for its declaration that "students [don't] shed their constitutional rights . . . at the school house gates."

In *Tinker*, the Supreme Court upheld the right of students at Iowa high schools and middle schools to wear black peace armbands to protest America's involvement in the Vietnam War. Because the armbands were a means of communicating an idea and not just an item of dress—because the armbands were a form of "symbolic speech"—wearing them raised a First Amendment issue.

The Supreme Court established in *Tinker* that in order to limit student expression, school authorities must reasonably forecast that the student expression would "materially and substantially" disrupt school work and school discipline or collide with the rights of others. The school must base its decision to limit speech on concrete facts showing that the expression would probably cause "substantial and material" disruption at school. Its decision must be motivated by more than the desire to avoid the discomfort that often accompanies an unpopular viewpoint. The court explained that school officials may not act on "undifferentiated fear or apprehension of disturbance."

According to the Supreme Court, the student armbands in *Tinker* didn't create any problems that substantially interfered with either school activities or the rights of the other students. Because the school district's no-armband rule couldn't be justified as a valid restriction on First Amendment rights, the Supreme Court declared it unconstitutional.

The basic analysis set out in *Tinker* applies to this day to cases involving the free speech rights of students.

According to *Tinker*, when can school officials prohibit students from engaging in certain expression?

There are two standards from the *Tinker* case that give public school officials the power to regulate student expression. The first is when public school officials can reasonably forecast that the student expression will cause a substantial disruption or material interference with school activities. This is called "the substantial disruption" test.

The second standard from *Tinker* that gives public school officials the power to regulate student expression is when the student expression infringes or invades the rights of other students. This is often called "the invasion of the rights of others" standard. For example, if a student engages in sexually harassing speech, a public school official could prohibit that speech, because the sexually harassing speech invades or infringes on the rights of the speech's recipients. The invasion of the rights of others standard is becoming more influential now, because of the phenomenon of cyberbullying.

What does the *Tinker* case have to do with viewpoint discrimination?

Many view the *Tinker* ruling as a case articulating the principle that government officials should not discriminate against private speakers based on viewpoint. In the *Tinker* case, school officials specifically prohibited the wearing of black armbands, but allowed students to wear other symbols such as Iron Crosses or political campaign buttons. The US Supreme Court justices feared that public school officials in Des Moines, Iowa, had punished the armband-wearing students because they disagreed with or opposed their antiwar political viewpoints.

What types of student expression does the First Amendment regulate?

The First Amendment regulates virtually every kind of communication, both verbal and nonverbal, including speeches, essays, leafleting, armbands and buttons, books in the library, school newspapers, underground newspapers, walkouts, and sit-ins.

In the area of free expression, what does "material and substantial" disruption really mean?

This is the million-dollar question, and there is no easy answer. Consider the following situation. A public school has had incidents of race-motivated violence. In order to curb the problem, the school passes a regulation prohibiting students from wearing racially inflammatory clothing, such as Confederate flag symbols. A reviewing court might determine that, because of the past incidents of race-motivated violence at the school, school officials could reasonably forecast that the wearing of Confederate flag clothing would cause a substantial disruption of school activities.

Students could probably distribute handouts between classes, unless doing so would seriously interfere with hall traffic. On the other hand, students could be prohibited from distributing such materials during class time. School officials could refuse to let students use the school's photocopiers to duplicate handouts if the students planned to use them instead of going to class. But the school would probably be required to let students use the copiers after school, whether or not school officials agreed with the content of the handouts.

Bulletin boards are a special case. Students may be able to post written materials such as newspaper articles and meeting announcements on school bulletin boards whether or not the subject matter was controversial, provided the posted material wasn't vulgar by standards that the community generally adheres to. But, students also may not be able to post materials to school bulletin boards if the school has reserved that bulletin board only for the transmission of official school speech. In other words, student access depends on whether the bulletin board has been opened up as a type of public forum or whether the board is reserved for the school's government speech.

Can a student be punished for openly criticizing a teacher or school policy?

It depends upon how the student criticizes the policy. On the one hand, a student would not have the right to utter a string of profanities to teachers or school officials in criticizing the policy. On the other hand, the First Amendment was designed to protect critical speech on important public matters. Thus, students generally do have the right to criticize school policies, as long as they don't cross the line into profane tirades or threats. In a 1973 case, a court upheld a high school's decision to confiscate signs that students planned to distribute to protest a certain teacher's dismissal. The court agreed that the school had a realistic basis for believing that the protest would interfere with school work and school discipline.

Although the school claimed victory in this situation, students have won many First Amendment cases. In 1972, an Illinois court upheld the actions of high school students who published and distributed an underground newspaper criticizing certain school officials. The newspaper, styled like the *National Lampoon*, urged the student body to discard reading materials relating to school policy that were intended for their parents. The students prevailed because the school couldn't prove that the newspaper caused material and substantial disruption or offended the rights of others.

Students also have the right to criticize public school officials online as long they don't degenerate into uttering true threats or causing a substantial disruption at school. In fact, in one case from Florida in 2010, a federal district court ruled that a student had a First Amendment right to criticize her teacher online.

Can a student insult a teacher and still be protected under the First Amendment?

It depends on the context. Certainly, a student may not utter direct, face-to-face personal insults against a teacher and receive free speech protection if that speech disrupts or interrupts class. However, the First Amendment does allow students to criticize school officials and teachers, as long as the criticism is respectful, does not involve profanity, and does not disrupt school activities. Students also have the right to criticize school officials online as long as it does not degenerate into a true threat.

But let's be clear: a student does not have a right to personally insult a teacher in the classroom. In those instances, the student may be punished. The teacher must have the ability to control her classroom.

Does the First Amendment protect students who libel or slander school officials?

The First Amendment doesn't protect anyone who defames others. Defamation refers to false statements that harm another person's reputation. There are two basic types of defamation: libel and slander. Libel generally refers to written defamation, while slander applies to oral defamation.

Both libel and slander are types of "defamatory" statements, and statements such as these are said to "defame" people. Defamatory statements are never protected by the First Amendment, and persons who defame others can be sued for damages caused by their defamatory acts. There are many more defamation lawsuits today, because of social media. The advent of social media has exponentially increased the amount of speech circulating in the world. Unfortunately, this also means that there is more defamation out there too.

School authorities always have the power to censor libelous material written by students and can stop its distribution, whether or not the material was prepared at school. In addition, school officials can punish students who make slanderous statements.

Students should also note that they may be liable for defaming someone on the Internet. Too many young people, view the Internet as a legal-free zone. It is not. There have been a few cases in which teachers actually have sued their students for posting defamatory comments online.

Can school officials prohibit profane language on school grounds?

Yes. Public school officials do not violate the First Amendment when they punish students for vulgar or lewd speech. The US Supreme Court firmly established this principle in *Bethel School District No. 403 v. Fraser* (1986). In this case, seventeen-year-old student Matthew Fraser delivered a speech, in which he made sexual references, to the school assembly of six hundred (600) students while nominating another student for elective office. School officials suspended Fraser for delivering the speech. He sued, contending that he had a free speech right to deliver his speech, which he claimed was not disruptive.

Fraser prevailed in the lower courts. However, school officials appealed successfully to the US Supreme Court. Chief Justice Warren Burger, in his last opinion for the Court, wrote the majority opinion. He emphasized that school officials have an interest in teaching students the boundaries of "socially appropriate behavior," including their manner of speech. He explained that "essential lessons of civil, mature conduct cannot be conveyed in a school that tolerates lewd, indecent, or offensive speech."

This rule doesn't apply just to "four-letter" words; in fact, the language that schools often prohibit wouldn't strike every high school student as vulgar or lewd.

Schools may prohibit the distribution of materials that are generally considered vulgar and lewd and may legally confiscate such materials. However, "vulgar and lewd" speech within the Supreme Court's *Fraser* ruling does not even come close to speech that qualifies as legally obscene. Obscenity refers to hard-core pornographic materials that have no serious artistic, literary, or other value. People trafficking in such material can face conviction and even prison time.

If a student can't use profanity on school grounds, are teachers and administrators held to the same standard?

They should be—and in fact, most schools explicitly forbid the use of vulgar language by everyone on campus. But these days a teacher probably wouldn't lose his or her job, and a student probably wouldn't be expelled, if a single profanity slipped out during a class discussion. A student might face a short-term suspension for profanity.

DISTRIBUTING MATERIALS ON SCHOOL GROUNDS

Can school authorities legally enforce a rule prohibiting students from distributing written materials on school property before, during, and after school?

Unclear, because legal cases orbiting around this issue have had different outcomes. As explained previously, the US Supreme Court declared that public school students do not "shed their constitutional rights to freedom of speech or expression at the schoolhouse gate." This means that students may distribute printed material, as long as that material does not libel someone, threaten someone, or qualify as vulgar or lewd. School officials may only enforce such a rule if they can show that distributing written materials at school would *always* interfere with school activities or the rights of others. That would be a tough case for school officials to win.

Can school authorities legally enforce a rule permitting students to distribute written materials before and after classes but not during school hours?

School officials can enforce such a rule only if the school is able to prove that the leafleting or distributing in question during school hours is likely to disrupt school work or school discipline materially. School officials would have to prove, for example, that the student leaf-letters would block the halls, disrupt classes, cause damage to school property, or interfere with the legal rights of others. That might be another tough case.

Can a school legally enforce a rule prohibiting students from bringing "controversial" or "distasteful" materials onto school property, regardless of the subject matter?

Probably not, though it depends on exactly what type of material. A policy banning "controversial" materials likely would be considered too broad or too vague and would not withstand First Amendment review. On the other hand, there could be controversial or distasteful material that bullies a particular student. School officials probably would have the power to prohibit the distribution of such material.

Because blanket rules like these fail to let students know what kinds of materials *in fact* are prohibited and what kinds of materials *in fact* are acceptable, the Constitution says they are "void for vagueness." If rules such as these could legally be enforced, a school could prohibit materials that the most oversensitive teacher or administrator might happen to have a problem with. The limits on the constitutional right of free speech don't reach this far.

If certain students distribute materials in an orderly manner but others react disruptively, can the school step in? Should the school step in?

These questions raise an important issue, because the disruption is being caused not by students who want to exercise their free speech rights, but rather by the reactions of others. This is referred to in legal circles as the "heckler's veto" problem.

In such situations, school officials must strike a balance between the rights of the student exercising free speech rights, the hecklers, and other students who bear the effects of the disruption. Officials have the authority to regulate the "time, place, and manner" of the students' leafleting activities to make certain that their right to distribute the materials isn't diminished. Officials may have to provide for the students' extra protection. They could only stop the leafleting if serious problems occurred, or if the activity tended to aggravate an already touchy situation.

Can a school forbid leafleting on a particular issue altogether?

No. This would be an unconstitutional restraint on the First Amendment rights of *all* students.

But, school officials may be able to prohibit leafleting in certain locations in schools. For example, the Sixth US Circuit Court of Appeals ruled in *M.A.L. v. Kinsland* (2008) that public school officials could prohibit a student from handing out leaflets in the public school hallway, as the hallway is a nonpublic forum with heavy student and teacher traffic. The appeals court explained that the limited ban on leafleting in the hallways was constitutional because the school allowed the student to leaflet in other areas, such as placing them on a bulletin board or handing them out during lunch hour at a cafeteria table.

But, school officials cannot flatly prohibit leafleting by students. This is a well-established principle. In one important case, a school policy prohibited the use of school facilities for all political activities, including activities relating to presidential politics. When a number of students were punished for distributing materials supporting Senator George McGovern's 1972 bid for the presidency, some of their parents took the issue to court. The parents won. The state high court refused to uphold the school's restrictive policy, stating that it violated the First Amendment rights of the entire student body.

Today, students may engage in a form of online leafleting. This would be a form of protected speech and beyond the purview of school officials to regulate unless they could somehow show that it was causing a substantial disruption at school.

If a school policy requires prior approval of materials to be distributed, how would a student go about obtaining that approval?

Ask a teacher or other school official for a copy of the school's approval procedures. These guidelines should always be in writing and should be precise. If they aren't clear enough or don't address important issues, the student should ask a school official for a more detailed explanation.

The approval procedures should require the school to decide on the student's materials right away. They shouldn't permit school officials to "sit" on a request for approval until the best time for the student to exercise his or her First Amendment rights has come and gone.

Approval procedures can be illegal when they are unclear or in any way tend to discourage students from exercising their constitutional rights.

If a school refuses to approve student material for distribution, what can be done?

The student should request a written copy of the school's decision, to test the reason for its refusal against the *Tinker* standard. Students always have a right to know why the school believes the rejected materials will seriously interfere with school activities or offend the rights of others.

If the student disagrees with the decision, he or she should consider appealing. Appeals are discussed later in this chapter.

STUDENT NEWSPAPERS

Can public school officials censor student material in school newspapers?

They can in certain situations. In a 1988 case, *Hazelwood School District v. Kuhlmeier*, the US Supreme Court created an exception to the *Tinker* rule for school-sponsored student newspapers and school-sponsored student speech in general.

The legal distinction between school-sponsored speech and student-initiated speech is very important. Many public school newspapers are considered school-sponsored, while the black armbands worn by the public school students in Des Moines, Iowa, were student-initiated speech.

In *Hazelwood*, student journalists produced a school newspaper called *The Spectrum* as part of a high school journalism class. Two of the articles in one issue of the school newspaper concerned the school's principal. These articles touched on the subjects of teen pregnancy and the effects of divorce on teens. The principal ordered those articles to be removed from the newspaper.

Three female students, who helped edit the newspaper, sued, contending that this amounted to unconstitutional censorship and a violation of their First Amendment rights. The students contended that they should prevail because, under the *Tinker* rule, their articles were in no way disruptive. The US Supreme Court ruled 5–3 in favor of the school and against the students.

The court applied a new rule for school-sponsored student speech. Under this rule, school officials can prohibit or censor school-sponsored student speech if they have a legitimate pedagogical, or educational, reason for doing so. This is a very broad standard that gives much deference to school officials.

Under the *Tinker* standard the articles probably would have been protected, because it would be difficult for school officials to show that the articles would cause any type of substantial disruption. However, the Supreme Court ruled that they could be censored because they conflicted with the school's overall educational goals.

Because of this decision, schools across the country now are able to censor articles in many school-sponsored student publications. They have the power to censor "poorly written, prejudiced or vulgar articles" and articles that are "not suited for immature audiences." They may censor material on teen sex and articles advocating the use of drugs or violence and other conduct inconsistent with the "shared values of a civilized social order." They may, according to the Supreme Court, even censor material that associates the school with "anything other than neutrality on political issues."

However, *Hazelwood* doesn't apply if the school-sponsored publication has consistently made a point of publishing student opinions—if the publication has been an "open or public forum" for student expression in the past. *Hazelwood* also shouldn't apply if student editors have control over the content of the newspaper.

Because of *Hazelwood*, school officials in Nevada were able to prevent a Planned Parenthood advertisement from running in a school-sponsored newspaper, even though the school had previously accepted ads from casinos, bars, churches, political candidates, and the US Army. The censorship was upheld because the school's decision was shown to be in keeping with sound academic concerns and because the newspaper had not been a public forum for student expression in the past.

What are anti-*Hazelwood* laws?

Anti-*Hazelwood* laws are state laws that provide greater protection to students than the US Supreme Court did in the *Hazelwood* decision. Under many of these state laws, students cannot be punished for their articles or other expression unless school officials can meet the *Tinker* standard of substantial disruption.

Fourteen states have such anti-*Hazelwood* or "New Voices" laws: Arkansas, California, Colorado, Illinois, Iowa, Kansas, Maryland, Massachusetts, Nevada, North Dakota, Oregon, Rhode Island, Vermont, and Washington. These laws grant public school students more free speech protection than the US Supreme Court provided in the *Hazelwood* decision.

The states' laws differ. California, for example, has a very broad law that applies to all public school students:

> Pupils of the public schools, including charter schools, shall have the right to exercise freedom of speech and of the press including, but not limited to, the use of bulletin boards, the distribution of printed materials or petitions, the wearing of buttons, badges, and other insignia, and the right of expression in official publications, whether or not the publications or other means of expression are supported financially by the school or by use of school facilities, except that expression shall be prohibited which is obscene, libelous, or slanderous. Also prohibited shall be material that so incites pupils as to create a clear and present danger of the commission of unlawful acts on school premises or the violation of lawful school regulations, or the substantial disruption of the orderly operation of the school.

Kansas's law, on the other hand, specifically addresses the free-expression rights of student journalists. It provides in its main part:

> The liberty of the press in student publications shall be protected.
>
> School employees may regulate the number, length, frequency, distribution and format of student publications.
>
> Material shall not be suppressed solely because it involves political or controversial subject matter.

Can schools prohibit students from distributing underground newspapers at school or require approval before passing them out?

In some cases, yes. Because "underground" newspapers and other materials aren't school sponsored, they aren't subject to *Hazelwood*'s restrictions. This means, in turn, that they retain greater First Amendment protections. School officials may forbid underground publications, but only if they have specific reasons for believing the contents will materially and substantially disrupt school activities, offend the rights of others, or aggravate a situation that is already tense. Courts are more likely to uphold a disciplinary action taken after the expression has occurred.

Do *Hazelwood*'s limits apply to forms of expression other than school newspapers?

Yes, the *Hazelwood* standard governs not just school-sponsored newspapers, but all school-sponsored speech. Courts have applied the *Hazelwood* standard to school plays, songs played by school bands, mascots, curricular matters, and other matters deemed school sponsored.

For example, the 2nd US Circuit Court of Appeals ruled in *Collins v. Pugh* (2020) that a public school college instructor did not violate the First Amendment rights of a student when she removed his blog post in relation to a class assignment in a virtual class. The appeals court reasoned that the student's "blog post bears the hallmarks of school sponsorship. It was made specifically in response to a class assignment, under the supervision of a college faculty member, and on a message board that was provided by the college offering the class." Even though this case involved a college student, the principle clearly applies to middle and high school students, where the authority of school officials is even greater.

CLOTHES AS A FORM OF EXPRESSION

Can public school officials prohibit students from wearing insignias, protest buttons, colors, T-shirts bearing special images, and other symbols of an idea?

It depends on the image and also the situation. In its *Tinker* decision involving black peace armbands, the US Supreme Court declared that forms of "symbolic speech" can't be banned merely because someone, such as a parent or teacher, thinks they are offensive. A symbol of expression only can be banned if school officials can predict that it will materially and substantially interfere with school, or if it is vulgar.

Wearing a protest button is a form of expression and therefore subject to the provisions of *Tinker*. Some courts have observed that if one student reacts disruptively to another's protest button, the school shouldn't impose an overall ban on buttons—the disruptive student should simply be disciplined. On the other hand, if students who wear buttons harass students who don't, school officials can probably prohibit them altogether.

Clothes are a separate issue. Dress codes that prohibit students from wearing clothes displaying biker and gang symbols and colors, beer ads, suggestive images, and vulgar language have been upheld by the courts upon proof that the clothing causes discipline problems. Schools have also been able to prohibit students from wearing T-shirts of particular sports teams, especially when students wear them to signify membership in a gang. Now school officials can forbid the wearing in school of T-shirts bearing such messages as "Drugs Suck!" and "See Dick Drink, See Dick Drive, See Dick Die, Don't be a Dick"—even if, as one court observed, "the message is laudable." In light of the *Tinker* case, these rules wouldn't violate the First Amendment.

Courts have also upheld school rules requiring students to wear underwear and regulating the length of slacks and skirts. Also, a school could legally require a student to cover up a tattoo. For more about laws relating to personal attire, see Chapter 6, "Your Personal Appearance."

Can school officials require students to wear uniforms?

Yes, many states have laws empowering school districts to require uniforms. School officials contend that uniforms create a level playing field across socioeconomic lines and help students focus more on learning than on what other students are wearing.

Several court decisions have upheld school uniform policies. These courts determined that the intent behind the adoption of school uniforms is not to suppress student expression but to create an environment that is more conducive to learning. Utah law provides that "a school may adopt a school uniform policy that requires students enrolled at that school to wear a designated school uniform during the school day." Arkansas has a similar law, which provides: "If a majority of the qualified electors of the district voting thereon at the election vote for the adoption of a school uniform policy, the school district board of directors shall prescribe appropriate school uniforms and implement the policy."

School uniform policies should provide exemptions for those with sincere religious objections and also provide financial assistance for those who cannot afford the school uniform clothing.

Can schools prohibit gang-related apparel?

Yes, and California's uniform law specifically mentions gang-related apparel as a reason for the adoption of uniforms for students. The law states: "The adoption of a schoolwide uniform policy is a reasonable way to provide some protection for students. A required uniform may protect students from being associated with any particular gang. Moreover, by requiring schoolwide uniforms teachers and administrators may not need to occupy as much of their time learning the subtleties of gang regalia." Tennessee has a similar law providing that school districts may adopt policies prohibiting students from wearing gang-related apparel. Generally speaking, school administrators have the ability to prohibit the wearing of certain clothing, if they can with reasonable certainty identify that the wearing of certain colors or symbols is clearly associated with gang affiliation.

However, this does not mean that students forfeit their free speech rights just because school officials have a policy against gang-related apparel. For example, a federal district court in Texas ruled that school officials violated the free speech rights of two students when they prohibited them from wearing rosary beads to school. School officials claimed that the rosary beads were gang-related symbols. However, the federal court in *Chalifoux v. New Caney Independent School District* (S.D. Tex. 1997) ruled that the students had a free speech right to wear the rosary beads, a protected form of religious expression.

Can public schools forbid students from wearing Confederate flag garb?

The answer depends on whether the school has a history of race-motivated violence or tension. Recall that the *Tinker* standard requires public school officials to show a reasonable forecast of substantial disruption before they can censor student expression. Many courts have determined that school officials could ban Confederate flag garb, noting incidents of disturbance.

For example, a federal appeals court ruled that public school officials in South Carolina could force a student to remove her "Southern Chicks," "Dixie Chicks," "Daddy's Little Redneck," and "Black Confederates" T-shirts, which depicted the Confederate flag, because of several incidents of race-based tension at school. The court ruled in *Hardwick v. Heyward* (4th Cir. 2013) that there was "ample evidence from which the school officials could reasonably forecast that all of these Confederate flag shirts would materially and substantially disrupt the work and discipline of the school."

On the other hand, another federal appeals court ruled in favor of two public school students in Kentucky who wore Hank Williams Jr. concert T-shirts, which depicted a Confederate flag, to school. The appeals court in *Castorina v. Madison County School Board* (6th Cir. 2001) ruled that school officials failed to show that the T-shirts would be disruptive. The court in that case reasoned that school officials had engaged in viewpoint discrimination by targeting the Confederate flag but allowing students to wear other racially charged symbols, such as Malcolm X T-shirts.

Can public schools legally forbid women students to wear pants or slacks on campus?

Such a rule would probably be found unreasonable and arbitrary because it couldn't be proved to promote safety, order, or discipline. But a school could legally enforce a rule prohibiting "too tight" pants.

Can a school prohibit a student from wearing clothing worn by the opposite sex?

The answer depends on the particular facts of the case and individual state law. In *Doe v. Yunits* (2000), the Massachusetts Superior Court determined that school officials could not prohibit a male student, who was diagnosed with gender identity disorder, from wearing female clothing to school. The court wrote that "a school should not be allowed to bar or discipline a student because of gender-identified dress but should be permitted to ban clothing that would be inappropriate if worn by any student."

SCHOOL LIBRARIES AND SCHOOL BOOKS

Can public school authorities legally ban books from school libraries because of the ideas in them?

No. In 1982, the US Supreme Court took up the issue of book banning in *Board of Education v. Pico*. In *Pico*, a school board attempted to remove certain books from a junior high school library that it claimed were "anti-American, anti-Christian, anti-Semitic and just plain filthy." Among the books it wanted to remove were *Soul on Ice* by Eldridge Cleaver, *Slaughterhouse-Five* by Kurt Vonnegut, *A Hero Ain't Nothing but a Sandwich* by Alice Childress, and *Black Boy* by Richard Wright—all modern American classics.

The Supreme Court ruled against the school board on First Amendment grounds. "The special characteristics of the school library," it stated, "make that environment especially appropriate for the recognition of the First Amendment." The court explained that public school officials could not remove books because they disagree with the ideas contained in the books. However, the court said that public school officials could remove books if they were "pervasively vulgar."

The court also cautioned that its ruling was narrow and only applied to the removal of books from school library shelves. The court emphasized that its decision did not apply to the acquisition of books by school libraries or curricular decisions.

Can a public school forbid younger students to check out a particular library book at school because school officials think the book is too "adult"?

The answer to this question is far from settled. It is true that there are certain materials suitable for older teens that may not be suitable for younger children. So, for example, a book acceptable at a high school may not be acceptable at a middle school and certainly not acceptable at an elementary school. But, it probably would be unconstitutional to limit a book only to seniors or to allow some high school students to view a book but not others.

The American Library Association's Bill of Rights prohibits libraries from discriminating on the basis of age when lending books. This document doesn't have the force of law, but it does assert an important First Amendment position.

Can school boards constitutionally restrict the types of reading material that teachers may use in class?

Yes. Although school boards can't have books removed from school libraries because of the ideas in them, they can prohibit the use of teaching materials that are considered vulgar or obscene by community standards.

In 1989, a federal appeals court in Florida in *Virgil v. School Board* upheld a high school's decision to remove a collection of essays from a school reading list because certain parents thought some of the essays were vulgar. The selections objected to were *Lysistrata* by the ancient Greek Aristophanes and "The Miller's Tale" from Chaucer's *Canterbury Tales*. Both selections contain references to sex. The appeals court applied the *Hazelwood* standard to curricular matters and determined that the removal of the books was reasonably related to legitimate educational concerns. The court explained: "In matters pertaining to the curriculum, educators have been accorded greater control over expression than they may enjoy in other spheres of activity."

The book censorship cases point to an odd distinction in the law, one that is troublesome to many. On the one hand, removing books from the shelves of a school library because someone disapproves of the ideas in them is a First Amendment violation. On the other hand, public school officials have legal authority to exercise almost total control over the curricula taught in their schools. Courts have permitted schools to bar even mildly offensive reading material from their lesson plans.

Are there laws that prohibit the teaching of racism and other controversial topics in public schools?

Several "red" states have passed laws that limit the teaching of what conservative critics call racially divisive topics. The laws are targeting so-called critical race theory, a theory that began in legal academic circles examining the pervasive impacts that race has had on law and society, both historically and today. Detractors assert that the teaching of critical race theory unfairly blames contemporary Americans for past racism in US society. Supporters of lesson plans that examine examples of institutionally or legally sanctioned racism argue that opponents of critical race theory are trying to "whitewash" American history.

Who is right? That is often in the idea of the beholder. North Dakota's law provides:

> A school district or public school may not include instruction relating to critical race theory in any portion of the district's required curriculum under sections 15.1-21-01 or 15.1-21-02, or any other curriculum offered by the district or school. For purposes of this section, "critical race theory" means the theory that racism is not merely the product of learned individual bias or prejudice, but that racism is systemically embedded in American society and the American legal system to facilitate racial inequality. The superintendent of public instruction may adopt rules to govern this section.

The American Civil Liberties Union (ACLU) has filed court challenges to anti-CRT laws in Oklahoma and New Hampshire at the time of this writing. There also is a challenge to

Florida's anti-CRT law. Still another group of plaintiffs, including several teachers, filed a challenge to a similar law in Tennessee in 2023. It remains to be seen whether these laws will stand or fall in America's courts.

FREE EXPRESSION AND MODERN TECHNOLOGIES

Are public schools legally required to train students on computers?

The answer depends in part on state law. Louisiana law mandates that public schools teach students safety instruction on both the Internet and cell phones. The law provides:

> The governing authority of each public elementary and secondary school shall provide age and grade appropriate classroom instruction regarding Internet and cell phone safety. Such instruction shall be integrated into an existing course of study and shall include but need not be limited to providing students with information on the following with respect to both cell phones and the Internet.

The instruction on safe use of the Internet must include safe usage of social networking sites.

Under the First Amendment, can teachers legally control access to certain types of computer images and information?

Yes, but this raises a thorny legal issue. Schools can prevent students from accessing information that is obscene or inappropriate by community standards—or try to. Even so, teachers, librarians, and lawyers are asking, "Wouldn't blocking be overbroad and therefore unconstitutional?" On the other hand, they also ask, "If teachers don't supervise access to obscene expression online, won't they provoke a public outcry? And won't they violate professional standards and school policies relating to the First Amendment?"

The US Supreme Court upheld a federal law known as the Children's Internet Protection Act (2000), which requires public libraries and public schools to install blocking technology on computers in order to receive federal funding for Internet hookups. The court's decision in *United States v. American Library Association* (2003) reasoned that public librarians often make content decisions in acquiring or not acquiring books. While the law was challenged by public libraries, it is clear that it is also constitutional as applied to public schools. This means that schools can legally use software filters to block access to selected online material. Often blocked are sites depicting or describing violence and profanity, nudity, sexual acts, racism and racist acts, satanism and cults, and drugs and drug cultures. But sometimes information that is harmless, and often valuable, is blocked unintentionally. For example, a student may be researching an article on the dangers in prison and come across an article on prison rape. A filtering product may block that article because it discusses rape. The problem is that the article may be quite useful and informative to the older teen writing a paper on dangers in prison.

Most school districts have specific written policies relating to online computer use. A teacher or school counselor should be able to guide any student through these policies.

When can school officials punish students for online speech created off campus?

The answer is not clear, because the law is not settled in this area. Some courts have determined that school officials can prohibit off-campus, online speech if there is a nexus, or connection, between the online speech and the school and they can satisfy the *Tinker* test by reasonably forecasting that the student speech would cause a substantial disruption at school. If there is no nexus, or connection, between the student online speech and activities at school, then the matter is beyond the control or jurisdiction of school officials.

If the matter involves threatening language, note that it may be a matter for law enforcement. If it involves purely inappropriate speech, that may be a matter of parental, rather than school, discipline.

Can school officials limit students' social media expression that is created off-campus?

It depends on the circumstances. The US Supreme Court finally addressed this issue in the case *Mahanoy Area School District v. B.L.* (2021). The case involved a high school student named Brandi Levy (identified in court papers as "B.L.") who was upset that she, as a member of the junior varsity cheerleading squad, did not make the varsity cheerleading squad. So, on the weekend, she and a friend went to a local convenience store where Ms. Levy posted to Snapchat a profane message that featured the "f-word" several times.

School officials learned of the profane social media post and suspended Levy from the junior varsity cheerleading squad for a year. Levy and her parents sued, alleging a violation of her First Amendment free speech rights.

The Supreme Court ultimately ruled in her favor, reasoning that her social media expression created off-campus on the weekend warranted parental discipline, not school discipline. The court explained that much student social media expression is off-limits for public school officials for three reasons:

(1) "First, a school, in relation to off-campus speech, will rarely stand in loco parentis." This means that much social media off-campus speech is for parents to regulate more so than school officials.

(2) "Second, from the student speaker's perspective, regulations of off-campus speech, when coupled with regulations of on-campus speech, include all the speech a student utters during the full 24-hour day. That means courts must be more skeptical of a school's efforts to regulate off-campus speech, for doing so may mean the student cannot engage in that kind of speech at all."

(3) "Third, the school itself has an interest in protecting a student's unpopular expression, especially when the expression takes place off campus. America's public schools are the nurseries of democracy."

However, the court also emphasized that public school officials retain authority over some types of student social media speech, including "serious or severe bullying or harassment targeting particular individuals; threats aimed at teachers or other students; the failure to follow rules concerning lessons, the writing of papers, the use of computers, or participation in other online school activities; and breaches of school security devices, including material maintained within school computers."

Are true threats protected by the First Amendment?

No, the US Supreme Court explained in *Watts v. United States* (1969) that true threats must be distinguished from constitutionally protected speech. The case involved an older teenager—nineteen-year-old Robert Watts—who was at an antiwar rally in Washington, DC, protesting the Vietnam conflict. Watts, who was African American, said out loud that if he got drafted the first person he would be in the scope of his rifle was "L.B.J."—the initials for President Lyndon Baines Johnson.

Watts had no real intent to harm President Johnson. He was just mad about the draft and also the way the draft was racially disproportionate against African Americans. Unfortunately, for Watts a federal agent heard his comments and he got prosecuted under a federal law that prohibits threats against the president.

The US Supreme Court reversed his conviction, reasoning that Watts had engaged more in crude political hyperbole rather than a true threat. However, the court's ruling stands for the principle that true threats are an unprotected category of speech.

The Supreme Court later explained in a case out of Virginia involving the burning of crosses:

> True threats encompass those statements where the speaker means to communicate a serious expression of an intent to commit an act of unlawful violence to a particular individual or group of individuals. The speaker need not actually intend to carry out the threat. Rather, a prohibition on true threats "protect[s] individuals from the fear of violence" and "from the disruption that fear engenders," in addition to protecting people "from the possibility that the threatened violence will occur."

In June 2023, the Supreme Court also clarified in *Counterman v. Colorado* that in order to convict an individual of uttering a true threat, the prosecutors must show that the individual at the very least had some subjective intent that his statement would be perceived as threatening.

The issue of true threats arises in the public school context, particularly in the last twenty-five years due to infamous mass shootings at schools including Columbine High School in Littleton, Colorado (1999); Sandy Hook Elementary School in Parkland, Connecticut (2012); and Marjory Stoneman High School in Parkland, Florida (2018). School officials have a duty to protect students from violence, so students who make threatening comments are subject to suspension, expulsion, and possibly even arrest.

What about violent-themed student writing—can that constitute a true threat?

It depends upon context. Some violent-themed student writing may rise to the level of a true threat. However, much violent-themed writing does not constitute a true threat. The California Supreme Court ruled in *In re George T.* (2004) that a student's dark poetry did not rise to the level of a true threat. The court emphasized that just because a piece of writing has dark themes does not mean that the student is making a true threat.

Can a school legally prohibit cell phones in school, even if the parents want their children to carry them?

Yes. Several states have laws that specifically empower school officials to prohibit the use of cell phones or pagers by students.

What is cyberbullying?

Cyberbullying refers to an unlawful course of action based on online harassment of one person by others that causes physical or emotional harm to the victim. Many states either have general criminal laws prohibiting cyberbullying or have passed laws ordering school districts to amend their antibullying codes to include cyberbullying.

For example, Arkansas law (A.C.A § 5-71-217(b)) defines cyberbullying as follows:

> A person commits the offense of cyberbullying if:
>
> 1. He or she transmits, sends, or posts a communication by electronic means with the purpose to frighten, coerce, intimidate, threaten, abuse, or harass, another person; and
> 2. The transmission was in furtherance of severe, repeated, or hostile behavior toward the other person.

Florida has a more comprehensive definition of cyberbullying that relates directly to bullying at any public K–12 school. This law (Fla. Stat. § 1006. 147(3)(b)) provides the following:

> "Cyberbullying" means bullying through the use of technology or any electronic communication, which includes, but is not limited to, any transfer of signs, signals, writing, images, sounds, data, or intelligence of any nature transmitted in whole or in part by a wire, radio, electromagnetic system, photoelectronic system, or photooptical system, including, but not limited to, electronic mail, Internet communications, instant messages, or facsimile communications. Cyberbullying includes the creation of a webpage or weblog in which the creator assumes the identity of another person, or the knowing impersonation of another person as the author of posted content or messages, if the creation or impersonation creates any of the conditions enumerated in the definition of bullying. Cyberbullying also includes the distribution by electronic means of a communication to more than one person or the posting of material on an

electronic medium that may be accessed by one or more persons, if the distribution or posting creates any of the conditions enumerated in the definition of bullying.

Some states have laws requiring school districts to provide training for school employees on Internet safety issues, including cyberbullying.

FREEDOM OF ASSEMBLY

Congress shall make no law . . . abridging the right of the people peaceably to assemble.

—First Amendment, US Constitution

Can a public school prevent students from forming a club at school that promotes an unpopular point of view?

Generally, no. Public secondary schools that receive any federal funding are subject to a 1984 federal law known as the Equal Access Act. This law prohibits schools from discriminating against noncurricular student groups based on the "religious, political, philosophical or other content of the speech at such meetings." This law means that school officials generally may not prohibit Bible clubs or gay and lesbian clubs.

This does not mean that public school officials must tolerate any type of group. For example, school officials could prohibit a group espousing racial hatred or violence from meeting on school grounds. The reason is that the Equal Access Act provides that student groups' meetings must not "materially and substantially interfere with the orderly conduct of educational activities within the school."

Can public school officials legally stop sit-ins, walkouts, and protest marches on school property?

It depends on the situation. Demonstrations raise free speech issues and also free assembly issues, and this makes them subject to the guidelines in the *Tinker* case, discussed previously in this chapter. This question assumed nationwide prominence in 2018 when students at Marjory Stoneman High School in Parkland, Florida, organized a march for gun control after a horrific mass shooting at their school in which seventeen people (fourteen students and three staff members) were murdered and another seventeen injured. Students across the country walked out of school in solidarity with the Parkland students' effort to force the nation to confront gun violence and get more serious about gun control.

Demonstrations and walkouts can indeed disrupt school work and school discipline, and when they do, school authorities can and should intervene and may legally suspend students for participating. However, some courts have said that students should be given less punishment for participating in nonviolent demonstrations, or shouldn't be punished at all, given the importance of free speech in our society.

Sit-ins aren't necessarily illegal because they occur inside school, but any demonstration has a better chance of coming within the First Amendment's right to assemble peaceably if it occurs outdoors and before or after school. School officials have the right to stop protests that block halls or make students miss class and may discipline students who damage property or cause injuries. Students may be arrested if a situation becomes so serious that property is damaged or laws are broken. But a school violates the Constitution if it enforces a rule banning demonstrations altogether.

RELIGION AND SCHOOL PRAYER

Congress shall make no law respecting an establishment of religion, or prohibiting the free exercise thereof.

—The religious liberty clauses of the First Amendment, US Constitution

What are the religious liberty clauses of the First Amendment?

There are two religious liberty clauses of the First Amendment: (1) the establishment clause and (2) the free exercise clause. The establishment clause comprises the first ten words of the First Amendment: "Congress shall make no law respecting an establishment of religion." The free exercise clause adds "or prohibiting the free exercise thereof."

The establishment clause is the part of the First Amendment that provides for separation between church and state. Many disagree about exactly how much separation there should be between religion and government. The free exercise clause is the part of the First Amendment that gives individuals the right to believe and practice whatever religious faith they wish, or none at all. It provides absolute protection for religious belief but not total protection for religious-based conduct. For example, religious practices that threaten a strong government, health, safety, or welfare interests may be prohibited.

How does a court determine whether there has been a violation of the establishment clause?

Courts use several different tests to evaluate whether governmental action violates the establishment clause. The US Supreme Court articulated perhaps the leading test in *Lemon v. Kurtzman* (1971), called the "Lemon test." Under the Lemon test, government officials must have a secular purpose for the law, the governmental law must not have a primary effect that advances or denigrates religion, and the law must not excessively entangle religion with government. These parts of the Lemon test are called the purpose, effects, and entanglement prongs. Sometimes the entanglement prong is folded into the effects prong.

Still other courts will employ a different test, first proposed by Justice Sandra Day O'Connor in *Lynch v. Donnelly* (1984), a case involving the display of a religious symbol surrounded by a number of secular Christmas symbols. O'Connor's endorsement test asks whether a reasonable observer, familiar with the history and context of the governmental law or policy, would believe that the government is endorsing or promoting religion. Other courts sometimes use other tests, including the "coercion test" or a "history and tradition" analysis. The establishment clause is one of the most difficult areas of constitutional law, in part because there are so many different legal tests.

However, in 2022, the US Supreme Court overruled the Lemon test in *Kennedy v. Bremerton School District*, a case involving a high school football coach who was disciplined for praying at the 50-yard line at the conclusion of football games. The court explained that "shortcomings [associated with the Lemon test] became so 'apparent' that this Court long ago abandoned Lemon and its endorsement test offshoot." Instead, the court instructed that "historical practices and understandings" should be the primary focus. Thus, if a practice has been used by history or tradition, it likely does not violate the Establishment Clause. In the *Kennedy* decision, the court held that the coach had a First Amendment right to engage in silent prayer as a private act of religious expression that took place at the conclusion of the games.

Many scholars regard this as a momentous change in the law and associated issues of church–state separation, but it remains to be seen just exactly how this will impact religious expression in schools in the years ahead.

Can public school teachers lead students in prayer?

No. The US Supreme Court determined in the early 1960s that teacher-led prayer in public schools violated the establishment clause. The court reasoned in *Engel v. Vitale* (1962) and *Abington School District v. Schempp* (1963) that teacher-led prayer or teacher-led Bible readings would place coercive pressure on religious minorities. In *Engel*, a Jewish man named Steven Engel and other parents challenged a New York policy that required public school students to recite a twenty-word nondenominational prayer. Mr. Engel believed that school officials should not be dictating a one-size-fits-all prayer to students of different religious faiths. The majority of the Supreme Court agreed with him and invalidated the practice. The *Schempp* case involved a Pennsylvania law that required public school teachers to recite ten Bible verses daily to their students. The court ruled that this policy had a clearly impermissible purpose of the state promoting religion.

Can public schools prevent students from praying during school hours?

Nobody can prevent anybody from praying. There is a misconception that public schools are complete religion-free zones. The First Amendment's establishment clause prohibits school-led prayer, but does not prevent students from praying by themselves.

Can schools set aside a time for students to pray or observe a moment of silence?

It depends. Under the establishment clause of the First Amendment (shown above), public schools can't take actions that appear to advance or promote religion. For this reason, giving students a special time during the day to pray or observe a moment of prayerful silence is unconstitutional if the clear purpose is to restore school-sponsored prayer or even to encourage students to pray. The US Supreme Court ruled in *Wallace v. Jaffree* (1985) that an Alabama moment of silence law violated the establishment clause, because the legislative history of the law clarified that legislators introduced the measure to bring prayer back into the public schools.

On the other hand, public schools may allow students a moment of silence. This gives students the chance to do what they want during that moment. They may pray or quietly reflect on issues confronting them that day. For example, a federal appeals court upheld a Georgia law known as the Moment of Quiet Reflection in Schools Act (1994). The court ruled in *Bown v. Gwinnett County School District* (11th Cir. 1997) that "the language of the statute as enacted reveals a clearly secular legislative purpose: to provide students with a moment of quiet reflection to think about the upcoming day." Another federal appeals court upheld a similar Texas law in *Croft v. Governor of Texas* (5th Cir. 2009).

Is it illegal for an instructor to teach about religion in a public school?

No. It is illegal for an instructor to *promote* prayer or religion. Discussing prayer and religion in the framework of a school subject such as social studies is acceptable and, in the opinion of many, quite appropriate.

Can schools release students from school during the day for religion classes?

Yes, public schools may "accommodate" religion by letting students leave school for religious instruction. According to the courts, these "release-time" programs don't advance religion illegally even though they do help students practice their faith.

Schools may also release students from sex education classes for religious reasons, but only if there are other ways (such as a health class) to satisfy the overall class requirements.

Why don't rules limiting religion in public schools violate the First Amendment right to the free exercise of religion?

Because in public schools the rule against government involvement in religion overrides the right of young people to exercise the religion of their choice. (The First Amendment, including the free exercise clause, is shown above.) To permit a student or teacher to practice his or her religion openly in public school would infringe on the personal rights of others.

The tension between these two rights has arisen when teachers have tried to promote their religious beliefs in class. For example, a public school teacher in Pennsylvania was dismissed for opening class with the Lord's Prayer and a Bible story. The teacher took the issue to court, arguing that he was dismissed because he had exercised his rights under the free exercise clause. The court upheld the teacher's dismissal, saying his right to practice his religion didn't entitle him to promote his personal beliefs in class.

If evolution is taught in a public high school, shouldn't "creation science" also be taught?

The US Supreme Court has ruled "no" on this issue in *Edwards v. Aguillard* (1987), which held that a Louisiana law requiring "equal time" for evolution and creation science was unconstitutional. The court noted that evolution has been a fully accepted *scientific* theory for decades. For a public school to allow equal time for creation science would be an instance of promoting a religious theory—and a violation of the establishment clause.

May student religious groups use public school facilities for meetings?

Yes, under certain conditions. In the past, student religious groups weren't allowed to meet in public schools—the school would be giving the appearance of advancing religion. But under the federal Equal Access Act of 1984, if a public school permits any student group to meet after hours on matters outside the regular curriculum, it can't forbid any other group from forming for religious, political, or philosophical reasons. This means that if a school permits any non-curriculum-related groups to use its meeting rooms, it can't forbid a religious group to do the same. The meetings must be voluntary, initiated by students, held during nonschool hours, and not sponsored or controlled by school personnel.

Would school-sponsored prayer at a public school graduation ceremony violate the establishment clause?

Yes. The US Supreme Court surprised many in 1992 by ruling 5–4 in *Lee v. Weisman* that a public middle school in Rhode Island violated the establishment clause when it arranged for a rabbi to give a short prayer at a high school graduation. In court, the school argued that the students hadn't been forced to participate in a religious event, because they could have skipped the ceremony. It also argued that it had sincerely attempted to come up with a nonsectarian prayer.

The Supreme Court rejected these arguments, saying that because each graduate was undoubtedly going to attend graduation, each was also required to participate in the prayer. The court deemed the students to be a captive audience to hear the prayer. The school therefore had violated the establishment clause.

Is it legal to broadcast prayers over the loudspeakers at public school athletic events?

The US Supreme Court ruled in *Santa Fe Independent School District v. Doe* (2000) that a Texas high school's practice of announcing prayers over the loudspeaker violated the establishment clause. The school district contended that the practice was constitutional because the students had voted on the prayer practice. However, the Supreme Court ruled 6–3 against the school district, saying that announcing prayers over the loudspeaker involved the school too much and sent a message that the school was endorsing or promoting religion.

Can students stay out of public school on religious holidays without risking punishment?

Yes, at least with respect to important holidays of major religions.

Can a student be punished for refusing to salute the American flag or recite the Pledge of Allegiance at school?

No, because refusing to salute the flag or recite the Pledge of Allegiance is a form of symbolic speech. The US Supreme Court proclaimed this in its famous ruling in *West Virginia Board of Education v. Barnette* (1943). When two Jehovah's Witness sisters refused to stand and salute the flag, school officials expelled them on the basis of a West Virginia law that not only called for the students' expulsion, but also provided that their parents could be fined and even spend time in jail.

The court invalidated the West Virginia law, reasoning that it invaded the students' individual religious liberties. In famous language, Justice Robert Jackson wrote that "if there is any fixed star in our constitutional constellation, it is that no official high or petty shall prescribe what shall be orthodox in matters of politics, nationalism, [or] religion." The *Barnette* ruling means that school officials must provide an opt-out for students who do not wish to participate in the Pledge of Allegiance.

Some states still have laws that require public school students to stand and recite the Pledge of Allegiance. However, because of the *Barnette* ruling many years ago, schools must give an opt-out to students who have sincere religious or philosophical objections to reciting the pledge.

DISCIPLINE AND DUE PROCESS

> *No State shall . . . deprive any person of life, liberty, or property, without due process of law.*
>
> —Fourteenth Amendment, US Constitution

What is "due process of law"?

Due process of law, or simply "due process," is the overall method by which a society decides whether someone's legal rights should be taken away. There are two types of due process, substantive and procedural. Substantive due process requires that a law, regulation, or policy must be reasonable and not arbitrary. In other words, the law must have some substance to it and not be arbitrary. Procedural due process requires that before the government may infringe on our "life, liberty, or property" interests, it must provide a fair procedure. This normally means that the government must provide some type of notice and some type of hearing.

This means that a public body can't punish someone or take away his or her rights without following specific procedures to determine whether the "taking" would be fair. The procedures almost always involve a hearing to give the "accused" a right to deny or defend his or her actions and hear the "accuser's" version of what happened. The clearest example of due process is a trial to determine whether a person has committed a crime and whether a particular form of punishment should be imposed.

Do students have an absolute right to be advised of their school's disciplinary rules?

Yes. The essence of due process is fundamental fairness. It is not fair for people to be punished without knowing the rules that they must obey. Most school districts require that their schools' disciplinary rules be written out and distributed to each student at the beginning of the school year. This makes sense, because students naturally have a better chance of knowing when they've broken a school rule if they have had an opportunity to read it. But whether or not a public school has written rules, school officials can't punish a student for breaking a school rule if the student had no reason to know it existed.

Does a school have to advise students of the punishment for violating a particular rule?

It depends on the offense. When it comes to serious violations, schools need to spell out in advance the types of punishment a student can receive. For less serious violations, schools don't have to specify the range of possible punishments.

Is a student entitled to a school hearing before being punished?

It depends on the seriousness of the offense. If a student faces suspension or other serious form of discipline, he or she is always entitled to "due process of law." This is an important concept—every adult and adolescent should know what it means.

What does due process mean in the high school setting?

It means that a student can't be seriously punished without being afforded at least an informal hearing to determine the offense and the surrounding circumstances. The amount of due process depends on the seriousness of the offense and therefore the seriousness of the possible punishment.

The US Supreme Court established in *Goss v. Lopez* (1975) that students have due process rights. In this landmark case, a number of students were suspended for demonstrating, participating in a fight, or engaging in similar misconduct at their public high school in Ohio. Their student records were unclear as to why the school took action against them, and none was given a due process hearing to either deny or explain his or her participation.

The Supreme Court ruled that the due process clause of the Fourteenth Amendment required the school to advise each student in advance that he or she was being suspended. Also, it ruled that the school should have advised each student of the facts supporting his or her suspension and should have provided each at least an informal hearing, with adequate prior notice, to either deny or defend the charges.

When does due process apply to students?

It applies whenever a student is accused of an act that could result in suspension, expulsion, a lowered grade, or other serious disciplinary measure. Due process doesn't mean the student will be found innocent. It simply means that procedures are in place and are used to ensure that the school treats its students fairly.

Sometimes states or school districts afford students more due process than is guaranteed under the Constitution. When this happens, the school must follow the state or school district's broader procedures.

What is the difference between a suspension and an expulsion?

The difference is the length of punishment. A suspension usually means that a student is temporarily removed and then can return to school. An expulsion means that the student has been expelled or removed from school for a long time and may have to meet certain obligations to be readmitted. Although school districts or individual schools establish their own time frames for suspensions and expulsions, a short-term suspension usually lasts up to ten days. A long-term suspension usually lasts longer and may extend as long as two semesters.

In an expulsion the student normally is dismissed from school permanently. Students can be expelled for being violent at school, damaging or stealing either school property or the property of another student, or having drugs or weapons on campus.

How does due process apply to expulsions?

Formal due process procedures are required for an expulsion. A student who faces the prospect of being expelled should receive adequate advance notice of the charges and adequate notice of the time, place, and nature of the hearing. The student is entitled to a fair hearing before an impartial person and may be represented at the hearing by an adult, and in some states by an attorney.

The student or adult representative should be entitled to introduce evidence, cross-examine the school's witnesses, and receive a written record of the school's decision. The decision always should describe the evidence it relied on in deciding to expel.

These procedures apply to all serious offenses. They should also apply if the school has proposed a long-term suspension.

What due process guarantees apply to short-term suspensions?

Short-term suspensions require less due process protection than expulsions and long-term suspensions. A student who faces a short-term suspension has a right to oral notice of the offense, an explanation of the evidence the decision maker is relying on, and a chance to disprove the charges. Advance notice of the school's intent to impose a short-term suspension can be shorter than for situations that could result in expulsion or long-term suspension. Cross-examination of witnesses usually isn't allowed, and the student normally can't be represented by a lawyer.

What is zero tolerance?

Zero tolerance refers to a get-tough approach to discipline in public schools for certain offenses, usually those involving weapons or violence. Zero tolerance means that if a student commits a particular offense, he or she is punished severely, even if there are extenuating circumstances. Critics believe that at least some zero-tolerance policies do not provide students with their due process rights. Other critics refer to zero tolerance as zero judgment.

In one extreme (and incredible) situation in 1999, an Ohio third grader actually received a two-day suspension for writing and placing an allegedly threatening message inside a fortune cookie. The youth was a fan of martial arts videos. The fortune read, "You will die an honorable death." Not only was the student represented by counsel at his suspension hearing, but the American Civil Liberties Union in Ohio took the case. Ultimately the decision was reversed. Many believe that the initial suspension probably was influenced by the mass shooting that had occurred earlier that year at Columbine High School in Littleton, Colorado.

If a student is expelled from high school, is he or she out "forever"?

Not usually. Most school districts have an "alternate education program" for expelled students, which may simply mean that the student is sent to another school. Courts rarely uphold the expulsion of a student who is too young to legally quit school.

Do students have due process rights whenever they get in trouble at school?

No. Due process is for serious school violations that may have serious consequences—for violations that could deprive a student of a valuable right and be a blot on his or her record. But as stated, a school board may permit a student to be heard on a disciplinary matter that federal or state law doesn't consider serious enough for due process. School authorities should always advise students of the types of offenses meriting due process, in addition to those that could result in a suspension or expulsion.

How can a student find out about the types of offenses meriting due process? How can a student find out about the school's due process procedures?

Most high schools give each student a handbook explaining the school district's disciplinary rules and its due process procedures. If no such handbook exists, the student should ask a teacher or school administrator for more information on the subject.

Can a student be suspended or otherwise disciplined for an off-campus activity?

Only if the student's actions pose a serious danger to other students, or the student's acts have a direct bearing on the well-being of the school. For example, a serious criminal charge, including a drug-related offense, can be the basis for a suspension. Because a suspension means that the student might be deprived of a valuable right, punishment for an off-campus activity can only occur after the student has been afforded a full due process hearing.

This area is contentious, particularly when it comes to cyberbullying or controversial online speech by students. Some student-speech advocates insist that much off-campus, online speech is not a matter for school discipline. However, school officials often assert that off-campus, online speech can have profound impact on school atmosphere and educational efforts, giving them both a right and responsibility to intervene in certain cases.

If a student is found guilty of a school offense, can the school impose any punishment it wants?

No. Courts will overturn a form of punishment that is too severe—punishment that is "arbitrary, capricious or oppressive." But schools do have extensive power when it comes to meting out punishment.

If a student is arrested, can he or she be suspended or expelled from school before trial?

Not for that reason alone. As Chapter 12 explains, an arrest is simply a police action based on an officer's reasoned belief that a person has committed a crime or is in the process of committing one. But an act resulting in a student's arrest can also be a school violation, and when this happens, the school can hold its own due process hearing on the offense.

An important concept applies here. The amount of evidence needed to discipline a student for a school offense may be less than the amount needed to convict the student for the same offense in juvenile court. As a matter of constitutional law, to convict and sentence a person for committing a crime, the state must prove its charges "beyond a reasonable doubt." But as in a noncriminal or "civil" case, the school only needs to prove it is "more likely than not" that the student violated a certain school rule to impose discipline. Its "burden of proof" is less weighty because the school is only disciplining the student for breaking an internal rule, not a public law.

If the school meets its burden of proof at the school hearing, it can punish the student before his or her courtroom trial. Also, the court may take the school's decision into account in reaching its own decision.

The student should be represented by a lawyer at both the disciplinary hearing and the trial.

Students can't be punished at school for the criminal acts of their parents, relatives, or friends.

If a student gets in serious trouble at school, is he or she entitled to receive the *Miranda* warnings from a school official?

No. Only the police give *Miranda* warnings. As explained in Chapter 12, the *Miranda* warnings advise individuals being arrested that they have a right to remain silent, that anything they say to the police may be used against them, and that they are entitled to the services of an attorney.

School officials aren't required to give the *Miranda* warnings, because they don't have the legal power to arrest. For more about arrests and *Miranda*, see Chapter 12, "Teens and Crime."

Can a student's grades be lowered because of particularly bad conduct?

Not in most schools, although in many, grades can be lowered for too many missed classes. Schools generally see disruptive behavior such as interfering with teaching activities and harassing classmates as behavior that needs to be addressed through methods other than grading, which is supposed to measure knowledge rather than behavior.

Without a due process hearing, can a student be forbidden to participate in extracurricular activities as punishment for a school offense?

No. The right to participate in extracurricular activities is valuable enough to merit a due process hearing.

Can a student appeal a disciplinary decision?

Yes, provided the offense is significant enough to trigger due process protections. For example, a school's decision to suspend or expel a student can always be appealed.

How do appeals work?

A student's appeal (or an appeal by the student's parents) usually goes directly to the principal. It must be in writing. The principal must conduct an appeal hearing within a short time (usually within five school days) and is required to rule on the appeal shortly after the hearing. That decision can then be appealed to the school superintendent, who must also provide a hearing and make a decision in a prescribed number of days.

If the "appellant," the person appealing an adverse decision, is dissatisfied with the decision of the superintendent, an appeal can be taken to the school board. An appeals hearing before the school board is always more formal.

If the appellant receives an "adverse" decision at every stage of the hearing process, the entire matter can be taken to federal or state court.

Any student who receives an adverse decision from the school principal should request written procedures for appealing. At every stage of the appeals process, the school's decision should be in writing.

CORPORAL PUNISHMENT

What is corporal punishment?

Corporal punishment is any type of punishment directed toward a person's body. Striking a student by slapping or paddling is the most obvious example.

Do school officials have a legal right to inflict corporal punishment on students?

The US Constitution doesn't forbid corporal punishment in public schools. The US Supreme Court ruled in *Ingraham v. Wright* (1977) that the use of corporal punishment by public school officials at Florida middle schools did not constitute "cruel and unusual punishment" within the meaning of the Eighth Amendment of the US Constitution. The court determined that "the pertinent constitutional question is whether the imposition [of corporal punishment] is consonant with the requirements of due process." The court applied what it deemed to be the controlling principle from the common law (case law) through the years: school officials may use corporal punishment only as it is "reasonably necessary for the proper education and discipline of the child."

Corporal punishment is prohibited in twenty-seven states as of 2023. For example, Delaware law prohibits school officials from using corporal punishment, which it defines as the "intentional infliction of physical pain which is used as a means of discipline," including paddling and slapping.

However, corporal punishment is either expressly allowed or not prohibited in twenty-three (23) states. Without a provision ruling corporal punishment out, a school district may approve its use. The laws of some states actually authorize it. For example, Arkansas law provides that school officials are entitled to immunity from civil claims for the use of corporal punishment, if school officials properly comply with school policies on its use.

Students usually aren't entitled to a due process hearing before corporal punishment is inflicted. The US Supreme Court has stated that a school suspension is more serious than corporal punishment, which is why a student is entitled to due process before being suspended but not before receiving bodily punishment.

Even so, a student's constitutional due process rights were violated in one case in which his injuries resulted in ten days' hospitalization, and in another case in which a student was injured after a teacher tied him to a desk. In both cases the school intruded on the students' personal privacy to the extent of committing a "taking" without due process of law.

Schools should make every attempt to rule out corporal punishment as a way to deal with problems. In fact, the US Secretary of Education wrote to state officials in March 2023, stating: "if the use of corporal punishment is permitted or practiced in schools and educational settings within your state or district, I urge you to move swiftly toward condemning and eliminating it."

Even in those jurisdictions that still allow corporal punishment, teachers first should exhaust all other means of disciplining a student. If corporal punishment is used, it should be witnessed by a second school official. In addition, parents should receive a written explanation of the nature of the punishment and why it was used.

Force can be used to break up fights on school grounds and to prevent property damage, but only to an appropriate degree.

How does a court determine if corporal punishment in schools crosses the line and becomes unconstitutional?

One federal appeals court (*Gottlieb v. Laurel Highlands School District*, 3rd Cir. 2001) evaluated the issue by asking the following four questions:

- Was there a pedagogical justification for the use of force?
- Was the force utilized excessive to meet the legitimate objective in this situation?

- Was the force applied in a good faith effort to maintain or restore discipline, or maliciously and sadistically for the very purpose of causing harm?
- Was there a serious injury?

SCHOOL SEARCHES

The right of the people to be secure in their persons, houses, papers, and effects, against unreasonable searches and seizures, shall not be violated, and no Warrants shall issue, but upon probable cause, supported by Oath or affirmation, and particularly describing the place to be searched, and the persons or things to be seized.

—Fourth Amendment, US Constitution

Do public school authorities have the legal right to search a student's clothing, backpack, gym bag, or purse?

In most circumstances, yes, although such searches *do* intrude on students' privacy. To search a student legally, two requirements must be met. First, there must be reasonable grounds for suspecting the search will turn up evidence that the student broke the law or a school rule. Second, the search can't be too broad in its scope and can't intrude on the student's privacy more than is necessary to carry out the purpose of the search.

This is a constitutional test, established in 1985 in the Supreme Court case *New Jersey v. T.L.O.* In this decision the Supreme Court did not require public school officials to have "probable cause" before conducting a search of a student. Instead, the court required a "reasonableness" test. Under this two-part test, (1) the search must be justified at its inception, or beginning, and (2) the search must be reasonably related in scope to the circumstances that justified the search in the first place. If the search is deemed unreasonable and too intrusive, it violates the Fourth Amendment's prohibition against "unreasonable searches and seizures." In the *T.L.O.* case, a female student's purse was searched after she was caught smoking in a restroom. As the principal was removing a pack of cigarettes from her purse, he saw a package of rolling papers. He searched further and found some marijuana, a pipe, some empty plastic bags, a number of dollar bills, a list of students who apparently owed the student money, and two letters suggesting that she might be selling drugs.

The Supreme Court ruled that because the school had "reasonable suspicion," the student's privacy rights hadn't been violated. This made the search legal. It stated that although students do have privacy rights, these rights must be balanced against the need of their schools to maintain a safe place for learning. According to the Supreme Court, this balance is achieved by applying a "reasonableness" standard to school searches.

Can school officials legally search lockers and desks?

Yes. Students are said to share control over their lockers and desks with school officials, so their privacy rights with respect to them are limited. In some states, lockers and desks may be searched at any time and for any reason, on the theory that the students' rights have been waived. Students in these states have no privacy rights whatsoever in desks and lockers.

Can school officials conduct strip searches?

It depends on the underlying circumstances and how intrusive the search is. The US Supreme Court ruled in *Safford Unified School District v. Redding* (2009) that public school officials in Arizona violated the Fourth Amendment rights of a middle school student when they strip searched her for allegedly possessing ibuprofen pills. The court noted that "the content of the suspicion failed to match the degree of intrusion." The court's ruling, however, does not mean that all strip searches are per se unconstitutional. Under certain circumstances, strip searches are constitutional. However, school officials must have a really compelling need to conduct a strip search. Otherwise, school officials will violate a student's constitutional rights. Body searches should be left to the police. For more about probable cause, see Chapter 12, "Teens and Crime."

Are mass searches of students legal?

No, because under the reasonable suspicion test, the school's suspicion must always relate to a particular individual. In other words, the Fourth Amendment generally requires individualized suspicion. In one case, school authorities did not have individual suspicion and therefore made unreasonable searches violating the search and seizure clause when they inspected each student's luggage as a condition of going on a field trip. In another case, strip searches of all members of a class to discover who stole $3.00 were also deemed illegal.

Can public school officials search the contents of a student's cell phone?

There is a difference of opinion on the circumstances under which public school officials can search a student's cell phone. Some courts hold that the standard from *New Jersey v. T.L.O.* (1985) controls in these instances. This standard asks whether the search of the cell phone was reasonable under the particular circumstances. More specifically, this standard says whether a search involving students is reasonable depends on both (1) whether the action was justified at its inception, and (2) whether the search as actually conducted was reasonably related in scope to the circumstances which justified the initial need to search in the first place.

Others argue that public school officials need a search warrant before they can search through a student's phone. These courts follow the Supreme Court's decision in *Riley v. California* (2014) in which the Supreme Court held that the police generally need a warrant before they can look through someone's phone.

Ultimately, the US Supreme Court may have to decide which standard applies in public schools with regard to searches of student cell phones—the flexible, deferential-to-school officials standard in *New Jersey v. T.L.O.* or the standard the court applied to an adult criminal defendant in *Riley v. California*.

Can public school officials look through a student's phone and force a student to unlock their social media accounts?

No, it is unlikely that public school officials can force public school students to unlock their private accounts by accessing their cell phones. Public school officials may be able to seize a phone temporarily if a student is disrupting class by talking on their phone. But, they cannot rummage through the contents of the student's phone and then force students to provide passwords to private accounts.

A federal district court in Minnesota reasoned in *R.S. v. Minnewaska Area School Dist.* (2012) that a student's Fourth Amendment rights were violated when school officials took his phone and forced him to disclose his private passwords to his Facebook account. The court reasoned that the student had a "reasonable expectation of privacy to her private Facebook information and messages."

Can a school require the entire student body or an entire class to take blood or urine tests to check for drug use?

No. Making students submit to urine or blood tests without individual suspicion puts all of their privacy rights in jeopardy. In a 1985 case, a New Jersey high school made each student submit to a urine test for twenty-six different drugs. When the matter went to court on a Fourth Amendment argument, the judge ruled that the school had conducted "searches" without reasonable suspicion, which meant the tests were illegal.

Can an individual student be required to take a urine test if the school suspects he or she has been using drugs?

Yes, provided the student is allowed to give the urine sample in the privacy of a bathroom stall.

Drug testing programs for high school athletes are also legal. On this issue, the post-1970s rights of young people are eroding. In *Vernonia School District v. Acton* (1995), an Oregon school district adopted a policy to randomly drug test 10 percent of its student athletes. The athletes' parents were required to sign a consent for the testing, and a student athlete couldn't play until his or her signed consent was returned. One seventh grader's parents refused to sign. They filed a lawsuit against the school district, claiming that the urine tests were suspicionless searches and therefore unconstitutional.

The case made its way to the Supreme Court—and the parents lost. Upholding the searches, the court stated that the school's interest in orderliness and safety could legally be balanced against the students' privacy rights. This ruling dealt a blow to the reasonable suspicion requirement outlined in the *T.L.O.* case, because the "suspicion requirement" has ceased to mean suspicion of a particular individual.

A few years later, the US Supreme Court in *Board of Education v. Earls* (2002) approved of an Oklahoma school district's policy mandating the drug testing of students who participated in extracurricular activities. The court majority concluded that "testing students who participate in extracurricular activities is a reasonably effective means of addressing the School District's legitimate concerns in preventing, deterring, and detecting drug use."

However, some random drug testing programs of athletes or other students may violate state constitutional privacy protections. For example, the Washington Supreme Court ruled in *York v. Wahkiakum School District* (2008) that a school district's random, suspicionless policy of drug testing student athletes violated the Washington State Constitution. The court noted: "Most troubling, however, is that we can conceive of no way to draw a principled line permitting drug testing only student athletes."

Can school officials use improperly obtained evidence against a student in a school disciplinary hearing?

In many states, yes. The *T.L.O.* decision didn't go so far as to rule out the use of improperly obtained evidence.

Most high school districts have explicit rules in their student handbooks about desk and locker searches, but not always. But whether or not published rules exist, a student should never keep anything in a locker or desk that he or she doesn't want someone else to see.

See Chapter 12, "Teens and Crime," for information about the use of evidence obtained in an illegal search.

WEAPONS

What happens if a student brings a gun or other weapon to school?

Carrying a weapon is always against school policy. Most school districts have a zero-tolerance policy with regard to weapons. The consequences of bringing a weapon onto school property can range from short-term suspension to automatic and permanent expulsion from the school district.

Schools can require students to pass through a metal detector before entering the school building and may legally "stop and frisk" a student who appears to be concealing a weapon. For more about stop-and-frisk searches, see Chapter 12, "Teens and Crime."

In school weapons cases, as in all serious disciplinary matters at school, the student is entitled to a due process hearing before being suspended, expelled, or otherwise punished.

What happens if a student accidentally brings a knife to school?

Unfortunately, that can be a real problem for the student. Most school codes have a strict no-weapons policy that specifically lists a knife as a weapon. It doesn't matter that the student did not have a subjective intent to use the knife as a weapon. If the student brings the knife to school, he is risking suspension or expulsion in many school districts.

What happens if a public school official sees a weapon at a student's home during remote learning? Can the student be expelled for that?

No, the public school officials do not have jurisdiction over weapons at a student's home. The weapon may well be a lawfully purchased weapon by the student's parents. Furthermore, the US Supreme Court has emphasized that the right to keep and bear arms is an individual right protected by the Second Amendment and that this right is at its zenith or peak with regard to self-defense of one's home.

Now, if a public school official sees a student brandishing a weapon during a school session, that may be something to report to the student's parents or to report to the police if the student makes a threat. But, again, school officials lack authority over what a student's parents possess in the confines of their own home.

STUDENTS AND THE POLICE

Can the police question students on school property?

Police have the right to question students anywhere, and school officials don't have the power to prevent it. But schools usually can require the police to give advance notice to a principal or teacher of their intent to question a student or interrupt class.

In fact, school authorities usually cooperate with police officers when it comes to student questioning. Students can be arrested on school grounds and be taken from school for questioning. The police arrest must be based on probable cause to believe that a crime has been committed and that the "arrestee" is the one who committed it. The process is easier these days, because many schools have school resource officers, trained police officers who work at the school to maintain safety and order.

If the police begin questioning a student, what should the student do?

Students are not required to answer police questions. If a student is the target of police questioning, the best thing to do is remain silent, except to give one's name and address, and request permission to call a parent or legal guardian right away. If the student is placed under arrest, he or she has a constitutional right to contact a lawyer, but should say nothing to either the police or any school official until both a parent/guardian and a lawyer arrive.

School officials shouldn't discourage a student from calling a parent or lawyer and should never encourage a student to answer questions. Not only would doing so put the school in a bad light; it might also make the student's confession inadmissible in court. School officials should leave such matters to the police and the student's attorney.

What if the student thinks he or she can answer police questions competently?

Legal experts still encourage students to remain silent. Young people often think they can clear up problems or misunderstandings on their own but that is a potentially perilous course of action. Never forget that the *Miranda* warnings, discussed in Chapter 12, remind every criminal suspect, including teens, that "anything you say may be used against you."

What if public school officials don't read a student his or her *Miranda* rights?

Public school officials generally do not have to read a student his or her *Miranda* rights before questioning the student. However, the police generally do. However, public school officials may need to read a student his or her *Miranda* rights if they question a student in the presence of a school resource officer (who is a police officer whose post is at the school). For, the North Carolina Court of Appeals recently ruled in *In re D.A.H.* (2021): "We agree that when a student is interrogated in the presence of an SRO—even when the SRO remains silent—the presence of the officer can create a coercive environment that goes above and beyond the restrictions normally imposed during school, such that a reasonable student would readily believe they are not free to go."

Can the police personally search a student on school property?

They can, but they generally need individualized suspicion to reasonably believe that the student has committed a crime or is harboring contraband. Some courts have ruled that if the police are simply assisting school officials in a search, they don't need full probable cause. If the police turn up evidence of a criminal act, it can be used in court.

For more about probable cause, see Chapter 12, "Teens and Crime."

Can student property that school officials find in a search be used in a criminal investigation?

School officials are always free to turn over evidence of a crime. In some states, even evidence uncovered in an illegal school search can be used in a later criminal investigation.

SPORTS

Are all-male and all-female high school athletic teams ever illegal?

Yes. If the school doesn't have a separate-sex team for a sport that doesn't involve bodily contact, it can't prohibit girl students from participating or at least trying out for boys' teams. Track, ski, golf, and tennis are examples of such sports.

Does this mean that separate-sex teams for noncontact sports can be legal?

Yes, although in some states if a school has both a women's and a men's team for a particular noncontact sport, a woman may try out for both. A local high school athletic association is an excellent source of information on gender-related sports issues.

Can female students play contact sports such as football or basketball on the same team as the male students?

Courts in a number of states have ruled that when it comes to contact sports, if no separate-sex team exists and the women can compete effectively against men, they can't be prohibited from playing unless doing so places their health and safety at risk. But if all the men who try out for a contact sport are better than all the women, the women who don't make the team haven't been discriminated against on the basis of gender.

The Washington Supreme Court ruled in *Darrin v. Gould* (1975) that a public high school discriminated against two girls when it tried to prohibit them from playing on the all-male high school football team. "Boys as well as girls run the risk of physical injury in contact football games," the court wrote.

A New York court faced the question of whether a woman student could try out for junior varsity football. It ruled in 1985 in *Lantz v. Ambach* that the school district failed to prove that prohibiting mixed competition serves any important objective. Although the school claimed the policy was needed to protect the health and safety of women students, its argument failed because no woman athlete was given the chance to prove that she was as fit as, or more fit than, the weakest man on the team.

If women shouldn't be competing in mixed play because of health or safety risks, a separate-sex team must be formed. The women's team must be equal to the men's team in terms of funding, available facilities, and coaching staff.

Can a female student be required to play on a women's team involving a contact sport if she is as good as the male students?

Yes, on the theory that separate-sex teams increase total participation in high school sports, especially the participation of women.

Can a male student be prevented from playing on a women's sports team?

Yes. Courts generally have ruled that males can be prohibited from playing on women's sports teams. Traditionally, it has been women and girls who have faced discrimination and exclusion. Males have had significant opportunities for athletic participation. Thankfully, female students now have more athletic options than they used to have.

TESTING

What are the most frequently cited advantages of academic tracking?

Tracking refers to the practice of placing students in different classes based on their performance on test scores. The idea behind tracking is that it is better for teachers and students for the latter to learn with other students on their same learning level. An advantage of tracking is that it allows teachers to modify their lesson plans and reach more students, since these students are on the same ability level in terms of learning. Another benefit of tracking is that it helps students to learn with students on the same level and avoids the possibility that some will become discouraged or lose self-esteem because they fall behind the progress of more advanced classmates.

Has tracking been challenged?

Yes, tracking—placing students in different classes, usually on the basis of test scores—has been challenged in the courts as unfair to racial and ethnic minorities. The challenges claim that the tests are culturally biased, which means that when they are drafted by members of a particular group, students from that group too often are the highest scorers. If it is proved that the tests are biased and therefore discriminate against minorities, the tracking system discriminates illegally.

A California court recently ruled that too many black students were placed in special education classes after the results of an IQ test were used to place them. On the basis of its finding, the court said the school's tracking system was discriminatory and therefore illegal.

Courts in a number of states have ruled that after forced school desegregation is ordered, schools can't group minorities in lower tracks until the disadvantages of their earlier discriminatory education have been corrected. Some courts have ruled that a minority student can't be put into a special class without first receiving a due process hearing.

What was No Child Left Behind?

No Child Left Behind (NCLB; 2001) was a federal law that requires states to establish testing of pupils to determine what percentage of students are making "adequate yearly progress" in terms of academic performance. The idea behind the law is to hold public schools more accountable and ensure that the schools are adequately teaching students the basic skills they need in reading, mathematics, and science. States can set their own barometers for determining what level of competency students must achieve. Schools that do not reach the stated goal of "adequate yearly progress" for two straight years are identified for what is called "school improvement." A school that continues to not meet the stated goals then can be subject to more governmental intervention. Some critics charged that NCLB has placed more emphasis in education on testing rather than on actual learning.

Eventually, the criticism of NCLB became even greater and it ended in 2015. Instead, a bipartisan Congress replaced NCLB with a new federal law known as the Every Student Succeeds Act, or ESSA.

What does ESSA do the same and differently than NCLB?

The ESSA, like the NCLB, is a reauthorization of an older 1965 federal law dealing with education, the Elementary and Secondary School Act. Furthermore, ESSA is also similar to NCLB in that it requires that public school students undergo annual standardized testing between the third and eighth grades. However, the major difference is that ESSA reduces federal control over student achievement and test scores and places primary control back to the states. Under ESSA, states have much greater control over schools' accountability than they did under NCLB.

Is competency testing discriminatory?

Critics charge that it can be. Minimum competency tests, or MCTs, are used by many schools to decide whether a student should pass to a higher grade or be awarded a diploma. Competency tests can be discriminatory if they are introduced into a school where, because their earlier public schooling was inadequate, minority students can't make passing grades. When this has happened, students have been permitted to advance to the next grade without taking the test.

States with MCTs often build in a series of required skills tests in earlier grades and require schools to provide remedial help to students who don't pass. On the basis of these early tests, schools are able to develop improvement plans for students who are behind, focusing on areas in which a particular student needs special help.

What happens if a student is denied a high school diploma because he or she can't pass the school's competency tests?

If the tests aren't discriminatory, the student would have to study for a GED. For more about GED tests, see the discussion at the beginning of this chapter.

OTHER DISCRIMINATION ISSUES

Are all-male or all-female classes still permitted in public high schools?

No in general, though there are two exceptions. A 2020 "Guidelines on Single Ed Classes and Schools" provides:

> Our current Title IX regulations generally prohibit single-sex classes or activities. The regulations in 34 CFR 106.34 state—
>
> A recipient shall not provide any course or otherwise carry out any of its education program or activity separately on the basis of sex, or require or refuse participation therein by any of its students on such basis, including health, physical education, industrial, business, vocational, technical, home economics, music, and adult education courses.

However, the guidelines identify two exceptions for this: (1) physical education classes that involve sports and physical bodily contact and (2) portions of classes in elementary and secondary schools that deal with human sexuality. In these two instances, single-sex education is considered appropriate.

Are single-sex high schools illegal?

No, provided the women's school has programs and facilities that are at least as good as the men's school, and vice versa. There remain proponents of single-sex educational programs. There are some public charter schools that are single sex.

Do schools have an obligation to prevent students from being sexually harassed at school?

Yes. School officials have a duty to prevent sexual harassment in school settings or activities. Unfortunately, the problem of sexual harassment afflicts most schools to at least some extent. According to a report from the American Association of University Women, nearly half of students between the grades of 7 and 12 experience some form of sexual harassment.

The US Supreme Court ruled in *Davis v. Monroe County School District* (1999) that public school officials can be held liable under Title IX for student-on-student harassment if the school officials know about the harassment and then do nothing to correct the problem. Title IX is a federal law that provides: "No person in the United States shall, on the basis of sex, be excluded from participation in, be denied the benefits of, or be subjected to discrimination under any education program or activity receiving Federal financial assistance."

The Supreme Court explained in the *Davis* case that school officials will be liable if they are deliberately indifferent to the plight of the harassed student. The court also explained that the harassment must be severe and pervasive and disrupt the victimized student's ability to obtain an education. The court explained that "in the context of student-on-student harassment, damages are available only where the behavior is so severe, pervasive, and objectively offensive that it denies its victims the equal access to education that Title IX is designed to protect."

Do noncitizens have a right to attend public high school in the United States?

Yes. They have just as much right to attend public high school as native-born young people. To attend school, a noncitizen just needs to live within the school's geographic boundaries.

Are schools required to offer classes in a student's native language if the student can't understand English?

Bilingual education—classes taught in one's own language while the same classes are taught in English—is not usually guaranteed. However, public schools must at least provide English-language classes for non-English-speaking students to bring down language barriers. These are called ESL classes: English as a Second Language. Students for whom English is not the primary language are referred to as English Language Learners (ELLs).

States with high numbers of non-English-speaking students (e.g., California, Arizona, and Florida) have extensive school programs to eliminate language barriers.

California law provides that "English language shall be the basic language of instruction in all schools." However, the law also provides that "bilingual instruction may be offered in those situations when such instruction is educationally advantageous to the pupils." Some states do use forms of "bilingual education" to help ELLs.

Are disabled students entitled to special benefits at school?

Yes, if they need them. Under important federal laws, including the Individuals with Disabilities Education Act (IDEA; 1990), public schools must provide for students who, because of a disability, can't learn their lessons through regular teaching methods. Each student with a disability must have a "free appropriate public education" in accordance with his or her special needs. States must establish programs to identify qualifying students and use nondiscriminatory tests to determine their achievement levels. If schools discriminate, they risk losing financial assistance from the federal government. The IDEA also provides that schools must adopt policies that provide basic rights to students with disabilities.

Under the IDEA, what qualifies a child as one with a disability?

The IDEA defines or identifies "children with disabilities" as those who have one of these categories of disabilities: intellectual disability, "hearing impediments which include deafness, speech or language impairment, visual impairment including blindness, learning disabilities, brain injury, emotional disturbance, orthopedic impairments, autism, traumatic brain injury, specific learning disabilities and other impairments who by reason of such conditions need special education and related services."

What is an IEP?

An IEP is an individualized education program, a basic requirement that schools must provide for children with disabilities. It is a detailed plan of action that the school must implement in order to provide specific educational services to children with disabilities. An IEP must be designed for each student who is evaluated and determined to qualify as a child with a disability. Each IEP must be evaluated on an annual basis.

Can students with disabilities always take classes with other students?

Students with disabilities must be integrated with general student population as much as possible, at the same time that their special needs are being provided for. This is called "the least restrictive environment" requirement or "mainstreaming."

To mainstream a student, a teacher may need special learning materials, speech services either in or outside of the classroom, or an aide to take care of the student's unique physical needs. Challenged students include, for example, those with hearing problems, speech problems, and emotional disturbances. For such students, special education plans are developed.

What happens if a student with disabilities struggles to adapt to mainstreaming?

He or she usually is transferred from some or all regular classes. Sometimes the student attends "special ed" classes or classes in a "resource room." But the student is still entitled to a "free and appropriate education"—at a special school or perhaps at home.

Can a special education student be suspended or expelled for particularly bad behavior?

The answer depends on whether the bad behavior is a manifestation of the student's disability. The US Supreme Court ruled in *Honig v. Doe* (1988) that public school officials could not remove handicapped (the term used in the ruling instead of disabled) students who engaged in bad behavior resulting from their disability. The court explained that the students could be suspended for up to ten days, however, if they were a danger to themselves or other students. A 1997 amendment to the IDEA provided that students with disabilities may be placed in an Interim Alternative Education Setting for up to forty-five (45) days, if that process is also employed for other students in the school.

Are students with HIV/AIDS considered disabled under these special laws?

Courts in a number of states have ruled that HIV/AIDS students must be regarded as disabled under the federal laws noted previously. In these states, students with HIV/AIDS can't be discriminated against at school because of their condition. Students with hepatitis B are also protected.

STUDENT RECORDS

Can parents see their children's high school records? Can high school students see their own records?

The answer to the first question is yes. Under a federal law, the Family Educational Rights and Privacy Act (FERPA) (1974), parents must be able to review their children's school records and transcripts. As to the second question, students may see their records when they reach age eighteen, although schools may elect to allow underage students to view them.

Public schools can't give out student records without parental consent, and state laws often provide added privacy protections. Federal law does, however, make certain exceptions. Information in student records can be legally used to compile transcripts, yearbooks, and student directories and can be made available for academic research. These privacy laws also apply to private schools, particularly if the school receives federal funds.

Can a student do anything about damaging information in his or her student file?

Sometimes. Negative information in a student file shouldn't necessarily be removed or changed. Schools have a duty to record information about students and provide information to colleges and technical schools when students apply to them for admission.

But school records shouldn't be gossip columns. To ensure that a school keeps fair and accurate records, a good rule of thumb would be for parents to inspect their children's records once a year. If information in a student file is incorrect, misleading, or otherwise unfair to the student, the parent should ask the school to remove or correct it. If the school decides not to take action on the request, the parents are entitled to a due process hearing. If the school wins, the parents can appeal the decision through the appeal process described previously.

Can police see student records if they want?

Law enforcement officials can't view a young person's academic file simply on request, although student records can be demanded or "subpoenaed" by a court. In addition, parents have the power to authorize persons such as relatives, lawyers, guardians, and psychologists to review their children's records.

PRIVATE SCHOOLS, CHARTER SCHOOLS, AND HOMESCHOOLING

Are private schools subject to state education laws?

To a great extent, yes. State laws regarding high school attendance, student health, and teacher certification apply to private as well as public schools.

Do students in private schools have the same kind of constitutional rights as public high school students?

No. Due process under the federal Constitution only protects students in public schools—only when "state action" is involved. Operating a private school is not a type of state action, so due process isn't a constitutional right. However, state constitutions, state laws, and private school policies sometimes grant due process rights to students in private schools.

Can a private school discriminate on the basis of race or gender?

A private school may not deny admission on the basis of race, gender, or nationality. If it does, it loses its tax-exempt status, which means it forfeits important tax advantages of operating as a nonprofit organization under the federal tax laws.

Can a private school discriminate on the basis of a disability?

No, private schools may not discriminate against students with a disability under the Americans with Disabilities Act of 1990 (ADA). These schools, though private, must provide all enrolled students with a "reasonable accommodation." There is an exception for religious schools, though even those schools may be covered under state law, which vary significantly from state to state.

What is a charter school?

A charter school is a public school that operate free of certain state or local rules and regulations, although they must still meet specific performance standards. They create and manage their own budgets and often design innovative curricula. Many charter schools are geared to special fields of study such as math and science, music and other arts, or computers.

Teachers in charter schools must have a college degree and a current teacher certification. In addition, specific "core" subjects must be taught for a specified number of days and hours each year.

The charter school movement is growing fast. According to the Center for Education Reform, there are more than 7,800 charter schools in the United States. Forty-five states and the District of Columbia have passed laws that allow for the creation of charter schools. The only five states that do not have charter schools, as of 2023, are Montana, Nebraska, North Dakota, South Dakota, and Vermont.

Could a charter school be created specifically for students of a particular religion?

No. In 1994, the Supreme Court ruled in *Village of Kiryas Joel v. Grumet* that a public school created for Hasidic Jews in New York was a violation of the First Amendment's establishment clause. This ruling is consistent with the court's rulings in earlier establishment clause cases.

What is a voucher program?

A voucher program is a state educational program giving parents the equivalent of tuition payments for a child's education in either a public or private school. Supporters of voucher programs claim they create competition, which they believe should improve public education overall. They point out that the state's role is to do more than support an educational system—that it must also provide a good one. Critics charge that vouchers drain money and resources away from public schools and sometimes lead to violations of the principle providing for separation of church and state. The US Supreme Court ruled in *Zelman v. Simmons-Harris* (2002) that an Ohio voucher program known as the Pilot Project Scholarship Program, which provided educational options for parents and students in the failing public school system of Cleveland, Ohio, did not violate the establishment clause of the First Amendment.

Voucher programs remain a hot political issue in many states.

Is homeschooling legal in every state?

It is now legal in every state, but state regulations regarding homeschooling vary considerably. In many states a parent (or related individual) who teaches his or her children at home must have a college degree and also a current teacher certification. State laws always require that certain subjects be taught for a specific number of days and hours each year. In some states only grade schoolers can be homeschooled.

States authorizing homeschooling usually require that the parents permit home visits by school personnel. If a homeschool teacher refuses to permit inspection of his or her curricula and school records or doesn't require the homeschooled student to take certain standardized tests, the parents can be charged with a criminal offense.

FOR FURTHER READING

In General

Driver, Justin. *The Schoolhouse Gate: Public Education, the Supreme Court, and the Battle for the American Mind*. New York: Pantheon, 2018.

Essex, Nathan L. *A Teacher's Pocket Guide to School Law*. 3rd ed. Upper Saddle River, NJ: Pearson, 2014.

Schimmel, David, Leslie Stellman, and Louis Fischer. *Teachers and the Law*. 9th ed. New York: Pearson, 2014.

Warnick, Bryan R. *Understanding Student Rights in School: Speech, Religion, and Privacy in Educational Settings*. New York: Teachers College Press, 2013.

First Amendment Issues

Hudson, David L., Jr. *Let the Students Speak: A History of the Fight for Free Expression in American Schools*. Boston: Beacon Press, 2011.

Johnson, John W. *The Struggle for Student Rights: Tinker v. Des Moines and the 1960s*. Lawrence: University Press of Kansas, 1997.

McWhirter, Darien. *Freedom of Speech, Press, and Assembly*. Phoenix, AZ: Oryx Press, 1996.

Ross, Catherine J. *Lessons in Censorship: How Schools and Courts Subvert Students' First Amendment Rights*. Boston: Harvard University Press, 2015.

Solomon, Stephen D. *Ellery's Protest: How One Young Man Defied Tradition and Sparked the Battle Over School Prayer*. Ann Arbor: University of Michigan Press, 2007.

School Newspapers

Fuller, Sarah Betsy. *Hazelwood v. Kuhlmeier: Censorship in School Newspapers*. Springfield, NJ: Enslow Publishers, 1998.

Osborn, Patricia. *School Newspaper Adviser's Survival Guide*. New York: Center for Applied Research in Education, 1998.

School Prayer

Alley, Robert S. *Without a Prayer: Religious Expression in Public Schools*. Amherst, NY: Prometheus Books, 1996.

Andryszewski, Tricia. *School Prayer: A History of the Debate*. Springfield, NJ: Enslow Publishers, 1997.

Dierenfeld, Bruce J. *The Battle over School Prayer: How Engel v. Vitale Changed America*. Lawrence: University of Kansas Press, 2007.

Soloman, Stephen D. *Ellery's Protest: How One Young Man Defied Tradition and Sparked the Battle over School Prayer*. Ann Arbor: University of Michigan Press, 2009.

Discipline and Due Process

Black, Derek W. *Ending Zero Tolerance: The Crisis of Absolute School Discipline*. New York: New York University Press, 2016.

Skiba, Russell J. and Gil G. Noam. *Zero Tolerance: Can Suspension and Expulsion Keep Schools Safe?* San Francisco: Jossey-Bass, 2002.

Van Jon, M. Dyke and Melvin M. Sakurai. *Checklists for Searches and Seizures in Public Schools*. Deerfield, IL: Clark, Boardman, Callaghan, 1996.

Sports

Coffino, Michael. *The Other Classroom: The Essential Importance of High School Sports*. Baltimore, MD: Rowman & Littlefield, 2018.

Fronske, Hilda. *Teaching Cues for Sports Skills for Secondary School Students*. 6th ed. London: Pearson, 2015.

Office of Juvenile Justice, US Department of Justice. *The Coach's Playbook Against Drugs*. Washington, DC: US Department of Justice – the federal government, 2012.

Students with Disabilities

Bateman, David F. and Jenifer L. Cline. *A Teacher's Guide to Special Education*. New York: ASCD, 2016.

Browder, Diane M. et al. *Teaching Students with Moderate and Severe Disabilities*. 2nd ed. New York: The Guilford Press, 2020.

Thomas, Stephen B. and Charles J. Russo. *Special Education Law: Issues and Implications for the '90s*. Dayton, OH: Education Law Association, 1995.

Wright, Peter W. D. and Pamela Darr Wright. *Wrightslaw: Special Education Law*. Hartfield, VA: Harbor House Law Press, 1999.

Private and Alternative Schools

Sarason, Seymour Bernard. *Charter Schools: Another Flawed Educational Reform?* New York: Teacher's College Press, 1998.

Shaughnessy, Mary Angela. *Catholic Schools and the Law: A Teacher's Guide*. 2nd ed. Mahwah, NJ: Paulist Press, 2000.

Wohlstetter, Priscilla, et al. *Choices and Challenges: Charter School Performance in Context*. Boston: Harvard Education Press, 2013.

OTHER INFORMATION SOURCES

Organizations

American Center for Law and Justice, P.O. Box 450349, Atlanta, GA 31145. (877) 989-2255. Home page: www.aclj.org.

American Civil Liberties Union for Students, 125 Broad Street, 18th Floor, New York, NY 10004. (212) 549-2500. E-mail: aclu@aclu.org. Home page: www.aclu.org/students.

National Center for Youth Law, 405 Fourteenth Street, Ste. 1500, Oakland, CA 94612. (510) 835-8098. E-mail: info@youthlaw.org. Home page: www.youthlaw.org.

National Education Association, 1201 16th Street, NW, Washington, DC 20036-3290. (202) 833-4000. Home page: www.nea.org.

The Rutherford Institute, P.O. Box 7482, Charlottesville, VA 22906. (434) 978-3888. E-mail: staff @rutherford.org. Home page: www.rutherford.org.

Student Press Law Center, 1608 Rhode Island Ave. NW, Suite 211 Washington, DC 20036. (202) 785-5450. E-mail: splc@splc.org. Home page: www.splc.org.

Online Sources

Coalition for the Separation of Church and State: www.coalition.freethought.org

English as a Second Language (ESL): www.lang.uiuc.edu/r-li5/esl/

Homeschooling Zone: www.homeschoolzone.com; E-mail: webmaster@homeschoolzone.com

Student Association for Freedom of Expression: www.mit.edu:8001/activities/safe/home.html

Y-RIGHTS (school privacy issues); E-mail: listserv@SJUVMÁBSTJOHNSÁBEDU [body: subscribe y-rights firstname lastname]

CHAPTER 3

At Home

This chapter covers the rights of young people at home and the extent of their parents' authority.

How much legal authority do parents have over their children?

Parents have the right to make decisions about what their children eat, wear, read, access on the Internet, and watch on television. They have the right to determine where their children will attend school, what kind of religious training they receive, and with whom they associate. Parents have broad authority to decide how to discipline a minor child. They can use corporal punishment, although they cannot engage in child abuse.

So is spanking allowed?

Yes, spanking by parents is allowed as long as it doesn't leave a mark on the child. If spanking leaves a mark on the child, then it likely crosses the line into unacceptable punishment and may even be considered child abuse. The social science literature in recent years has called into question the efficacy of spanking as a positive form of behavioral modification.

Why do parents have so much control?

The right to have children and to raise them without substantial interference from the government is a fundamental right in America. Parents are the "natural guardians" of their children. Over the years, both Congress and the US Supreme Court have gone to great lengths to preserve the parent–child relationship.

Minor children are inexperienced and vulnerable to exploitation, and parents are expected to protect them from life's sinister forces. But state and local governments watch out for young people as well. School attendance laws, child labor laws, harmful-to-minors legislation, statutory rape laws, and juvenile courts exist to protect minors—from their parents. These types of laws affect the parent–child relationship, regardless of a particular parent's opinions about work, school, sex, "porn," or parental authority.

For more about school attendance laws, see Chapter 2, "At School"; for more about child labor laws, see Chapter 4, "On the Job"; and for more about statutory rape, see Chapter 8, "Your Sexual Life."

When did the Supreme Court recognize parental rights as a fundamental right?

The US Supreme Court emphasized the importance of parents' fundamental rights to control the education and upbringing of their children in some early decisions—*Meyer v. Nebraska* (1923) and *Pierce v. Society of Sisters* (1925). In *Meyer*, the court invalidated a Nebraska law that prohibited the teaching of foreign languages in public schools. The court recognized a liberty interest in parents providing an education for their children and found that the law infringed on that interest without a proper "police power" rationale.

In *Pierce*, the court invalidated an Oregon law that mandated children must attend public schools, not private schools. The court found this to be an infringement of parental rights and added that "the child is not the mere creature of the State; those who nurture him and direct his destiny have the right, coupled with the high duty, to recognize and prepare him for additional obligations."

TEENS, PARENTS, AND MONEY

Does a teen have a right to an allowance?

No. But parents are responsible for a minor child's support until the child reaches the age of majority, and children have a corresponding right to be taken care of.

Does a minor have a legal right to have a part-time or summer job?

No. Parents can legally forbid an unemancipated teen to work for pay outside the home. (Emancipation is discussed in Chapter 5.)

Are minors legally entitled to keep the money they earn?

Not necessarily. Because parents are entitled to the services of their children, in most states they have a legal right to their children's income. If this idea seems outdated or even wrong, it is because it evolved when children were considered a type of property—when each child was regarded as another hand on the farm. If the minor was earning money instead of contributing to the upkeep of the household, his or her earnings would be the parents' pay for providing care and shelter.

Many states now have laws permitting minors to keep their earnings unless the parents notify the employer that they want to claim the earnings separately. When this happens, the employer must pay the parents, and the parents must declare the earnings on their own tax returns.

If a teen controls his or her money, can the teen independently decide how to spend it?

Again, not necessarily. Parents also have the right to forbid a minor child to buy, for example, a particular book or magazine, video or computer game, or other amusement. They have the legal authority to forbid a teen from going to a certain movie or rock concert. They can also make a teen's purchase of certain styles of clothes or footwear off-limits.

Is there any way a minor can prevent a parent from taking his or her earnings?

Yes. Parents can agree, orally or in writing, that they have no claim to their child's earnings. Or the minor's right to his or her separate earnings can be understood, although not expressly stated. Nowadays this is almost always the case.

Are teenage children legally required to work in order to help support the family?

No. Parents are required to support their family without assistance from their children. But nothing prevents parents from requiring a teenager to work at a part-time job. If the teen refuses to look for one, nothing in the law prohibits parents from punishing the teen in a manner that doesn't constitute abuse or neglect.

However, there are legal limits on children and work. These are called child labor laws. For example, under the federal Fair Labor Standards Act (FLSA), an employer may not employ a child under fourteen years of age. There are restrictions on the number of hours children under sixteen may work. You should also check your individual state law on child labor. States vary in how they regulate child labor.

DISCIPLINE

Can a parent legally throw a teen out of the home?

No. Parents have a legal responsibility to provide for their minor children, including hard-to-handle teens. They must give each child adequate food, shelter, clothing, schooling, and medical care. Parents should not discipline a child in a manner that constitutes physical, sexual, or psychological abuse or use neglect as a form of punishment. In other words, teens have a right to live at home.

If parents don't live up to their responsibilities—if, for example, they force a child to live on the streets—the state can enforce the teen's rights in "abandonment" proceedings in family court. (Abandonment is discussed later in this chapter.)

What should a minor do if he or she feels parental discipline methods are abusive?

Discuss the matter with a trusted teacher, minister, medical person, or adult friend, or call the state child protective agency. Action should be taken immediately.

Can parents legally prevent a child from calling the police in a family violence situation?

No. Anyone can call the police when violence erupts, although sometimes it's impossible to get to the phone before somebody gets hurt. To prevent injury and to subdue the violent family member, the police should always be called—by another family member or by someone outside the family such as a neighbor or relative.

For more information about abuse and neglect at the hands of parents and relatives, see Chapter 10, "Your Right to Be Healthy and Safe from Abuse."

If a minor's parents are divorced, who is legally responsible for the minor's discipline?

Both parents remain responsible. However, unless the parents have joint custody, day-to-day decisions regarding the child are made by the custodial parent. With joint custody, the parents continue to share these responsibilities.

For more about the rights of young persons when parents split up, see Chapter 7, "If Your Parents Divorce."

If a minor's parents have never married, which parent is responsible for the minor's discipline and care?

Both are, in every state.

Are grandparents or brothers and sisters ever legally responsible for a minor?

Only if the minor's grandparents or his or her siblings have agreed to be responsible. This often happens when a minor's parents are elderly.

TOBACCO

At what age can teens buy tobacco products: cigarettes, chewing tobacco, and snuff?

In most states a person must be eighteen to buy any form of tobacco. Although some states prohibit minors from using tobacco in public places, it usually isn't illegal for a minor just to possess or use it.

Tobacco products are known to cause cancer and other serious diseases, and high schoolers are foolish to spend their earnings on them. It might be wiser to save the money for college, for this reason. In a 2014 survey, the CDC's National Youth Risk Behavior Survey noted that 15.3 percent of teens had smoked in the previous year (in 2013).

Can minors purchase marijuana legally?

No. Even states that allow for recreational marijuana, such use is limited to those who are twenty-one years of age or older. In Connecticut, a teen can obtain marijuana for medicinal purposes, but they have to be least eighteen years of age.

ADULT BOOKS AND ADULT MOVIES

Why aren't laws prohibiting the sale of pornography to minors a violation of the First Amendment?

Courts have said that society has a strong interest in protecting minors from harmful material, particularly of a sexual nature. In *Ginsberg v. New York* (1968), the US Supreme Court upheld a New York law prohibiting the sale of pornographic materials to persons under age seventeen, even though some of the materials reviewed in the case weren't considered legally obscene for adults. In other words, the Supreme Court recognized that material may be legal to sell to adults, but illegal to sell to minors. This is sometimes referred to as the concept of "variable obscenity." The Supreme Court stated that although there is no sure way to prove that a minor's exposure to pornography is harmful, New York could assume that such a link exists. Nearly every state has a law that is based on the concept of variable obscenity. These are called harmful-to-minor laws.

Every state controls the sale of "porn" to minors. Furthermore, every state prohibits the production and sale of child pornography, which is visual or printed material that depicts children engaged in explicit sexual conduct. This type of pornography is often called "kiddie porn."

What is obscenity?

This is sometimes a difficult question to answer. Justice Potter Stewart wrote in *Jacobellis v. Ohio* (1964):

> I shall not today attempt further to define the kinds of material I understand to be embraced within that shorthand description; and perhaps I could never succeed in intelligibly doing so. But I know it when I see it, and the motion picture involved in this case is not that.

Obscenity is a narrow category of hard-core pornography that is not protected by the First Amendment right of free speech. Most pornography is protected by the First Amendment.

In fact, the only two types of pornography that are not protected by the First Amendment—at least regarding adults—are (1) obscenity and (2) child pornography.

The US Supreme Court detailed the legal definition of obscenity in *Miller v. California* (1973). The so-called Miller test has three parts:

1. The material must appeal predominantly to a prurient interest in sex as judged by contemporary community standards. A prurient interest in sex means a morbid or shameful interest in sex, as opposed to a healthy interest in sex.
2. The material must depict or describe sexual conduct in a patently offensive way. This is also judged by contemporary community standards.
3. The material must have no serious literary, artistic, political, or scientific value.

In the early part of the twentieth century, obscenity prosecutions were brought against booksellers for selling books that might have a racy or sexually explicit passage. Today, the vast majority of obscenity prosecutions are brought for extremely hard-core pornography that is considered deviant.

What is child pornography?

Child pornography is a separate category of sexual expression that is not protected by the First Amendment. Child pornography involves materials showing minors engaged in sexually explicit activity or lascivious exhibition of the genitals. Child pornography is very harmful—both to any actual children involved in the creation of the material but also to children in general. The Supreme Court recognized this unprotected category in *New York v. Ferber* (1982), noting that such material was not protected—even if not *obscene*—because of its link to the sexual abuse of children.

For more about First Amendment rights under the federal Constitution, see Chapter 2, "At School."

Can a minor go to an X-rated movie?

No, minors are not allowed to attend X-rated films. The current designation for X-rated movies is "NC-17." Minors are not supposed to even be able to attend an "R"-rated movie without a parent or guardian accompanying them, although this rule is not always enforced by movie theatres. Parents do, however, have the power to forbid their children to go to all types of movies, under their authority as parents.

What did the US Supreme Court rule about a law restricting minors' access to violent video games?

The US Supreme Court invalidated a California law that imposed criminal penalties on those who sold violent video games to minors, in *Entertainment Merchants Association v. Brown* (2011). The state of California attempted to characterize violent video games as a form of obscenity. However, the Supreme Court rejected this, finding that obscenity was confined to materials that were sexual in nature. The court explained that minors are entitled to a significant degree of free speech protection. "No doubt a State possesses legitimate power to protect children from harm, but that does not include a free-floating power to restrict the ideas to which children may be exposed," the court explained.

Writing for the court majority, Justice Antonin Scalia stated that there is a long history of violence in expressive works, such as children's fairy tales, such as the stories of Cinderella and Hansel and Gretel. He also noted that many mythological tales, such as Homer's *Iliad* and *Odyssey*, contain violent themes. The court also found that the state of California admitted that it could not "show a direct causal link between violent video games and harm to minors."

THE AGE OF MAJORITY

What is meant by the term "the age of majority"?

This is the age at which a person legally becomes an adult. The age of majority is eighteen in forty-seven states. The only three states that are different are Alabama, Nebraska, and Mississippi. The age of majority in Alabama and Nebraska is nineteen, while the age of majority in Mississippi is twenty-one.

When a young person reaches the age of majority, does all parental authority end?

Yes, but this doesn't mean the young person is entitled to all the rights of adulthood. For example, it is illegal to purchase alcoholic beverages before age twenty-one, regardless of the state's legislated age of majority. In addition, states have the power to set a higher legal age for special activities such as voting in local elections and serving on a jury.

What rights does a young person gain at the age of majority?

The right to work at almost any job, marry, or enlist in the armed forces without parental consent; enter into all types of contracts; consent to all types of health care; and buy adult books. On the other hand, at the age of majority a minor no longer is subject to the "jurisdiction" of the juvenile court.

Can parents' legal responsibilities toward their children ever extend beyond the age of majority?

Yes, but these extensions occur in connection with divorce decrees and custody agreements and not by virtue of public laws. For example, a custody decree might require a parent to pay for a child's college education through age twenty-four.

In one Ohio case a divorce court ordered a wealthy father to pay for his nineteen-year-old son's $17,000 education at a local technical school. The court interpreted the divorce decree to require this, even though it stated that the father had to pay for his son's *college* education.

A young person with divorced parents is rarely in a position to make his or her parents pay for college if the divorce decree doesn't order it. This is partly because a young person usually can't afford a lawyer. However, a divorced parent might be willing to cosign or guarantee a higher education loan.

LEGAL GUARDIANS

If parents can't care for their minor children, who helps out?

Usually this depends on factors such as the age of the children and the parents' financial worth. If the parents don't have much in savings, the children are often cared for by relatives, particularly if the children are older. Sometimes this type of relationship presents difficulties if parental consent is needed for medical care.

If a minor child is quite young or needs special treatment, a family court might appoint a "legal guardian" to be responsible for the child. The adult files a petition in the local family court to obtain his or her appointment. The petitioner is often a sibling or other relative.

Once appointed, the guardian makes decisions about the minor's overall care and discipline, plus his or her education, medical care, and religious life. The "ward" almost always lives with the guardian. The appointment doesn't relieve the parents of their legal duty of support, however, and usually the guardian is entitled to be paid for serving.

Unlike a court-appointed foster parent or custodian in abuse or neglect cases, neither the parents nor the child needs to have gotten into trouble for a guardian to be appointed. Guardians also serve when parents have died, can't be found, or don't reside with the child for some other reason.

Again in contrast to custody proceedings involving a child either at risk or in trouble with the law, the state's involvement in a guardianship diminishes after the appointment is made. This means the legal guardian isn't under the continuing supervision of the family court. Even so, a guardian is considered an "officer of the court" and must act in "the best interests of the child."

Does a minor have to obey a guardian?

Yes, unless the guardian asks the minor to do something illegal. The specific powers of legal guardians are spelled out in state law.

How long does a guardianship last?

Until the minor reaches the age of majority, unless the court believes it should continue longer. A guardianship might be extended beyond the age of majority if, for example, the young person can't manage in the adult world because of a physical or mental disability.

Can a teen arrange for an elderly parent's medical care?

No. As a rule, a doctor can't treat a sick or injured adult without his or her consent. If a parent is unable to consent to treatment, only a spouse or adult child may legally do so. But nothing prevents a minor from calling an emergency medical team to help a sick or injured parent, and nothing prevents a minor from arranging for a parent to be taken to the emergency room for immediate care.

If a person, young or old, needs emergency treatment, that person's consent is legally *presumed*. This is why doctors and medics may give treatment in an emergency without obtaining consent from anyone.

TERMINATION OF PARENTAL RIGHTS

In cases of serious abuse or neglect, can parental rights be terminated completely?

Yes, although to do so the state must establish by clear and convincing evidence that the parents are not fit to rear the children. State laws provide the grounds on which a parent's rights can be terminated. These generally include abandonment, serious physical abuse or torture of the child, drug abuse by the parent that renders the parent unfit to meet the needs of the child, or imprisonment. When parental rights are terminated, the parent–child relationship ends by court order. Once this happens, a parent has no legal right to see his or her child or know the child's whereabouts. This makes termination of parental rights dramatically different from custody and foster-parent arrangements. (For more about the circumstances in which the state can take custody of a minor, see Chapter 10, "Your Right to Be Healthy and Safe from Abuse.")

In parental termination cases, are the parents in question entitled to legal representation?

Yes, in the vast majority of states, a parent who is facing a termination of their parental rights has the right to an appointed attorney to represent their interests. Legal representation is seen as essential in these cases because the right of a parent to rear her or his child is a paramount constitutional right protected under the Fourteenth Amendment of the US Constitution. However, a word of caution is in order here. In some states, a parent is not entitled to the effective assistance of counsel. In other words, the aggrieved parent in some states may not be able to file a motion for ineffective assistance of counsel.

What is abandonment?

In contrast to "neglect," abandonment is a *conscious* failure to perform parental responsibilities for a specific period of time—often six months or a year. Examples of abandonment include failing to keep in contact with a minor child; failing to provide care, love, and affection for a child; leaving a child with another person for a long time for no good reason; failing to provide support for a child; and totally ignoring a child in foster care. Abandonment most definitely is a cause for terminating parental rights.

Abandonment doesn't require that a parent have left the child on the steps of the local orphanage. In fact, family courts are now more willing to declare an abandonment than in years past. They now look for facts showing "disinterest and total lack of concern" for the child. Courts are less likely to hold parental rights sacred when the parents have obviously and deliberately ceased to care. Claims of parental love and affection don't hold much weight in such circumstances.

Sometimes circumstances of abandonment can be traced back to a parent's serious physical or emotional illness. In these instances, foster care or a legal guardianship arrangement is frequently the court's first course of action.

Will a court only terminate parental rights when the child is an infant?

No. It often happens in the case of teens.

Can the state seek to terminate the parental rights of one parent but not the other?

Yes. This often happens, for example, in cases where only one parent is engaging in physically or emotionally abusive behavior.

Why might the state seek to terminate parental rights in some cases but not others?

Because the focus of a termination case isn't just a parent's current inability to provide care, but whether his or her obligations can be fulfilled in the years ahead. If the parent's problem is serious but not hopeless, the child protective agency might take custody of the child and possibly make a foster care placement.

Must the state assist a family with its problems before it can terminate parental rights?

Yes. Usually the family court or child protective agency will require the parent (or parents) to undergo counseling or take parenting classes. Here the goal is to keep the family intact. If the parent fails to cooperate or rehabilitation doesn't prove worthwhile, the state can initiate termination proceedings in family court.

In most states a family court will terminate parental rights only if the parent has already been separated from the child for six months to one year.

Does a parent have any constitutional rights in a termination case?

Yes. Parental rights can be terminated only if the parent has received procedural due process. Procedural due process means that before the state may infringe on a parent's liberty interest to rear one's child, the state must provide notice of the grounds and a hearing at which the parent can contest the charges and present evidence. The essence of procedural due process is both notice and a hearing. The parent's goal will be to retain or resume custody of the child.

Most states provide legal counsel for indigent parents in termination cases. However, the right to counsel may depend on the complexity of the case and whether the parent faces criminal charges (such as abuse or neglect charges) in connection with the parent–child relationship.

What must the state prove in order to terminate parental rights?

It must present facts establishing one or more of the following situations: extreme lack of interest in a child, extreme or repeated neglect or abuse, severe deterioration of the parent–child relationship, failure to show an ability to care about the child, and failure to improve an already serious negative family situation. Also, the state must prove that severing the bonds between parent and child is in the best interests of the child. The state must prove its case by "clear and convincing evidence," which is a higher burden of proof than the normal standard in civil cases, a mere "preponderance of the evidence." Preponderance of the evidence means more likely than not. Clear and convincing evidence is a much greater burden of proof.

Obviously a state can only sever these bonds in very grave cases. In most, the state will already have the child in custody or foster care, and it probably will have intervened on previous occasions. In fact, revoking parental rights of one or both parents after a first incident is unusual, and in some states it is illegal. Again, see Chapter 10, "Your Right to Be Healthy and Safe from Abuse," to read about "dependency" actions to protect young people.

Is a minor entitled to a lawyer in a termination of parental rights case?

In certain states, yes.

Can parents give up parental rights voluntarily?

Yes. This actually is the way parental rights are most often terminated. When a minor child is placed for adoption, the child's "birth parents" already have agreed to give up parental rights.

Can parental rights be terminated because the parents don't have enough money—are too "indigent"—to raise the child?

The rights of indigent parents can be terminated only if there is a serious reason *besides* poverty to justify terminating their rights, such as abuse or abandonment. Failure to support a minor child will rarely be the sole reason for terminating parental rights, especially if the parent and child are close.

Can parental rights be terminated if the parent has been convicted of a serious crime?

Yes. Some states also permit parental rights to be terminated if a parent has been convicted in adult court of "debauchery" or if the parent has been involved in prostitution.

Can parental rights be terminated because a parent is mentally ill or has some other emotional disability?

In some states, yes, but only if the mental problem is so serious that the parent is unable to care for the child. These days, many mental disorders (even grave ones such as schizophrenia) can be treated with medication and therapy. For this reason, a family court's ruling that a parent is mentally disabled, without strong proof that he or she isn't fit to parent, won't be sufficient to terminate parental rights.

Can the parent–child relationship be terminated if the minor child would be better off in another situation and environment?

Family courts don't exist to find perfect homes for minors—their purpose has always been to protect young persons in danger. Parents have a fundamental right to raise their children; they don't have a legal obligation to be models of parenthood.

Even so, courts in some states have considered using the child's "best interests" as the only basis for terminating parental rights. When this approach is used, the state doesn't have to show that a parent repeatedly committed a serious wrong such as child abuse or abandonment. It has to prove only that the child would be better off in other circumstances.

US Supreme Court decisions in the early 1980s suggest that states may violate the federal Constitution if they allow parental rights to be terminated without proof that the parents truly are unfit. Before long, the Supreme Court may have to decide whether parental rights can be lawfully terminated simply because the child's "best interests" aren't being served.

Can parents be charged criminally for abandoning or neglecting their children?

Yes, in many states parental neglect or abandonment of a child constitutes a crime, not just grounds for termination of parental rights. In many states, abandonment of a child, child neglect, and criminal nonsupport are criminal offenses. Abandonment of a child is often classified as a felony. Courts may suspend the sentences of such parents if they begin supporting their children.

OTHER FAMILY ISSUES

Can a minor carry or use a firearm or other weapon with parental consent? Without parental consent?

The answer to the first question is a qualified yes. Federal, state, and local laws govern the possession and use of weapons. Federal law prohibits the sale of handguns to persons under age twenty-one and the sale of rifles and shotguns to persons under age eighteen. A minor can receive a handgun as a gift but can't legally buy ammunition until age twenty-one.

States and cities regulate weapons within their borders, and the scope of their laws always includes the possession and use of firearms by young people. In some states minors can possess rifles or shotguns at age sixteen or seventeen. However, nearly every state prohibits possession of handguns by minors. In most states an unemancipated minor can carry a handgun only if he or she has written permission from a parent. But even in these states, if a law forbids weapons in certain places such as a retail store or public auditorium, or if a high school forbids weapons on school grounds, parental permission will never make the weapon legal.

Recent illegal uses of handguns and other firearms by minors have focused national attention on the issue of weapons issue.

Can a minor legally take illegal drugs at home or elsewhere with parental permission?

Never.

FOR FURTHER READING

In General

Barber, Nigel. *Why Parents Matter: Parental Investment and Child Outcomes.* Westport, CT: Bergin & Garvey, 2000.

Gardner, Martin R. *Understanding Juvenile Law.* 5th ed. Durham, NC: Carolina Academic Press, 2018.

Guggenheim, Martin, et al. *The Rights of Families: The Authoritative Guide to the Rights of Family Members Today (ACLU).* Carbondale: Southern Illinois University Press, 1996.

Marsh, Toni. *Juvenile Law.* Clifton Park, NY: Thomson Delmar, 2007.

Stahl, Rebecca and Philip Stahl. *Representing Children in Dependency and Family Court: Beyond the Law.* Chicago: American Bar Association, 2019.

Money

Bijlefeld, Marjolijn and Sharon K. Zoumbaris. *Teen Guide to Personal Financial Management.* Westport, CT: Greenwood Press, 2000.

Burkholder, Steve, et al. *I Want More Pizza: Real World Money Schools for High School, College, and Beyond.* Schenectady, NY: Overcome Publishing LLC, 2015.

Chatzky, Jean and Kathryn Tuggle. *How to Money: Your Ultimate Visual Guide to the Basics of Finance.* New York: Roaring Book Press, 2022.

Covey, Sean. *The 7 Habits of Highly Effective Teens: The Ultimate Teenage Success Guide.* New York: Simon & Schuster, 1998.

Adult Books and Movies

Geltzer, Jeremy. *Dirty Words and Filthy Pictures: Film and the First Amendment.* Austin: University of Texas Press, 2016.

Hixson, Richard F. *Pornography and the Justices: The Supreme Court and the Intractable Obscenity Problem.* Carbondale: Southern Illinois University Press, 1996.

Legal Guardians

Field, George W. *Legal Relations of Infants, Parent and Child and Guardian and Ward*. New York: William S. Hein & Company, 1981.

Hurme, Sally Balch. *The Fundamentals of Guardianship: What Every Guardian Should Know*. Chicago: American Bar Association Book Publishing, 2017.

Shapiro, Michael. *Solomon's Sword: Two Families and the Children the State Took Away*. New York: Times Books, 1999.

Guns

Dunbar-Ortiz, Roxanne. *Loaded: A Disarming History of the Second Amendment*. New York: City Lights Publishing, 2016.

Kates, Don B., Jr. and Gary Kleck. *The Great American Gun Debate*. San Francisco: Pacific Resource Institute for Public Policy, 1997.

Roleff, Tamara. *Gun Control: Current Controversies*. San Diego: Greenhaven Press, 1997.

Waldman, Michael. *The Second Amendment: A Biography*. New York: Simon & Schuster, 2015.

OTHER INFORMATION SOURCES

Organizations

Americans for a Society Free from Age Restrictions (ASFAR). E-mail: asfar@oblivion.net. Home page: www.asfar.org.

National Guardianship Association, Inc., 1604 North Country Club Road, Tucson, AZ 85716. (520) 881-6561. Home page: www.guardianship.org.

Parents Anonymous, 675 West Foothills Boulevard, Ste. 220. Claremont, CA 91711. (909) 621-6184. E-mail: parentsanon@msn.corn. Home page: www.parentsanonymous-natl.org.

Teens 411—National Help Resources, Streetcats Foundation, Box 191396, San Francisco, CA 94119. Home page: www.child.net/teenhelp.

Online Sources

Campaign for Tobacco Free Kids: www.tobaccofreekids.org

Parenting Today's Teen: www.parentingteens.com

US Bureau of Alcohol, Tobacco and Firearms: www.atf.treas.gov

CHAPTER 4

On the Job

TEENS AND THE JOB MARKET

At what age can a young person work outside the home?

It depends on the type of work. At age eighteen, any person can be employed at any job. However, federal and state child labor laws regulate the types of work that persons under eighteen can legally perform.

Young people under age eighteen can't be hired for work that is hazardous, such as in mines, steel mills, quarries, foundries, and butcher shops. Working with explosives, dangerous chemicals, radioactive materials, power-driven machinery, and earth-moving equipment is also off-limits for those under eighteen.

Persons under age sixteen almost always are prohibited from working in factories unless the job involves office work. Teens between the ages of fourteen and sixteen are permitted to work only after school, on weekends, and during vacation and aren't allowed to hold jobs that are dangerous or unhealthy. They can do office and sales work, wait on tables, be shelvers and baggers at retail stores, and hold similar positions.

Minors above age twelve (above age ten in some states) can have newspaper routes and work as golf caddies, but only during nonschool hours. They can also do yard work, babysit, and perform certain types of nonhazardous farm work. As a rule, children under age twelve can't work outside the home, although special child labor laws in each state permit minors of any age to do stage and screen work. Table 4.1 lists state laws on children working as entertainers.

TABLE 4.1: State Laws on Child Entertainers

State	*Regulates Child Entertainment*	*Work Permit Required*	*Law/Comments*
Alabama	Yes	No	Alabama requires “written consent” to employ Child Actors, Performers, and Models, and if it is a film production, the consent must be signed by the Alabama Film Office. The work may not be detrimental to the minor’s life, health, safety, welfare, or morals and cannot interfere with the minor’s schooling. Minors under age 16 must be accompanied by a parent or guardian at all rehearsals, appearances, performances, or sessions, and for minors under age 16 working as actors or performers, provisions must be made for full-time equivalent education.
Alaska	Yes	Yes	Extensive requirements for theatrical employment. 8 AAC 05.300 requires any child under 18 employed in the entertainment industry to have a work permit. Regulations also establish hours of work, working conditions, and prohibited practices. A waiver is available from the Studio Teacher requirement if it can be shown that the working conditions are safe for the minor child.
Arizona	No	No	Sec. 23-235: Minors employed as stars or performers in motion picture, theatrical, radio, or television productions are exempt from the law governing persons under the age of 16 if before the beginning of production, the production company provides the Department of Labor with the name and address of the person; the length, location, and hours of employment; and any other information required by the Department.
Arkansas	Yes	Yes	11-12-104: A child under 16 employed in the entertainment industry must have a permit and the written consent of a parent or guardian for issuance of the permit; written statement from principal as to academic standing of child.

California	Yes	Yes	Extensive requirements for theatrical employment: The labor commissioner issues permits to minors to work in the entertainment industry with required documentation from appropriate school districts as applicable and/or permits permitting employment of minors in the entertainment industry. Sec. 6-1308.7: Work permit to work not more than 5 consecutive days in the entertainment or allied industries; excused from school for up to 5 absences per school year; school districts are to allow pupils to complete all assignments and tests missed during absence. Sec. 6750 Family Code: Courts may require a portion of earnings be set aside for the minor in a trust.
Colorado	Yes	No	C.R.S. 8-12-101 et. seq. regulates the employment of minors in Colorado. Colorado law provides for some exemptions from youth employment relating to, for example, actors, models, and performers.
Connecticut	Yes	No	Sec. 31-23: Minors under the age of 16 are permitted to work in the theatrical industry with the authorization of the labor commissioner. Must have a certificate of age.
Delaware	Yes	Yes	Sec. 508: Special permit issued by Department of Labor allows child under age 16 to be employed in the entertainment industry for a limited time.
Florida	Yes	Yes	450.132: Employers or agents must make application to the Division and notify the Division showing the date, number of days, location, and date of termination of the work performed by minors in the entertainment industry.
Georgia	Yes	Yes	39-2-18: For minors employed in the entertainment industry a permit is required. The commissioner of labor must give written consent.
Hawaii	Yes	Yes	Sec. 12-25-22: Minors under the age of 14 may be permitted to work in theatrical employment with written consent filed with the director by guardian or parent; certificate is kept on file by employer. Sec 12-25-23 establishes limits on daily and night work hours.

(*Continued*)

TABLE 4.1: (Continued)

State	*Regulates Child Entertainment*	*Work Permit Required*	*Law/Comments*
Idaho	Yes	No	Sec. 44-1305: Prohibits children under the age of 16 from certain entertainment activities.
Illinois	Yes	Yes	Sec. 205/8, 8.1: Minors under the age of 16 appearing in theatrical productions must have a certificate authorized by the superintendent of schools; minors employed in entertainment industry may be employed subject to conditions imposed by DOL.
Indiana	Yes	No	IC 22-2-18.1-14 and 16: For minors less than age 18, employment in listed activities must not be detrimental to the life, health, safety, or welfare of the minor or interfere with their schooling; employment or appearances cannot be in a cabaret, dance hall, night club, and so on; and if the minor works as an actor or performer and certain provisions are met, they are exempt from the hours per day/week, days per week, and time of day restrictions. For minors less than age 16, provisions must be made for full-time equivalent education, and they must be accompanied by a parent at all rehearsals, appearances, and performances.
Iowa	Yes	No	Sec. 92.17: Children under age 16 may be employed as models, outside of school hours, for up to 3 hours a day between 7:00 a.m. and 10:00 p.m., not exceeding 12 hours in a month, with parental permission. Special order issued by labor commissioner, to exempt from restrictions any child employed as a performer.
Kansas	No	No	Sec. 38-614 and 616: Children employed in the entertainment industry are exempt from child labor requirements, except that infants under one month must have written certification from a licensed physician stating that they are at least 15 days old and that they are physically capable of handling the work. Sec. 38-622: Rules and regulations may be adopted setting standards for minor children on motion picture sets. Sec.21-3604: Courts may require a portion of earnings be set aside for the minor in a trust.

Kentucky	No	No	Sec. 339.210: Children employed in the entertainment industry are exempt from child labor requirements.
Louisiana	Yes	Yes	Sec. 253: Minors under the age of 16 must have permit issued by state DOL to participate in employment in the entertainment industry.
Maine	No	Yes	Sec. 26-773 to 775: Minors under age 16 working as theatrical or film actors are exempt from the child labor law except that they must have work permits and approval by local superintendent of schools. No restrictions at ages 16 and 17.
Maryland	Yes	Yes	Sec.3-207 (a): Special permit must be issued by the labor commissioner. The permit must be signed and notarized by parent or guardian and employer.
Massachusetts	Yes	Yes	Chap. 149, Sec. 60: Minors under the age of 16 may take part on the stage in a theater where not more than 2 performances are given in one day and not more than 8 performances are given in any one week, with written permission from the attorney general. The Attorney General's Office has the authority to issue temporary waivers of time restrictions for children working in entertainment, theater, or film (M.G.L. c. 149, § 60 & M.G.L. c. 149, § 104).
Michigan	Yes	Yes	Application for Performing Arts Authorization form must be approved by the Michigan Dept. of Labor and Economic Opportunity for ages 15 days to 17 years.
Minnesota	Yes	Yes	181A.07. Exemptions: Minors are subject to the child labor law except for the minimum age provisions. The labor commissioner may issue waivers from the hours limitations.
Mississippi	No	No	
Missouri	Yes	Yes—for under 16.	Sec. 294.022 and 294.030: Need: proof of age, written parental consent, and written statement of employer stating nature and duration of job. Waivers of time and hour restrictions may be issued by the director of the division of labor standards.

(*Continued*)

TABLE 4.1: (Continued)

State	*Regulates Child Entertainment*	*Work Permit Required*	*Law/Comments*
Montana	No	No	41-2-104: All minors, regardless of age, may be employed as an actor, model, or performer.
Nebraska	Yes	Yes—special permit for a child.	Special permit: Issued by Dept. of Labor, to exempt from restrictions any child employed as a performer. Need: written parental consent.
Nevada	No	No	Ch. 392: Casinos or resort hotels employing minors in the entertainment industry for more than 91 school days must, upon request, pay for tutoring or other equivalent educational services. Ch. 609: Courts may require a portion of earnings be set aside for the minor in a trust.
New Hampshire	No	No	
New Jersey	Yes	Yes—for under 16.	Sec. 34:2-21.59: Need: parental consent, good health, workplace approved by DOL, minor under direct care of adult named in application, not attending public school, receiving approved instruction, and not during summer vacation. Number of performances and hours permitted are specified.
New Mexico	Yes	Yes	A work permit is required at all times when employing children under the age of 16, issued only by school superintendents, school principals, other appropriate school officers, or the director of the labor and industrial division. The work must also be certified as not dangerous to the child or prohibited as outlined in the FLSA hazardous list. The maximum number of hours allowed for children under the age of 16 to work is 18 hours a week during the school week and 40 hours a week in nonschool weeks.

				With respect to employing and protecting child performers in the entertainment industry, including motion pictures, theatrical, radio, and television productions, employers are required to follow educational and safety requirements and they are responsible for obtaining a Pre-Authorization Certificate for any child performing under the age of 18 before the employment begins. The certificate is valid for one year or until the specific project is completed, whichever time period is shorter. The employer must provide a certified teacher for each group of 10 or fewer children and must provide a New Mexico certified trainer or technician at the place of employment at all times when a child performer may be exposed to potentially hazardous conditions. The statutes governing child entertainment within New Mexico can be found at the New Mexico Department of Workforce Solutions—Child Labor Section—11.1.4.10—11.1.4.14.
New York	Yes		Yes—models under 18 need permit from educational authorities. Performer 16–17 needs employment certificate. Performers under 16 need permit from mayor or chief executive.	To obtain certificates and permits need: written parental consent (exceptions for emancipated children), proof of age, and a certificate of physical fitness; separate procedures are in effect for New York City and for the remainder of the State. Sec. 7-7.1: Estates, Powers and Trusts Law: Courts may require a portion of earnings be set aside for the minor in a trust.
North Carolina	Yes		Yes—for under 18 need Youth Employment Certificate from county social services.	To obtain certificate need: proof of age. Sec. 48A-13: Courts may require a portion of earnings be set aside for the minor in a trust.
North Dakota	Yes		Yes—for under 16 need parental permit and commissioner of labor permit.	Permits issued if appearance of such minor will not be detrimental to the minor's morals, health, safety, welfare, or education.
Ohio	No		No—performers need parental consent.	Performers must be without remuneration and performance must be given by a church, school, academy, or at a concert or entertainment given solely for charitable purposes or religious institution.

(*Continued*)

TABLE 4.1: (Continued)

State	*Regulates Child Entertainment*	*Work Permit Required*	*Law/Comments*
Oklahoma	No	No	Minors who entertain are exempt from all laws because they are considered independent employees with agents.
Oregon	Yes	Yes—employer must register with the Bureau of Labor for jobs of short duration (5 or fewer days). Babies under 15 days can't work. Longer duration: minors 14–17 need work permits/under 14 need special permit from Bureau of Labor and Industries.	To obtain work permits need: parental and minor's signature and Social Security number and proof of age.
Pennsylvania	Yes	Yes—minors 7 to under 18 need special permits from Dept. of Labor and Industry, and can't work where there is alcohol.	To obtain special permits need: application signed by parent and employer, and with the seal of notary. Includes provisions for educational instruction, supervision, health, welfare, and the safeguarding and conservation for the minor of the monies derived from such performances.
Rhode Island	No	No	With one exception, the state doesn't regulate such employment because entertainers are not employees on a payroll, but are rather independent employees with agents. Therefore, regulation is left up to the localities. The state does not permit minors under the age of 18 to work in commercial adult entertainment establishments.
South Carolina	No	No	71-3105-d: The provisions of this Article do not apply with respect to any employee engaged as an actor or performer in motion pictures, radio or television productions, or theatrical productions.
South Dakota	No	No	60-12-1: The provisions of this section do not apply to children employed as actors or performers in motion pictures, theatrical, radio, or television productions.
Tennessee	No	No	50-5-107: The provisions of this chapter shall not apply to any minor who is a musician or entertainer; minors under 16 may model.

			Sec. 50-5-201: Courts may require a portion of earnings be set aside for the minor in a trust.
Texas	Yes	No	Minors under 14 need to submit application for authorization signed by agency and parent, proof of age, and a photograph. 13-5(H)-902 & 904: Contracts limited to no more than 7 years. Courts may require a portion of earnings be set aside for the minor in a trust.
Utah	No	No	
Vermont	Yes	Yes—minors under 16 need a certificate from commissioner of labor and industry except for certain work done outside of school hours.	To obtain certificate need: written parental consent, commissioner of labor and industry consent, proof of age, and school record. Children employed as actors or performers in motion pictures, theatrical productions, radio, or television, or employed as a baseball bat girl or bat boy may be employed until midnight or after midnight if a parent or guardian and the commissioner of labor have consented in writing.
Virginia	Yes	Yes—work permits for minors under the age of 16 for theater or other public place where a performance, concert, commercial presentation, or entertainment is to take place No such permit is required for any nonprofit dance, or music recital or noncommercial television or radio broadcast. Nonprofit schools of performing arts are not required to obtain Theatrical Permits for performances related to classes.	Child labor provisions do not apply to children employed as actors or performers in motion pictures, theatrical, radio, or television productions. To obtain permit one needs: a completed employer intention to employ form, a permission to employ form signed by parent and school, and proof of age.
Washington	Yes	Yes—work permit for all minors issued by Dept. of Labor.	Work permits required for all minors employed as actors or performers in film, video, audio, or theatrical productions. Employers must obtain Theatrical Minor Variance for the minor to work additional hours, earlier or later than usually allowed, or during school hours.
West Virginia	No	No	Minors of any age may be legally employed without a permit or certificate in acting or performing in motion pictures, theatrical, radio, or television productions.

(*Continued*)

TABLE 4.1: (Continued)

State	*Regulates Child Entertainment*	*Work Permit Required*	*Law/Comments*
Wisconsin	No	No—employment can't be in a roadhouse, cabaret, dance hall, night club, tavern, or other similar place.	No work permits needed between 12 and 18 for public entertainment. Nothing contained in sections 103.64–103.82 shall be construed as forbidding any minor under 18 to appear for the purpose of singing, playing, or performing in any studio, circus, theatrical or musical exhibition, concert or festival, in radio and television broadcasts, or as a live or photographic model.
Wyoming	Yes	No	Minors of any age may perform in radio, TV, movie, or theatrical productions. Under 16 can be actors or performers in any concert hall or room where there is no alcohol or malt present. Also, under 16 must entertain for charity and in reputable place.

Source: Division of Communications Wage and Hour Division, US Department of Labor, "Child Entertainment Laws as of Jan. 1, 2023," https://www.dol.gov/agencies/whd/state/child-labor/entertainment (accessed August 15, 2023).

Some states have fairly extensive restrictions on the employment of younger minors. For example, Louisiana prohibits the employment of minors under fourteen unless the following conditions are met: (a) the minor is at least twelve years of age, (b) the minor's parent or legal guardian is the owner of the business in which the minor is employed, (c) the minor works only under the direct supervision of the parent or legal guardian, (d) the younger minors have the same protections as older minors, and (e) the minor obtains an employment certificate under state law.

Can a minor work full-time?

In most states, minors between ages fourteen and sixteen are prohibited from working more than 40 hours per week. Furthermore, this age group in many states often can't work for more than 3 hours on school days and more than 8 hours on nonschool days and during the summer.

Minors between the ages of fourteen and sixteen also are prohibited from working the "graveyard shift"—between 9:30 p.m. and 7:00 a.m. In some states, however, teens can work these hours if school isn't in session the next day.

Couldn't a teen just lie about his or her age to be hired for a particular job?

No, because in most states, job applicants under age sixteen (under age eighteen in some states) must present an "employment certificate" or other proof of age in order to be hired.

Who issues employment certificates?

If state law requires them, the superintendent of schools usually is the issuer. The state board of education may designate someone else to issue these certificates. To obtain an employment certificate, the minor must be able to produce

1. a statement from the prospective employer describing the type of work;
2. a statement that the minor's parents don't object to the job;
3. a birth certificate or other proof of age; and
4. a statement, signed by a doctor, that the minor is physically fit for the job.

Employment certificates are called "work permits" in some states.

Is it illegal for a minor to work without an employment certificate?

If one is required, yes. In states that require them, an employer can't hire a young person who is unable to produce one.

Who, then, is regulated by child labor laws—the minor or the employer?

The employer. When a federal or state child labor law is violated, the employer commits the offense.

Can the government punish a minor for working without an employment certificate—or for working under age if a certificate isn't required?

No.

Can an employment certificate be revoked?

Yes, if the minor's job interferes with school work or adversely affects his or her physical or mental health. The school principal usually is the person with the power to revoke. Some state laws are quite broad on this subject. Minnesota's law provides that "the issuing officer is authorized to cancel an employment certificate, if the issuing officer determines that such action would be in the best interest of the minor." In other words, in some states, if the school official determines that it is not in the best interest of the minor to continue working, the employment certificate can be revoked.

Does a minor need a Social Security card to work outside the home?

Yes. A person's Social Security card shows his or her lifetime Social Security number. Employers need their employees' Social Security numbers to make advance Social Security payments and income tax deposits to the federal government on their employees' behalf. Employers are legally required to make these payments, which is why they always ask for a person's Social Security number at the time of hiring.

Who issues Social Security cards?

The local Social Security Administration office issues these cards. To obtain a card, call the closest office and ask to be sent a Social Security card application. Fill it out, have a parent sign it, then send it back with an original copy of your birth certificate and one of the other forms of identification requested on the application. Your Social Security card will arrive in about two weeks. Most teens probably already have Social Security cards, since children need Social Security numbers if their parents wish to claim them as dependents on their income tax forms.

Can minors who aren't US citizens legally work here?

It depends on whether the minor has the required legal documentation. To be legally eligible for work, a person born abroad—an "alien"—must at least have a "visa." The various types of visas are issued by the Immigration and Naturalization Service, or INS.

An INS immigrant visa permits an alien to live in the United States for a work-related purpose. Obtaining this type of visa is often an alien's first step toward getting a "green card." Because there are many types of visas, an alien who wants to work here should consult an INS agent or other immigration expert to determine the best visa for his or her job skills.

It is a violation of federal law to hire an undocumented worker. However, it is also a violation of federal law for an employer to discriminate on the basis of nationality or noncitizen status, provided the alien has a right, by virtue of his or her visa or green card, to work in this country.

What is a "green card"?

A green card is the document needed by aliens to travel to and from the United States and to work here legally and without restrictions. Although its official name is the "Alien Registration Receipt Card," everybody uses the term "green card." When it was introduced in the 1940s, the ID card with the alien's photo, registration number, birth date, entry date, and port of entry was green. However, the cards were changed to blue in the 1960s and 1970s, changed to white in the 1980s, and in the 1990s they became pink. Even so, they're still called "green cards."

THE MINIMUM WAGE

Are minors entitled to the minimum wage?

Yes. Congress increased the minimum wage to $7.25 per hour in 2009. It remains at this rate. Most states have minimum wage laws as well. Some of these state laws require the payment of more wages than the federal law. For example, the minimum wage in Connecticut is $14.00, in Oregon it is $13.50, and in Washington it is $14.49. When an employer is covered by both federal and state minimum wage laws, employees must be paid the higher of the two minimum wages.

What state has the highest minimum wage?

California has the highest minimum wage of any state at $15.00 per hour. California's law originally applied to employers with more than twenty-five employees but in 2023, it will apply to all employers. Washington, DC—though not a state—has an even higher minimum wage of $17.00.

See Table 4.2 for a listing of minimum wage laws state-by-state.

Are certain jobs outside the minimum wage laws?

Yes. "Exempt" positions such as executive and professional positions aren't covered because persons with these types of jobs usually aren't paid by the hour. Certain administrative positions are also exempt. The best way to find out whether a job is exempt is to call the local Wage and Hour Division of the Department of Labor.

Do people have to work full-time to receive the minimum wage?

No.

TABLE 4.2: State Minimum Wage Laws

Alabama	No state minimum wage law (employers subject to Fair Labor Standards Act must pay the current Federal minimum wage of $7.25)
Alaska	$10.85
Arizona	$13.85
Arkansas	$11.00
California	$15.50
Colorado	$13.65
Connecticut	$15.00
Delaware	$11.75
Florida	$11.00
Georgia	$7.25 ($5.15 for those not covered under the Fair Labor Standards Act)
Hawaii	$12.00
Idaho	$7.25
Illinois	$13.00
Indiana	$7.25
Iowa	$7.25
Kansas	$7.25
Kentucky	$7.25
Louisiana	No state minimum wage law (employers subject to the Fair Labor Standards Act must pay the federal minimum of $7.25)
Maine	$13.80
Maryland	$13.25 (for employers with more than 15 employees)
	$12.80 (for employers with fewer than 15 employees)
Massachusetts	$15.00
Michigan	$10.10
Minnesota	$10.59 (for employers with a yearly revenue of more than $500,000 per year)
	$8.63 (for employers with revenue less than $500,000 per year)
Missouri	$12.00
Mississippi	No state minimum wage law (those employers subject to the Fair Labor Standards Act must pay the federal minimum of $7.25)
Montana	$9.95 (for businesses with annual revenue of more than $110,000)
	$4.00 (for businesses with annual revenues of less than $110,000 and not subject to the Fair Labor Standards Act)

TABLE 4.2: (Continued)

North Carolina	$7.25
North Dakota	$7.25
Nebraska	$10.50 (employers with four or more employees)
New Hampshire	$7.25
New Jersey	$14.13
New Mexico	$12.00
Nevada	$11.25 (if health insurance not offered by employer)
	$10.25 (if health insurance offered by employer)
New York	$14.20 or $15.00 depending on location
Ohio	$10.10 (if employer has gross receipts totaling more than $372,000)
	$7.25 (if employer has gross receipts less than $372,000)
Oklahoma	$7.25
Oregon	$14.20 (standard state rate)
	$15.45 (in Portland metro area)
	$13.20 (nonurban counties)
Pennsylvania	$7.25
Rhode Island	$13.00
South Carolina	No state minimum wage law (employers subject to the Fair Labor Standards Act must pay the federal minimum of $7.25)
South Dakota	$10.80
Tennessee	No state minimum wage law (employers subject to the Fair Labor Standards Act must pay the federal minimum of $7.25)
Texas	$7.25
Utah	$7.25
Virginia	$12.00
Vermont	$13.18
Washington	$15.74
Wisconsin	$7.25
West Virginia	$8.75 (applicable to employers with 6 or more employees at one location)
Wyoming	$5.15 (employers subject to the Fair Labor Standards Act must pay $7.25)
District of Columbia	$17.00

Source: US Department of Labor, https://www.dol.gov/agencies/whd/minimum-wage/state (accessed August 15, 2023).

Are tips treated as wages under the minimum wage laws?

It depends on the state. Some states—such as California, Minnesota, Montana, Nevada, Oregon, and Washington—do not allow tip credits at all. Other states do allow them. Other states follow the so-called 80-20 rule. This rule provides that restaurants can only use the tip credit if a worker spends 80 percent of their time on tip-producing work and no more than 20 percent—or more than 30 continuous minutes—on tasks that "directly support" tip duties.

Can minors draw overtime pay?

No, but this is because most minors can't legally work more than 40 hours per week.

Under the Fair Labor Standards Act of 1938, hourly employees must be paid extra for each hour worked over 40 in any week. The overtime rate is 1½ times the worker's regular hourly rate. But under state child labor laws, persons under age sixteen can't work more than 40 hours per week, and persons under age eighteen who attend school can't work more than 3 hours on school days and 8 hours on nonschool days. Because of these limits, minors usually don't qualify for overtime pay.

SUMMER JOBS

Can teens work full-time during the summer?

Yes, but only up to 40 hours per week under federal and state child labor laws. Although the FLSA's minimum wage and overtime rules don't apply to certain seasonal work such as jobs at resorts, summer camps, and swimming pools, the 40-hour-per-week limit nevertheless does.

For more about part-time and summer jobs, see the section "Teens, Parents, and Money" in Chapter 3.

THE OBLIGATIONS AND BENEFITS OF EMPLOYMENT

What is employment at will?

The employment at will doctrine provides that either the employer or the employee may terminate the employment relationship at will. In other words, the employee may decide to leave a job to take another job, and the employer may decide to fire the employee and hire someone else. Much of modern employment law focuses on exceptions to the employment at will doctrine. For example, an employer generally can't fire an employee because that person files a workers' compensation claim, serves on a jury, or blows the whistle about illegal activity on the job or because of the employee's race, sex, color, religion, or national origin.

What do employee and employer "owe" one another?

Every employee has a duty to work hard, be loyal, follow the employer's rules and directions, and work for the employer and no one else while on the job. In return, the employer must pay the employee for performing his or her job and refrain from discriminating against the employee because of race, color, nationality, gender, age, or religion with respect to pay, promotions, and working conditions. These duties and obligations apply across the board—to teens as well as adults.

What are "fringe benefits"? Are minors entitled to them?

A fringe benefit is any benefit other than pay that an employee receives for working. Examples of fringe benefits are paid holidays, paid or unpaid vacation time, maternity and sick leave, and pensions.

If an employer provides fringe benefits to adult workers, minors are entitled to them also. But employers usually restrict fringe benefits to full-time nonseasonal employees, so most minors aren't able to qualify for them.

What is a pension? Can a minor be in a pension plan?

A pension is a payment from a "pension plan" or "retirement plan," which is a company program for setting aside money for employees and their spouses for their later years, when they are no longer employed by the company. The federal Social Security program is a retirement program. Because employers aren't required to establish and maintain their own pension or retirement plans, Social Security is the only retirement program that many American workers ever participate in.

Company pension plans are governed by complex federal laws. Under a company plan, either the employer makes a yearly contribution to the employee's pension account or the employee makes a yearly contribution and the employer matches it. The accounts are invested and reinvested over the years. Unless the employee quits, he or she doesn't receive any payments from the pension plan until retiring.

Nothing prohibits an employer from including minors in a pension plan. But if eligibility in the plan is based on age and length of service (as almost always happens), under federal law the employer doesn't have to let employees participate until they reach age twenty-five and work at least 1,000 hours in twelve months. This means that although the law doesn't prohibit minors from participating, the terms of the plan rarely permit it.

Is health insurance a fringe benefit? Are employers required to provide health insurance for their employees?

Health insurance is indeed a fringe benefit, and a very important one. It pays an employee's medical expenses (or a large part of them) and often pays the medical expenses of the employee's family. An illness or injury doesn't have to be job related to be covered by employer-provided health insurance.

For many years employers weren't required to provide health insurance for their workers; many believe that federal law should require employers to cover at least their full-time people. However, the Affordable Care Act or "Obamacare" (named after President Barack Obama) was signed into law in 2010. It generally requires that individuals receive health care. Numerous legal challenges to various aspects of the law have been filed. It remains controversial. However, an important aspect of the law is that it prevents health insurance companies from denying people coverage because of preexisting health conditions.

What is workers' compensation?

It is a payment from an employer that "compensates" an employee for medical expenses and time off due to a job-related injury or illness. In this respect it differs from employer-provided health insurance.

The amount of wage compensation normally is a percentage of the disabled person's regular pay. If a job-related injury results in the loss of a body part such as a hand or foot, the employee usually receives a lump sum based on a payment schedule. The more serious the loss, the greater the lump sum. Keep in mind that like so many other areas of law, workers' compensation laws vary significantly from state to state.

Workers' compensation is "no-fault," which means that an employee can qualify for it regardless of who, if anyone, was at fault for the injury or illness. The problem—the "disability"—just has to be job related. But the employer also benefits: under a workers' compensation program, an employee cannot demand and receive additional payment for "pain and suffering" and can't receive "punitive damages." For more about damages resulting from an injury or illness, see Chapter 17, "Taking Matters to Court."

The laws of most states provide workers' compensation. Depending on the state, workers' compensation payments are made by an insurance company, the employer, or the state where the employee works.

Are minors entitled to workers' compensation benefits?

Minors as well as adults can receive workers' compensation. Extra benefits are often payable if the injured person is a minor who was employed in violation of a child labor law.

What should a minor do if he or she is injured on the job?

Report the accident to the employer right away. This is referred to as a "notice" requirement. Sometimes employers try to deny workers' compensation coverage by claiming that they did not receive proper or timely notice. So make sure that you report the work-related injury to the appropriate person. In turn, the employer must report it to the state workers' compensation board. All employers are required by law to post reporting and filing requirements at an easy-to-find location at work.

IF YOU LOSE YOUR JOB

Can an employer fire an employee for "no good reason"? Does it depend on whether the employee is a minor?

If an employee hasn't entered into a written contract with the employer to work a certain length of time or for a specific purpose, that person is an "employee at will." This refers to the employment at will doctrine mentioned early in this chapter. Employees at will can be fired or laid off for any reason and at any time, so long as the reason doesn't violate "public policy." In fact, an employee at will can be fired for no apparent reason at all.

These rules apply to employees of all ages. But since minors are almost always hired as employees at will, they usually can be fired for what may seem like no good reason.

Does the law ever prohibit an employer from firing an employee?

Yes, there are many exceptions to the employment at will doctrine, including numerous public policy exceptions. This means that an employer generally may not terminate an employee if such a termination would violate an important public policy. For example, society wants its citizens to fulfill their civic duty and serve on juries. Thus, states have laws that prohibit employers from firing employees simply because those employees had to miss work for jury duty. Another public policy exception is that an employer cannot fire an employee simply because the employee files a workers' compensation claim.

Perhaps the biggest exceptions to the employment at will doctrine are federal and state antidiscrimination laws. These laws prohibit employers from terminating people's employment because of their race, sex, color, religion, or national origin. Other laws prohibit terminating employees because of their age or disability. The major federal antidiscrimination provision in employment law is Title VII of the Civil Rights Act of 1964. This law prohibits employers with 15 or more employees from dismissing an employee solely for reasons of race, color, gender, age, national origin, or religion. If an employee is in any one of these "protected classes," Title VII requires that if the employee is discharged, it must be for the same reason or type of conduct that workers not in a protected class can be discharged for.

Other landmark items of legislation also prohibit employers from firing an employee. First, the ADA prohibits discrimination in hiring and firing for no other reason than the existence of a disability; second, the Age Discrimination in Employment Act of 1967 (ADEA) prohibits an employer from firing an employee for no other reason than that the employee is over age forty; and third, the National Labor Relations Act of 1935 prohibits an employer from firing an employee for either joining a union or refusing to join one. Also, an employee can't be fired for refusing to perform an unlawful act at work, for reporting a violation of the law, or for filing a workers' compensation claim.

Discrimination on the job is discussed later in this chapter.

If a minor gets fired, can he or she collect "unemployment"?

In some cases, yes. Unemployment compensation is a weekly payment that is meant to hold people over until they find another job. Unemployment compensation is a matter of federal law, although the states administer the system.

Some unemployed persons simply don't qualify. To be eligible, an applicant must have held a job for a specific number of weeks before being let go, and he or she must be actively looking for new work. In addition, the employee cannot have quit or have been fired for misconduct. This is often a disputed issue. Often, the employer will contest the awarding of unemployment benefits by saying that the former employee engaged in misconduct.

Minors aren't prohibited from receiving unemployment compensation, but part-time employees and persons under age fourteen don't qualify. (Part-time work includes work after school and during summer vacation.) For this reason, minors who are still in school usually can't collect it.

Each state has an unemployment office with detailed information available about how the system works.

INCOME TAXES

Do minors have to pay income taxes?

Yes. Everyone who has an income may have to pay income taxes, even babies. A person's income may take the form of wages, dividends from corporate stock, or a debt that has just been forgiven.

Income taxes are imposed by the federal government and most states. Annual federal and state tax returns for the previous calendar year and any unpaid taxes are due from every individual taxpayer on April 15.

To ensure that income taxes are paid, both the federal government and the states require employers to "withhold" certain amounts from their employees' pay. The employer then pays the withholding amount to the government. The payment serves as an advance deposit against income taxes owed by the employee.

Employers must withhold Social Security (FICA) taxes and federal unemployment (FUTA) taxes in addition to state and local income taxes. These withholding amounts are paid to the federal government.

Does this mean a minor's pay is subject to withholding?

Yes.

What happens if the taxes withheld during the year turn out to be more than the total taxes owed?

The taxpayer shows the amount of the overpayment on his or her annual tax return. If the "taxing entity" agrees with the taxpayer, the excess is refunded. So even if a person doesn't earn enough in a calendar year to have an income tax liability, returns are required in order to obtain the refunds owed.

Are FICA and FUTA withholdings ever refundable, either in whole or in part?

No.

Is babysitting money taxable?

Although earnings from babysitting and technically income that are taxable under federal and state tax laws, most teens don't earn enough from these pursuits to have to pay taxes on the money they take in. Even so, teens should let their parents know when their earnings from babysitting, cutting lawns, or similar part-time jobs have exceeded $500 in any single year.

PRIVACY

Can a minor be required to submit to a drug or urine test as a condition of employment?

Yes, though this depends on particular state laws. In many states a private employer can require all job applicants to be tested for drugs and also can make periodic, random drug testing a condition of continued employment. But employers can't legally test either employees or job applicants for HIV/AIDS without their explicit permission.

Government employees enjoy greater privacy protections. A drug or urine test by a governmental employer would be considered a "search and seizure" under the federal Constitution and would therefore need to satisfy the Fourth Amendment's "reasonableness" standard in order to be legal.

The results of drug and urine tests must remain confidential. Furthermore, if an employee tests positive for drugs, state law may require that there be a so-called confirmatory test to screen out the problem of a "false positive," in which the test falsely indicates someone has taken illegal drugs.

Can an employer legally require an employee to submit to a search?

Yes. Employers sometimes search employees or their personal belongings to prevent theft, seek evidence of suspected theft, or prevent drugs and weapons from coming onto company property. On-the-job searches are usually legal. There isn't much an employee can do about a search provided it isn't too "invasive." Strip searches are the most intrusive type of search and generally are illegal.

Both minors and adults can be searched. Again, government employees enjoy more privacy protections, due to the Fourth Amendment's search and seizure rules.

Can an employer legally enforce rules relating to employees' clothes, tattoos, or hairstyles?

Yes. It is almost always legal for an employer to forbid a certain style of dress or hairstyle, provided the rule doesn't discriminate on the basis of gender. An employer can require a particular uniform and type of footwear for the job, can prohibit excessive jewelry, and can require that tattoos be covered up. For more about related issues, see Chapter 6, "Your Personal Appearance." However, courts have determined that an individual may have a free exercise of religion right to wear particular clothing.

Can an employer legally use a video camera to monitor a working employee? Can an employer legally monitor telephone conversations between its employees and third parties?

The answer to both questions is yes. However, employees still retain some measure of privacy. For example, an employer would violate privacy rights if it installed a hidden camera and recorded employees using the restroom and undressing.

Can an employer legally access an employee's e-mail, voice mail, or private computer files?

Some states have laws that prohibit "computer theft," "computer trespass," or "computer invasion of privacy." However, these offenses generally require that the employer not have authorization to access the employee's computer. A federal court in Connecticut recently determined that a public school principal had a reasonable expectation of privacy in her work e-mails. The court determined that the public school principal, as a public employee, had privacy interests protected by the Fourth Amendment's guarantee against unreasonable searches and seizures.

Whether an employee has privacy interests in work may depend on the employer's computer usage policy. Most employers retain the right to inspect employees' computers, reasoning that the computers are the property of the employer, not the employee. Many employers address the issues of e-mail, voice mail, and computers in their employee handbooks, particularly when these technologies can be used by employees for personal matters as well as for work. To learn about your employer's position on these issues, look first to the employee handbook. If the answers to your questions aren't addressed, don't be afraid to pose them to a supervisor or human resource person.

DISCRIMINATION IN EMPLOYMENT

What, if anything, prevents an employer from discriminating against employees and job applicants?

Important federal legislation—including Title VII of the Civil Rights Act of 1964, the ADEA, and the ADA—prevents employers from discriminating for certain reasons in the hiring process. These laws make it illegal for employers to discriminate at work on the basis of race, color, religion, gender, age, national origin, or disability. Title VII, the ADEA, and the ADA apply to hiring, firing, promotions, pay, and benefits.

But these federal laws don't require employers to hire people who aren't qualified for a particular position or to keep people who can't handle the work. Nor do these laws prohibit employers from basing differences in pay on job performance or length of service. Pay differences based on these reasons are actually examples of lawful discrimination.

States have similar antidiscrimination laws in employment that are modeled after these federal laws.

For Title VII to be violated, must the employer have intended to discriminate against the job applicant or employee?

No, Title VII prohibits more than just intentional discrimination. Intentional discrimination is sometimes described using the legal term "disparate treatment." This means that an employer intentionally treated an employee worse than other employees. However, Title VII prohibits more than just disparate treatment. It also prohibits certain forms of "disparate impact" discrimination.

Disparate impact means that a facially neutral law has an adverse impact on certain types of employees. For example, let's say a police department has a rule that requires all police officers to be 5 foot 10 inches tall and weigh 150 pounds. This policy, though neutral on its face and applied to all employees, would impose an adverse impact on females.

As another example, if an employer requires all applicants to take a test to determine who has a particular job skill, and members of a racial minority consistently perform worse than others, a court may declare the test discriminatory if the test has no reasonable relationship to actual job performance, because it has the effect of imposing an adverse impact on a particular racial group. The impact of the test would be discriminatory, even if it appeared fair on its face.

In this situation the employer must prove that a job-related purpose justifies the test—that the skills being tested for are needed for the successful operation of the business. In addition, the employer must show that no other testing method would have a less discriminatory impact. If this can't be proved—if the employer can't carry its "burden of proof"—the test must be either revamped or discontinued.

Does Title VII prohibit employment discrimination on the basis of sexual orientation?

Yes, the US Supreme Court ruled in *Bostock v. Clayton County, Georgia* (2020) that an employer violates Title VII if they discharge or discriminate against an employee because of their sexual orientation or gender identity. It was a watershed ruling, as for many years Title VII only prohibited discrimination in employment on the basis of race, color, religion, sex, or national origin. It does not prohibit discrimination based on sexual orientation. This means the major federal antidiscrimination law in employment did not offer protection for gays and lesbians. A measure to address this, called the Employment Non-Discrimination Act (ENDA), was repeatedly been introduced in Congress, but it has never cleared both houses and has not become law.

Twenty-nine states and the District of Columbia have laws that prohibit employment discrimination based on sexual orientation. See Table 4.3 for more detail.

Do these federal laws like Title VII apply to all employers?

No, they only cover employers with a certain number of employees. For example, Title VII applies only to employers that have fifteen or more employees. Some state laws apply to smaller employers as well. For example, the Tennessee Human Rights Act, passed in 1978, applies to employers with at least eight employees.

Is it illegal to discriminate against young persons on the basis of age?

No, the ADEA doesn't prohibit discrimination against persons under age forty. In other words, the "protected class" of individuals for purposes of the ADEA includes all individuals who are forty years of age or older. The federal law only protects older workers, because young people don't have a history of being unfairly discriminated against—in contrast to women, the elderly, and racial and ethnic minorities. However, some state laws prohibit discrimination against age groups that aren't covered by federal legislation.

What racial groups are protected by Title VII?

Title VII applies to all racial groups, including blacks, whites, Asians, Hispanics, and American Indians. The US Supreme Court ruled in *McDonald v. Santa Fe Trail Transp. Co.* (1976) that Title VII applies to all racial groups, including whites.

What is "reverse discrimination"? Is it legal?

Reverse discrimination occurs when an employer gives an unfair advantage to a class of people who have historically been discriminated against—African Americans or women, for example. It occurs when a person is hired for a job or promoted because of minority status and not because he or she is the best candidate or has the best job record.

Reverse discrimination is prohibited under Title VII when it illegally favors a Title VII protected class. For more about discrimination issues, see Chapter 13, "Equal Protection and Employment Discrimination."

What is "affirmative action"?

Affirmative action occurs when an employer hires or promotes an employee in a manner that *legally* favors a protected class. For example, it would be legal for an employer to recruit black candidates to *compete* for a particular job, or set hiring goals to place women in positions in which they have been underrepresented. The justification for affirmative action is that it creates a more diverse job force. Many businesses support the idea behind enhancing diversity.

Can a woman be discriminated against because she is pregnant? Because she is pregnant and unmarried?

The answer to both questions is no. A 1978 amendment to Title VII, called the Pregnancy Discrimination Act (PDA), makes it illegal to discriminate at the workplace on the basis of pregnancy, childbirth, or a related medical condition such as abortion. In other words, an employer must treat a pregnant woman or a woman with a related condition the same as other employees, based on her ability to work.

These rules apply to minors as well as adults.

Can a teenage parent take paternity or maternity leave without placing his or her job at risk?

The federal Family and Medical Leave Act of 1993 (FMLA) permits a parent (father or mother) to take leave from work to care for a newborn child or tend to a family medical emergency—but only under certain conditions.

Under the FMLA, if an employee has worked at least 1,250 full-time hours for the employer in the last twelve months, he or she may take up to twelve weeks of unpaid leave to care for a newborn without losing his or her job. The employer must employ at least fifty people for the FMLA to apply. Because of these conditions, many teenage parents fail to qualify for leave in connection with the birth of a child and therefore risk their jobs if they take time off.

However, a father does not have to be married to the newborn's mother to take paternity leave under the FMLA.

Some states have their own laws regarding maternity and paternity leave, which apply when the FMLA doesn't.

What is sexual harassment?

It is any unwelcome sexual advance, a request for a sexual favor, or any other words or actions of a sexual type that interfere with work, especially if submitting to or rejecting the advance or request becomes the basis for a job-related decision. If the behavior is really unwelcome, it doesn't matter that the employee may have eventually decided to put up with it to save his or her job. There are different types of harassment. One type is sometimes referred to as "quid pro quo" harassment. Under this form of harassment, a harasser, for example, might say "sleep with me or you lose your job." Another type of harassment is called "hostile workplace" harassment. Under this form of sexual harassment, the hostility and sexually charged comments make it more difficult for the victim to perform her or his job duties.

Sexual harassment is illegal discrimination under Title VII. However, proving sexual harassment sometimes can be quite difficult. The rule is that the employee must also show that the harassment was not only unwelcome but that it was "severe" and "pervasive." This means that a stray comment or a few inappropriate sexual remarks may not rise to the level of sexual harassment.

If an employer knows or has reason to know that sexual harassment of an employee is going on and doesn't do anything about it, both the person causing the harassment and the employer can be found responsible.

TABLE 4.3: State Employment Discrimination Laws for LGBT Workers

State	*Prohibits Employment Discrimination Based on Sexual Orientation*	*Prohibits Employment Discrimination Based on Gender Identity*
Alabama		
Alaska	Enforcement authorities accepting complaints on both sexual orientation and gender identify because of the Bostock decision)	
Arizona	Enforcement authorities accepting complaints on both sexual orientation and gender identify because of the Bostock decision)	
Arkansas		
California	X	X
Colorado	X	X
Connecticut	X	X
Delaware	X	X
Florida	Enforcement authorities accepting complaints on both sexual orientation and gender identify because of the Bostock decision)	
Georgia		
Hawaii	X	X
Idaho		
Illinois	X	X
Indiana	Public employees only	(prohibits such discrimination for public employees only)
Iowa	X	X
Kansas	Enforcement authorities accepting complaints on both sexual orientation and gender identify because of the Bostock decision)	
Kentucky	Enforcement authorities accepting complaints on both sexual orientation and gender identify because of the Bostock decision)	
Louisiana		
Maine	X	X

TABLE 4.3: (Continued)

State	*Prohibits Employment Discrimination Based on Sexual Orientation*	*Prohibits Employment Discrimination Based on Gender Identity*
Maryland	X	X
Massachusetts	X	X
Michigan	Public employees only	Public employees only
Minnesota	X	X
Mississippi		
Missouri	Public employees only	Public employees only
Montana	Public employees only	Public employees only
Nebraska	Enforcement authorities accepting complaints on both sexual orientation and gender identify because of the Bostock decision)	
Nevada	X	X
New Hampshire	X	
New Jersey	X	X
New Mexico	X	X
New York	X	
North Carolina	Public employees only	Public employees only
North Dakota	Enforcement authorities accepting complaints on both sexual orientation and gender identify because of the Bostock decision)	
Ohio	Public employees only	Public employees only
Oklahoma		
Oregon	X	x
Pennsylvania	Enforcement authorities accepting complaints on both sexual orientation and gender identify because of the Bostock decision)	
Rhode Island	X	x
South Carolina		
South Dakota		
Tennessee		

(*Continued*)

TABLE 4.3: (Continued)

State	*Prohibits Employment Discrimination Based on Sexual Orientation*	*Prohibits Employment Discrimination Based on Gender Identity*
Texas	Enforcement authorities accepting complaints on both sexual orientation and gender identify because of the Bostock decision)	
Utah		
Vermont	X	x
Virginia		
Washington	X	x
West Virginia		
Wisconsin	X	
Wyoming		

Source: Human Rights Campaign, Employment Section of "State Equality Index 2021," https://www.hrc.org/resources/state-equality-index (accessed December 12, 2022).

Can discriminatory sexual harassment occur between persons of the same sex?

Yes, the US Supreme Court ruled in *Oncale v. Sundowner Offshore Services, Inc.* (1998) that discriminatory sexual harassment on the job can occur between persons of the same sex.

Does it matter who does the sexual harassing?

Yes, there are different rules in place depending on whether the alleged harasser is a co-employee or a supervisor. If an employee is harassed by a co-employee, the employer is liable for such harassment if the employer knew or should have known about the co-employee's harassing conduct. Generally, this means that the person harassed must report the harassment to the employer, pursuant to the employer's policy. That places the onus on the employer to take immediate, corrective action to prohibit further harassment.

If the harassment is committed by a supervisor, then the employer automatically has notice of the harassment. This is because employers act through their supervisors. It is much more difficult for an employer to defend against a claim of sexual harassment by a supervisor than by a co-employee. If the supervisor harasses an employee and for example that causes the employee to quit (what the law sometimes calls a "constructive discharge"), then the employer is automatically liable. If the employee is not subject to an adverse action, then the employer has a defense, but must meet certain requirements.

The US Supreme Court explained the difference between coworker and supervisor harassment in *Vance v. Ball State* (2013), writing:

Under Title VII, an employer's liability for such harassment may depend on the status of the harasser. If the harassing employee is the victim's coworker, the employer is liable only if it was negligent in controlling working conditions. In cases in which the harasser is a "supervisor," however, different rules apply. If the supervisor's harassment culminates in a tangible employment action, the employer is strictly liable. But if no tangible employment action is taken, the employer may escape liability by establishing, as an affirmative defense, that (1) the employer exercised reasonable care to prevent and correct any harassing behavior and (2) that the plaintiff unreasonably failed to take advantage of the preventive or corrective opportunities that the employer provided.

If a young person believes he or she has been discriminated against at work or in applying for a job, what can be done?

Sometimes the matter can be resolved by talking to the hiring person, the supervisor, or another individual in charge. If this doesn't help, the "complainant" may file a charge against the employer with the local Equal Employment Opportunity Commission (EEOC) or state civil rights office. Many cases are settled at this level. If no settlement is reached, the complainant at that point is granted the right to sue the employer in court.

If a young person is being sexually harassed at work, he or she should tell the harasser to stop and report to human resources or management/ownership. Also, he or she should keep an accurate written record of the harassing incidents, including the date, time, and place they occurred and the names of any witnesses. Again, the supervisor should be notified.

This area of law is complex, and it constantly changes. If a person, regardless of age, believes he or she has been illegally discriminated against in connection with work or sexually harassed, it is best to discuss the matter with a parent, who may want to contact a lawyer versed in employment law. This can be expensive, so most communities have legal service organizations that provide help with discrimination and civil rights cases at low cost.

What does a complainant have to prove in order to win a Title VII job discrimination case (other than a sexual harassment case)?

These four things:

1. That the complainant belongs to a "protected class": a particular race or sex, or persons over the age of forty, for example.
2. That the complainant was qualified for a position that the employer wanted to fill, or for a promotion, or the complainant was meeting the legitimate business expectations of the job.
3. That despite these qualifications, the complainant was denied the position or the promotion, or faced another sort of adverse employment action.
4. That after the person was rejected, the employer continued to seek applications and didn't change the job qualifications.

What is an adverse employment action?

An adverse employment action is any action taken by an employer that negatively impacts the status of the employee in a significant way. Firings, demotions, suspensions, transfers to less desirable jobs with less responsibility, and denial of promotion are classic examples of adverse employment actions.

Does the law protect those who complain about or oppose discriminatory practices in employment?

Yes, Title VII and other employment discrimination laws prohibit employers from retaliating against those employees who oppose discriminatory acts in employment or who participate in an employment discrimination proceeding filed by another employee. For example, an employer would violate the antiretaliation provision of Title VII if the employer fired an employee who complained that the employer tolerated sexually harassing conduct in the workplace. An employer also would violate the antiretaliation provision of Title VII if the employer fired an employee who testified by deposition in another employee's discrimination lawsuit.

JOB SAFETY

Are employers required to provide a safe place to work?

Yes, although this wasn't always the case. Under the federal Occupational Safety and Health Act of 1970 (OSHA) and also under state laws, employers must maintain a workplace that is safe and healthy for employees.

What should a person do if working conditions on the job appear unsafe?

Workers exposed to health or safety hazards have the right under OSHA to ask the employer to correct the problem or to report it to the closest OSHA office. Workers also have the right to talk privately to OSHA inspectors about what appear to be health and safety hazards. Under federal law, it is illegal for an employer to punish or discriminate against any worker who exercises these rights.

FOR FURTHER READING

In General

Barreiro, Sachi. *Your Rights in the Workplace: An Employee's Guide to Fair Treatment*. 11th ed. Berkeley, CA: NOLO, 2018.

Covington, Robert N. and Robert Seiner. *Employment Law in a Nutshell*. 5th ed. St. Paul, MN: West Publishing Company, 2022.

Immigration

Cohen, Susan and Steven Taylor. *Journeys from There to Here: Stories of Immigrant Trials, Triumphs, and Contributions*. Austin, TX: River Grove Books, 2021.

Simon, Elissa. *US Citizenship Test Study Guide 2021–2022: Comprehensive Review with Practice Questions for the United States Naturalization Civics Exam*. Houston, TX: Trivium Test Prep, 2021.

Privacy

Alderman, Ellen and Caroline Kennedy. *The Right to Privacy*. New York: Vintage Books, 1997.

Doss, April Falco. *Cyber Privacy: Who Has Your Data and Why You Should Care*. Dallas, TX: BenBella Books, 2021.

Gajda, Amy. *Seek and Hide: The Tangled History of the Right to Privacy*. New York: Viking Books, 2022.

Discrimination/Sexual Harassment

Bingham, Clara and Laura Leedy Gansler. *Class Action: The Landmark Case That Changed Sexual Harassment Law*. Harpswell, ME: Anchor Publishing, 2003.

Corcoran, Augustus B. *Sexual Harassment and the Law: The Mechelle Vinson Case*. Lawrence: University of Kansas Press, 2004.

England, Deborah C. *Essential Guide to Handling Workplace Harassment & Discrimination*. Berkeley, CA: NOLO Press, 2021.

Guerin, Lisa. *Essential Guide to Workplace Investigations*. Berkeley, CA: NOLO Press, 2021.

Disability Issues

Davis, Lennard. *Enabling Acts: The Hidden Story of How the American with Disabilities Act Gave the US Its Largest Minority*. Boston: Beacon Press, 2015.

Heumann, Judith and Kristen Joiner. *Being Heumann: An Unrepentant Memoir of a Disability Rights Activist*. Boston: Beacon Press, 2021.

OTHER INFORMATION SOURCES

Organizations

American Immigration Lawyers Association (AILA), 1400 Eye Street NW, Ste. 1200, Washington, DC 20005. (202) 216-2400. Home page: www.aila.org.

Americans United for Affirmative Action, 1201 Peachtree Street NE, Atlanta, GA 30361. (404) 870-9090. Home page: www.auaa.org.

Equal Employment Opportunity Commission (EEOC), 131 Main Street, Washington, DC 20507-1000. (202) 663-7022. E-mail: info@EEOC.gov. Home page: www.eeoc.gov.

National Organization for Women (NOW), 1100 H Street NW, Suite 300, Washington, DC 20005. (202) 628-8NOW. E-mail: now@now.org. Home page: www.now.org.

Online Sources

EDLAW, Inc. (disability law): www.edlaw.net

EEOC's listing of employment discrimination laws: http://www.eeoc.gov/laws/statutes/index.cfm

Employment discrimination laws that prohibit discrimination on the basis of sexual orientation: https://www.aclu.org/maps/non-discrimination-laws-state-state-information-map

Information on ENDA: https://www.aclu.org/maps/non-discrimination-laws-state-state-information-map
Laws Restricting Working Hours of Minors: http://www.dol.gov/whd/state/nonfarm.htm
Legal Information Institute (LII): www.law.comell.edu/topics/employment_discrimination
State Minimum Wage Laws: http://www.dol.gov/whd/minwage/america.htm
US Department of Justice—ADA: www.doj.gov/crt/ada
US Department of Labor: http://www.dol.gov/
Women's Bureau (800-827-5335): www.dol.gov/dol/wbz

CHAPTER 5

On Your Own

EMANCIPATION

Can minors legally live beyond their parents' control?

In certain cases, minors can live on their own as emancipated minors. They can be "emancipated" from their parents under the laws of most states.

What exactly is "emancipation"?

Emancipation refers to the process by which a minor becomes free from the control of his or her parents and operates as an adult in the eyes of the law. It is an act or course of conduct that terminates the right of parents over a minor child and also terminates the child's right to receive parental support. The Mississippi Supreme Court in *Pass v. Pass* (1960) defined emancipation as "the freeing of a child *for all the period of its minority* from the care, custody, control, and service of its parents; the relinquishment of parental control, conferring on the child the right to its own earnings and terminating the parent's legal obligation to support it."

Minors are automatically emancipated when they reach the age of majority (in the vast majority of states, age eighteen), but emancipation can occur for younger teenagers under a process defined by state law.

The result of emancipation is that these emancipated minors can work a job without parental permission, enter into valid contracts, buy or rent real property, keep the money they earn, enlist in the military, and marry. There are many legal ramifications of emancipation.

How does a minor become emancipated?

A minor can become emancipated in various ways. One way is that a minor can marry with parental consent and court approval. A valid marriage can emancipate a minor. A second way is that a minor can enlist in the military. A third way is that a minor can petition a family law court in his or her jurisdiction and obtain court approval of emancipation.

How old must a minor be to seek emancipation from a court?

The age varies from state to state. In many states the age is either fourteen or sixteen. For example, in New Mexico a minor must be at least sixteen years of age. However, in California a minor must only be at least fourteen years of age.

Does emancipation always occur at the request of the minor?

No, often it is parents of the minors who argue for the minors' emancipation. When this occurs, it is often because a judge confirms or denies the emancipation as part of a larger issue in a court case, such as a child support issue. But a court won't declare an emancipation simply because a minor can't stand his or her folks or because they can't stand their child. It only happens if a minor already has been living apart from his or her parents and is clearly self-sufficient—if the minor's emancipation already has been "implied."

Consider the following situation. An Iowa doctor went to court to recover payment from the father of a teenage girl after having given her extensive medical treatment. The young woman had previously left home, with her father's permission, to live and work in another town. She supported herself and paid her bills until she contracted typhoid fever.

The young woman's father argued that his daughter had been emancipated, so he shouldn't have to pay her medical bills. After reviewing the facts of the case, the Iowa court said there was no emancipation. Its ruling meant the young woman's father continued to be responsible for her medical costs.

This case was decided in 1890, and the daughter was only fourteen years old when she left home, but it demonstrates what emancipation really means.

If parents throw a teen out of the house, is his or her emancipation automatic?

Not in the vast majority of cases, because the teen usually won't have the income or maturity to live independently. Emancipation doesn't happen unless it's clear that the child is living an independent life and will be able to do so in the future. If this can't be shown, the child remains the parents' responsibility and continues to be under their authority.

If a minor runs away from home, is he or she emancipated?

Not usually. Parents are responsible for their minor children, including runaways. But if parents allow a runaway child to live independently for a long time and the child develops a reliable means of support or completely abandons the parents, a court may decide that emancipation has been implied.

For what reasons do parents seek to establish emancipation for minor children?

Often this will be done in relation to a child support order in a divorce settlement. For example, in one case a divorced mother went to court to collect past due child support from her former husband. After their daughter was age fifteen she briefly lived with her mother, but sometimes she lived with friends, worked odd jobs, and was even jailed on two occasions. Neither parent knew where she was, although both had tried to help her by offering special schooling and psychiatric care.

The mother wanted past due support payments because she had legal custody of the runaway daughter. The court refused, stating that the daughter was legally emancipated because she had completely abandoned both parents.

Even though many parents seek emancipation, the general principle of law is that parents cannot use the emancipation process simply to avoid their parental responsibilities.

For more about divorce and child support, see Chapter 7, "If Your Parents Divorce."

What factors will a court use to decide whether a minor is emancipated?

Some important ones are

- whether the minor still lives at home;
- whether the minor pays room and board at home;
- whether the minor has a job, and whether the minor is allowed to spend his or her earnings without parental interference;
- whether the minor owns a car or house;
- whether the minor pays his or her own debts; and
- whether the minor is being claimed as a dependent on his or her parents' tax return.

If a minor is emancipated, does he or she gain all the rights of adults?

No. For example, an emancipated minor still cannot vote until he or she turns eighteen and cannot drink alcohol until he or she turns twenty-one. Traditionally, emancipation didn't enable a minor to manage or convey property, bring a lawsuit, vote, change his or her name, or consent to medical care—the emancipated minor was still too young to engage in these adult activities. In some cases, however, states have given teens these rights when emancipation can be established by the parents or is evident in the minor's actions and housing and employment situation.

When a minor marries, is he or she instantly emancipated?

Yes, provided the marriage is legal. In most states a person under age eighteen must obtain parental consent and must be at least age sixteen in order to marry.

Does enlisting in the armed forces constitute automatic emancipation?

Yes. Serving in the armed forces is said to be inconsistent with the idea of parental control. To enlist in any branch of the armed forces except the army, a high school diploma currently is needed.

If a minor is emancipated, is he or she still required to obey the state's school compulsory attendance laws?

Yes, except in cases in which marriage was the basis for emancipation.

Once a minor is emancipated, are the parents relieved of liability for the child's negligent or reckless acts?

Not in every case. In California, for example, parents are responsible for a minor's negligent or reckless acts while driving, even if emancipation has occurred. For more about the responsibility of parents for a child's negligence while driving, see Chapter 1, "Behind the Wheel."

Can a minor be emancipated and still live at home?

The answer to this question is unclear. But if a minor pays room and board and has an independent source of income, a court might declare an emancipation. As a rule, it depends on the facts of the particular case.

Are there alternative options to emancipation?

Yes, there are other alternatives for minors instead of filing petitions for emancipation. A minor might be able to live with other relatives, go to counseling with his or her parents, or seek a formal guardian from the local family court.

If a minor really wants to become emancipated, where can he or she turn?

Many state court systems maintain emancipation forms and information about the emancipation process in that state on their online sites.

HAVING YOUR OWN APARTMENT

Can a teenager legally rent an apartment?

Teens may enter into contracts, and this includes lease and rental contracts. But many landlords refuse to rent to them—they don't want teens as tenants.

Although minors can walk away from or "disaffirm" contracts they enter into, this probably isn't the reason landlords refuse to rent to them. Some landlords worry that teens who want their own apartments might be troublemakers, "party animals," or unlikely to be able to regularly make rent payments on time. On the other hand, some landlords will rent to a teen if a parent or guardian cosigns the lease or rental agreement.

Age discrimination against a minor who wants to rent an apartment isn't against the law, although refusing to rent to someone on the basis of race, color, gender, religion, nationality, or disability clearly is. Some state constitutions or state laws prohibit landlords from renting to "adults only" because such policies discourage families from living together. To date, however, no state prohibits landlords from refusing to rent to teens.

If you do succeed in finding an apartment to rent or lease, don't be surprised if the landlord requires you to prepay both the first and last month's rent and also make a security deposit. For more about teens and contracts, see Chapter 16, "Entering into Contracts."

SERVING YOUR COUNTRY

Do men still have to register for the armed forces? Do women have to register?

With narrow exceptions, all men who are US citizens and all foreign-born males living in the United States and its territories must register for the draft within thirty days of their eighteenth birthday. The Selective Service's registration page indicates that late registrations are accepted and that all men living in the United States between ages eighteen and twenty-five need to register. Women aren't required to register but may enlist.

What is the procedure for registering for the draft?

Each registrant must complete and return a Selective Service draft registration form, available at any post office. Registrants receive notice within ninety days of the date the Selective Service receives it.

Does everyone who registers for the draft end up in the armed forces?

No. The last year anyone was drafted in the United States was 1973. We now have a stand-by draft and voluntary service. No one can be drafted involuntarily unless Congress and the president determine that inducting persons previously registered is necessary because of war or other national emergency.

When can a young person volunteer for the armed forces?

At age eighteen, although persons under eighteen may enlist if they have parental consent. Most branches of the armed forces require a high school diploma, however, and some won't consider an applicant who has a juvenile record. To find out more about the US Army, Navy, Air Force, Marines, Coast Guard, or National Guard, contact your local armed forces recruiter.

What is a conscientious objector?

A person who holds a sincere religious, moral, or ethical opposition to war. If the person's objection is only to participating in combat, he is assigned noncombat military duties if called to serve. If the person's objection is to participating in all military service, he may be excused from active or combat duty but may be required to perform civilian work related to the national interest.

THE RIGHT TO VOTE

What is the legal voting age?

The age for legal voting in federal elections is eighteen. The US Constitution established this in the Twenty-Sixth Amendment to the US Constitution, which provides:

> **Section 1.** The right of citizens of the United States, who are eighteen years of age or older, to vote shall not be denied or abridged by the United States or by any State on account of age.
>
> **Section 2.** The Congress shall have the power to enforce this article by appropriate legislation

The US Congress approved this amendment in 1971, shortly after the US Supreme Court's decision in *Oregon v. Mitchell* (1970), which held that the US Congress had the power to lower the age limit in federal elections to eighteen, but that the US Congress did not have such power to lower age limits in state elections. A few states would not lower their voting age from twenty-one to eighteen. The Twenty-Sixth Amendment changed that.

HOLDING PUBLIC OFFICE

Can a minor run for public office?

Age limitations bar minors from holding most public offices; however, it depends on the minor's place of residence, because age and residency requirements for particular offices vary from state to state and across municipalities. For example, most state constitutions set a minimum age for holding a seat in the state legislature, though that age varies widely, from eighteen to thirty. City laws also vary in age requirements for holding public office on bodies such as city councils.

FOR FURTHER READING

On the Streets

Kozol, Jonathan. *Rachel and Her Children: Homeless Families in America*. New York: Broadway Books, 2006.
Phelps, Carissa and Larkin Warren. *Runaway Girl: Escaping Life on the Streets One Helping Hand at a Time*. New York: Viking Press, 2012.
Plaster, Joseph. *Kids on the Street: Queer Kinship and Religion in San Francisco's Tenderloin*. Durham, NC: Duke University Press, 2015.
Wakin, Michele. *Homelessness in America: A Reference Handbook*. Santa Barbara, CA: ABC-CLIO, 2022.
Portman, Janet and Marcia Stewart. *Renters' Rights*. 7th ed. Berkeley, CA: Nolo Press, 2012.

The Armed Forces

Huffman, Amanda. *A Girl's Guide to Military Service*. St. Paul, MN: Elva Resa Publishing, 2022.
Ostrow, Scott. *Guide to Joining the Military*. Albany, NY: Peterson's, 2013.

OTHER INFORMATION SOURCES

Organizations

Rock the Vote, 1001 Connecticut Avenue, NW, Washington, DC 20036. (202) 719-9910. E-mail http://www.rockthevote.com/contact-us.html. Home page: www.rockthevote.org.
Selective Service System, Box 94638, Palatine, IL 60094-4683. (847) 688-2576 or 1-888-655-1825.

Online Sources

About elections and voting: www.fec.gov/pages/electpg
Selective Service: http://www.sss.gov/FSwho.htm
US military: usmilitary.about.com

Hotline

National Runaway Switchboard, (800) 621-4000 or (800) 621-0394 (TDD)

CHAPTER 6

Your Personal Appearance

AT HOME

Do parents have a right to decide how their children can dress and style their hair?

Yes. Although some parents give their children plenty of leeway when it comes to personal appearance, they do have the right to forbid particular types of clothes and hairstyles. Parents can forbid a teen to shave his or her head, use hair dye, or wear torn jeans or revealing tops. They can also forbid tattooing and body piercing.

What happens if a minor ignores his or her parents' requirements in matters of personal appearance?

Nothing in the law prevents the parents from punishing the minor. However, as discussed in Chapter 10, parents may never punish children in a manner that amounts to abuse or neglect. If they do, the state can take them to court.

AT SCHOOL

Can a school legally enforce a dress code?

Yes, schools can impose dress codes and even uniform policies. However, these policies must allow for those with sincere religious objections to opt-out. The policies also must have a provision that allows financial support for teens whose families don't have the money to buy mandated school uniforms.

Many students and parents have challenged the constitutionality of dress codes and uniforms, contending that they violate students' First Amendment rights to free expression and the parents' due process right, or liberty interest, to rear their children as they see fit. The courts, for the most part, have ruled that dress codes are a reasonable way for school officials to foster an environment more conducive to learning.

Many states have laws that specifically empower school districts to pass dress codes or require uniforms. This does not mean that all provisions in a dress code or uniform policy are constitutional. Some provisions in a dress code may be either too vague or too broad. For example, let's say that a dress code provision prohibits students from wearing "inappropriate clothing." If the code does not explain or provide examples of "inappropriate clothing," this provision is too vague. It doesn't provide students with fair notice of what clothing is allowed or disallowed.

For a discussion about clothes as a personal or political expression at school, see Chapter 2, "At School."

AT WORK

Can an employer require its employees to follow a dress code?

Yes. Courts rarely interfere with business policies relating to dress and hairstyle unless the policies are shown to discriminate on the basis of gender, race, or religion. But even employees asserting such discrimination claims don't prevail all the time. Courts routinely find that both dress and grooming requirements imposed by employers are bona fide requirements.

A federal court in Massachusetts ruled in 2004 that Costco did not violate the rights of a former cashier who was terminated for refusing to cover up her body piercings. The employee contended that the application of the dress code policy infringed on her beliefs as a member of the Church of Body Modification. The court found that there was no evidence that Costco's grooming policy was targeted at a specific religion.

A federal appeals court in Kentucky ruled in 2006 that a state park could impose a dress code on its employees that prohibited them from displaying tattoos or body piercings (other than earrings) and required them to tuck in their shirts. The employees contended that the ban on the display of tattoos and the "tucking in" policy infringed on their rights. The court sided with the park and against the employees.

Can company dress code provisions be applicable only to women?

In most cases this discriminates illegally. Rules requiring women employees to wear makeup or making women flight attendants stay below a certain body weight also discriminate illegally, unless the employer can prove the rule serves a very important business purpose.

IN PUBLIC

Is it legal for a business to place tattoos on minors?

In many states, tattoo parlors are forbidden by law from providing tattooing services to minors. For example, Illinois has a law that criminalizes the tattooing of a minor: "A person, other than a person licensed to practice medicine in all its branches, commits tattooing the body of a minor when he or she knowingly or recklessly tattoos or offers to tattoo a person under the age of 18." The law provides that such illegal tattooing is a Class A misdemeanor. See Table 6.1 for a state-by-state rundown of tattoo laws.

Florida law prohibits placing a tattoo on a teenager under the age of sixteen, although it allows tattoos for minors who are at least sixteen years of age if the teen is accompanied by a parent and legal guardian. Tennessee law is even stricter, prohibiting the tattooing of any minor or teenager under the age of eighteen. In many of these states there are criminal penalties for tattooing a minor.

While some states do allow older teenagers (usually sixteen or older) to receive tattoos, these states usually require the written consent of a parent or legal guardian. It usually is not a valid defense for the person making the tattoo to claim that he or she did not know the person was a minor. For example, Washington law provides:

> Every person who applies a tattoo to any minor under the age of eighteen is guilty of a misdemeanor. It is not a defense to a violation of this section that the person applying the tattoo did not know the minor's age unless the person applying the tattoo establishes by a preponderance of the evidence that he or she made a reasonable, bona fide attempt to ascertain the true age of the minor by requiring production of a driver's license or other picture identification card or paper and did not rely solely on the oral allegations or apparent age of the minor.

The general trend in state laws is to allow older minors (those sixteen years of age or older) to receive tattoos if they have the authorization of a parent or guardian.

Do these tattoo laws apply to a minor teen who tattoos another minor teen?

These laws may not apply to minors under the age of eighteen who tattoo other minors; it depends on the individual state. For example, the aforementioned Illinois law has an exemption for minors. It provides that the law "does not apply to a person under 18 years of age who tattoos or offers to tattoo another person under 18 years of age away from the premises of any business at which tattooing is performed."

What about body piercings of minors?

The general trend regarding body piercing of minors is that it is allowed for older minors in most states as long as they have the permission of a parent or legal guardian.

TABLE 6.1: Tattoo Laws by State

State	*Age Restrictions (w/o Parental Consent)*	*Consent Requirements*
Alabama	18	Written consent
Alaska	18	Prohibited
Arizona	18	Parent/guardian presence
Arkansas	18	Written consent
California	18	Parent/guardian presence
Colorado	18	Parent/guardian presence
Connecticut	18	Written consent
Delaware	18	Written consent
Florida	18	Written consent (for minors 16–17)
Georgia	18	Written consent
Hawaii	18	Written consent
Idaho	18	Consent of parents (for minors 14–17)
Illinois	18	Parent/guardian presence
Indiana	18	Parent/guardian presence
Iowa	18	Prohibited
Kansas	18	Written and notarized consent and presence
Kentucky	18	Written and notarized consent (for minors 16–17)
Louisiana	18	Written consent and presence
Maine	18	Prohibited
Maryland	18	Prohibited
Massachusetts	18	Prohibited
Michigan	18	Written consent
Minnesota	18	Prohibited
Mississippi	18	Prohibited
Missouri	18	Written consent
Montana	18	Parent/guardian presence
Nebraska	18	Written consent
New Hampshire	18	Prohibited
New Jersey	18	Written consent and presence
New Mexico	18	Written and notarized consent

TABLE 6.1: (Continued)

State	*Age Restrictions (w/o Parental Consent)*	*Consent Requirements*
New York	18	Prohibited
North Carolina	18	Prohibited
North Dakota	18	Written consent and presence
Ohio	18	Parent/guardian presence
Oklahoma	18	Prohibited
Oregon	18	Authorization of a physician
Pennsylvania	18	Written consent and presence
Rhode Island	18	Prohibited
South Carolina	21	Written consent (for ages 18–20)
South Dakota	18	Written consent
Tennessee	18	Parental/guardian presence (for minors 16–17)
Texas	18	Parental/guardian consent
Utah	18	Written consent
Vermont	18	Written consent and presence
Virginia	18	Parent/guardian presence
Washington	18	Prohibited
West Virginia	18	Parent/guardian consent (for minors 16–17)
Wisconsin	18	Authorization of a physician
Wyoming	18	Parent/guardian presence

Source: Adapted from World Population Review, https://worldpopulationreview.com/state-rankings/tattoo-laws-by-state (accessed August 15, 2023).

For example, Arizona prohibits the tattooing or piercing of a minor unless a parent or guardian is present. Arkansas allows body piercings but requires the written permission and presence of a parent or guardian. California law allows for piercings of minors but requires the written permission and notarization of a parent or guardian and the piercing must be done in front of the parent or guardian. The California law does not apply to emancipated minors and does not apply to ear piercings.

Can a restaurant legally refuse to serve persons who aren't dressed in a certain manner?

In most states a business can require a particular type of dress only if the rule doesn't discriminate on the basis of gender. For example, "no shoes, no shirt, no service" policies enforced by many restaurants and other business establishments are legal because forbidding bare feet and bare chests promotes cleanliness, which is considered good business policy. Restaurants and other businesses also have to follow a wide range of public health regulations which can come into play. In addition, such rules promote a positive business image and don't discriminate on the basis of gender. (Women dressed "topless" would be subject to the rule as well.)

Can a store or restaurant legally keep out "long hairs" or "biker types"?

Under federal law, yes, because the rule doesn't discriminate on the basis of gender, color, religion, national origin, or disability. A person challenging such a policy would have to rely on a state or local law that may provide greater protection for individuals than federal law. For more about discrimination, see Chapter 13, "Equal Protection and Employment Discrimination."

Is public nudity legal?

Not in very many places, as most states have laws that prohibit public nudity. States, cities, counties, and other legal subdivisions may legally forbid public nudity at beaches and parks as both a health measure and a means of upholding community standards of morality. However, California and Florida do have a few nude and topless beaches.

FOR FURTHER READING

Angel, Elayne. *The Piercing Bible: The Definitive Guide to Safe Body Piercing*. Berkeley, CA: Crossing Press, 2009.

Brunsma, David, ed. *Uniforms in Public Schools: A Decade of Research and Debate*. Lanham, MD: R & L Education, 2005.

Gilbert, Steve. *The Tattoo History Source Book*. New York: Juno Books, 2000.

Hamilton, Jill. *Dress Codes in School*. Farmington Hills, MI: Greenhaven Press, 2009.

Rollin, Lucy. *Twentieth-Century Teen Culture by the Decades*. Westport, CT: Greenwood Press, 1999.

OTHER INFORMATION SOURCES

Online Sources

National School Safety and Security Services on dress codes and uniforms: http://www.schoolsecurity.org/resources/uniforms.html

Tattoos

Surdi, Paul-Anthony. "The 2022 State-by-State Definitive Guide to Tattoo Laws." tattooschool.com, April 8, 2022.

CHAPTER 7

If Your Parents Divorce

CUSTODY

If a minor's parents plan to divorce, who decides where the minor will live after the divorce is final?

Usually parents determine who will have "primary custody" of the child. If they can't decide on their own, the court decides for them. Its decision must be "in the best interests of the child," a term often applied in relation to legal matters involving young people.

Married parents have both "physical" and "legal" custody of their minor children. Physical, or residential, custody means the parents are responsible for their children's immediate personal needs such as food, clothing, and shelter; legal custody means they are responsible, legally and financially, for their children's safety, education, and actions with respect to others. When parents divorce, one parent—the primary "custodial parent"—usually receives both primary physical custody and primary legal custody of the children, except when the parents agree to share physical custody, legal custody, or both. This is often called joint custody. Some states, such as Alabama, have a presumption in favor of joint custody.

What do divorce courts consider in determining which parent should be the custodial parent?

As a rule, the court consider the child's moral, physical, mental, spiritual, and financial needs; the parents' physical, mental, and moral fitness; and the parents' love and concern for the child. In addition, they take into account who has most recently been the primary custodian for the child and whether that situation has been in the child's best interests. These courts also consider the character and fitness of any other person who resides with either one of the parents and who has contact with the children. Some courts will consider the preferences of the minor or of particular minors. For example, a relevant child custody factor in Tennessee is the "reasonable preference" of minors who are least twelve years old.

Needless to say, states consider quite a few factors in the best interest of the child determination. Tennessee weighs more than a dozen factors, including:

- The love, emotional bonds, and affection that exists between the child and the parents.
- The ability of each parent to give the child medical care, food, clothing, education, and other care.
- The need of the child for stability, except in cases where child abuse was or is a reason for relocating.
- The stability of the family unit.
- The physical and mental health of each parent.
- The child's past education record and home and community involvement.
- The child's reasonable preferences if the child is twelve years old or more. The preferences of younger children may also be considered, but the younger the child, the less weight his/her opinion has.
- Evidence of emotional or physical abuse by the other parent.
- The character of anyone else who lives in the parent's home and how that person interacts with the child.
- The general ability to be a good parent, including promoting relationship between the child and the other parent.

Does a young person have a right to a lawyer at his or her parents' divorce?

Many states permit their courts to appoint a special representative for a child when parents disagree on custody, and many of these states require the representative to be an attorney. For example, Michigan has a law that provides: "If, at any time in the proceeding, the court determines that the child's best interests are inadequately represented, the court may appoint a lawyer-guardian *ad litem* to represent the child." The representative or "lawyer-guardian *ad litem*" can assist the child in expressing which parent he or she prefers to live with, can be effective at mediating problems, and can collect important information for the court. In some states the representative can also bring a support action on the child's behalf if a parent isn't obeying a child support order. The parents pay for the representative in most of these states, although the state or county will pay if they can't afford it.

Does a child of divorcing parents have a right to choose which parent he or she wants to live with?

Not usually. Even so, divorce courts in many states are required to take the child's preference into account. The older and more mature the child, the more weight his or her preference is likely to receive, especially if the child can give a good reason for preferring one parent to the other. For example, if an older child has been living with a grandparent and wants to continue to do so, his or her preference is given serious weight.

In Ohio, a child age twelve or older can choose which parent he or she wants to live with—its courts will respect the child's preference unless living with the chosen parent isn't in the child's best interests. Other states' divorce courts have been taking the child's preference into account for decades.

Does the mother usually win custody in a divorce?

Historically, America's legal system typically favored mothers in custody disputes. Most states recognized a principle of law known as the "tender years presumption," which held that in a child's earlier (or "tender") years, the mother was the most suitable guardian and protector. The tender years presumption, sometimes called the "maternal preference," has been declared unconstitutional by courts in some states for depriving fathers of due process rights. The District of Columbia Court of Appeals rejected the tender-years presumption in 1978, noting: "A rule of law providing that a mother has the strongest claim to the custody of her child obscures, and indeed may be inconsistent with the basic tenet, overriding all others, that the best interest of the child should control."

This viewpoint has become much more prevalent in America's family courts, which now determine custody disputes on a case-by-case basis by evaluating the best interests of the child, rather than presuming that the mother would be the superior caregiver. For more about the maternal preference, see Chapter 9, "Marrying and Having Children."

What is "joint custody"?

This is a type of custody arrangement in which the divorced parents continue to share physical custody, legal custody, or both. Joint custody gained popularity in the 1980s. The child might spend weekdays with one parent and weekends with the other, or live with one parent during the school year and stay with the other during summer vacation. When the parents share both legal and physical custody, both continue to make important decisions about the child's education, religious upbringing, and extracurricular activities. Sometimes both parents will be awarded joint legal custody, but just one will have physical custody.

Joint custody arrangements are usually more flexible than traditional custody arrangements, and most experts believe that joint custody cushions children against the traumas often associated with their parents' divorce. Also, many contend that joint custody cuts down on parental kidnapping (discussed later in this chapter).

But joint custody has its critics. If the parents couldn't get along during their marriage, how will they ever be able to agree on what is best for their child once they split up? This can be a problem—one that sometimes requires the divorce court to act as the parties' referee.

Can parents continue to have legal custody over a person who is over the age of majority?

No, because that is the age at which a young person can live independently. Under the terms of a support decree, however, parents can be required to support a child who is beyond the age of majority. (Child support is discussed later in this chapter.) In addition, some states allow minors to be legally emancipated when their parents divorce if the minor is self-supporting. For more about the age of majority, see Chapter 3, "At Home," and for more about emancipation, see Chapter 5, "On Your Own."

In custody matters, is a parent's sexual behavior relevant?

It can be, although most courts don't give sexual conduct that much weight unless the parent's behavior is likely to have an adverse impact on the child. For example, some courts have awarded custody to one parent when the other parent was having extramarital affairs regularly.

Will a divorce court award custody to a gay or lesbian parent?

Yes. Gay and lesbian parents certainly can obtain custody of children. Some states have laws similar to that of Kentucky, which provides: "The court shall not consider conduct of a proposed custodian that does not affect his relationship to the child." Under this provision, the sexual orientation of a parent does not factor into the child custody determination unless it is shown that the parent's sexual orientation somehow has an adverse impact on the child.

Can a divorce court award custody to a parent with a disability?

They certainly can—and often do. In some states there are laws that prohibit discrimination against parents with disabilities. Generally, "the best interests of the child" is the standard to be applied. A physical or mental disability would be just one factor to weigh, although if the disability is substance abuse, the best interests of the child might motivate a court to award custody to the other parent.

If one parent makes a lot more money—through employment or an inheritance, for example—is that parent more likely to obtain primary custody?

Not necessarily. Although divorce courts take the separate financial status of the parents into account, this isn't a controlling factor. Even a parent's poverty won't determine who receives custody unless the lack of money or steady income has resulted in child neglect.

Can a young person "divorce" his or her parents: bring a lawsuit to terminate their parental rights?

In 1992, a Florida judge permitted a young boy to go to court to do just this. The boy had been in foster care, and life at the foster home was stable. His foster parents wanted to adopt him, so he filed a lawsuit to terminate parental rights in order to clear the way for adoption proceedings. The boy won. This case is important because it is the first time a court permitted a young person to *personally* seek a termination of parental rights.

Does a child of divorced parents have a legal right to visit the parent he or she isn't living with?

Not exactly. Visitation rights belong to the noncustodial parent, not the child. Courts grant visitation to the noncustodial parent except in cases in which it wouldn't be in the child's best interests.

What happens if a child doesn't want to see the noncustodial parent?

In most situations the child can be required to, particularly if the custodial parent has turned the child against the other parent. In a Pennsylvania case, a court permitted a father to visit his eleven-year-old daughter against her wishes after the court declared that the mother had been "poisoning her daughter's mind against her father." As a practical matter, however, it can become difficult to enforce these visitations on uncooperative teens as they get older.

Will a court forbid a noncustodial parent to visit a minor child because that parent is "living with someone"?

Not for that reason alone. Courts will forbid a parent to have contact with a child only if spending time together isn't in the child's best interests. These days, a court would not limit visitation rights solely because the noncustodial parent lives with someone outside of marriage.

If it appears that the noncustodial parent might not return the child at the end of a visit, the court has the power to suspend the parent's visitation rights or revoke them altogether. Courts will also suspend or revoke visitation rights if the noncustodial parent physically injures the child or threatens to do so. If the noncustodial parent abused a child during marriage, his or her visits usually are both short and supervised.

In custody determinations, does a young person have the right to continue living with his or her siblings?

No, but courts try to keep brothers and sisters together unless there is an important reason not to.

What happens if a parent wishes to relocate?

Generally, state law requires that the parent proposing relocation file a petition with the court seeking approval of the relocation. The issue usually involves a parent with primary custody who seeks to move. This is a tough issue, because it could upset the visitation rights of the parent who doesn't have primary custody of the child. That is why the relocating parent often tries to obtain approval from the other parent.

The parent seeking relocation has to include several things in the petition to approve relocation. For example, Florida law provides: "If one of the reasons [for the relocation] is based upon a job offer that has been reduced to writing, the written job offer must be attached to the petition."

Once a custody determination is made by a court, can it be modified?

Certainly custody determinations can be modified by courts. In fact, often custody battles are protracted affairs that take years and years of litigation. Usually the parent seeking to obtain custody from the parent who has primary custody has to show a "material" or "substantial" change in circumstances that justifies a change in custody. For instance, if one parent has recently started cohabitating with a former felon convicted of violent crimes, the other parent could petition for a change in custody and may well be able to show a material change in circumstances.

What is virtual visitation?

Virtual visitation refers to a form of visitation whereby a parent and child use the Internet and other technological advancements to have quality time with each other. Courts in New Jersey, Utah, and other states have been experimenting with creative ways of allowing parents who do not have primary physical or residential custody to communicate with their children.

CHILD SUPPORT

Are both parents legally required to support their minor children after a divorce?

Yes, unless the parental rights of one or both parents have been terminated in a separate court case. For more about terminating parental rights, see Chapter 3, "At Home."

What is child support?

It is an amount of money that the noncustodial parent is required to pay to fulfill his or her legal support obligations. Usually these payments are made to the custodial parent, although they may be made through the divorce court. Child support must cover food, clothing, shelter, medical expenses, and education.

Who decides how much child support the noncustodial parent must pay?

The divorce court usually decides. The actual amount depends on how much each parent earns; the number of children in the family; its standard of living; and any child's unique physical, educational, and psychological needs. Each state has "child support guidelines" that set the appropriate amount. Parents can agree on a figure, but if they do, it must be approved by the court. Generally, child support is based on gross income and the number of children the individual needs to support.

If the court refuses to grant visitation rights to the noncustodial parent, is that parent relieved of his or her child support obligations?

No. Child support must be paid by the noncustodial parent regardless of whether visitation rights are granted.

Aren't most children worse off financially after their parents' divorce?

Studies show that the majority do experience lesser standard of living. The purpose of child support is to allow the children to enjoy the same standard of living that they enjoyed before the divorce, but even so, support is often inadequate.

Does the noncustodial parent have to pay child support if the custodial parent works outside the home?

Yes, although in some cases the amount the custodial parent earns will reduce the noncustodial parent's support payments.

Can child support continue after a child reaches the age of majority?

Yes. As part of many divorce settlements, one parent may be required to pay child support until each child reaches age twenty-one and may have to pay for each child's college education. In 1989, an Illinois court required a father who earned $77,000 annually to pay $11,000 each year for his son to attend a four-year private college.

Can a custodial parent take a noncustodial parent to court to enforce a child support order?

Absolutely. In addition, state child welfare agencies, with substantial help from the federal government, always pursue "deadbeat parents." Furthermore, a noncustodial parent's income tax refund can be seized for nonpayment of child support. In some states (and in narrow and extreme circumstances), courts can even hold a nonpaying parent "in contempt of court." This means the noncustodial parent can be ordered to sit in jail until he or she pays up.

Can a young person take a parent to court to recover child support?

Only if he or she is above the age of majority and continues to be entitled to support (such as tuition for a college education) under the parents' divorce decree.

Are there any special ways to track down deadbeat parents in order to enforce current or overdue support obligations?

Yes. Special laws help parents collect child support from noncustodial deadbeats who live within the state's boundaries. In addition, the federal government assists state welfare agencies in locating absent, nonpaying parents out of state. In many states, individuals who owe large arrearages of child support (back child support) can be found in criminal contempt and go to jail unless they pay the support.

What's the difference between child support and alimony?

Alimony or "spousal maintenance" is a payment made by one former spouse to the other to reduce the latter's financial hardships after a divorce. Women who have never worked outside the home during a lengthy marriage often are awarded monthly or annual alimony after divorcing. The recipient of the alimony doesn't need to have legal custody of minor children to receive it, as payments are separate and distinct from child support. Nothing prevents a court from awarding both child support and alimony, but these days it doesn't happen that often.

GRANDPARENTS AND STEPPARENTS

Do grandparents have a legal right to visit their grandchildren after the divorce?

Visitation by grandparents used to be decided by the custodial parent. Through the years, states have passed so-called grandparent visitation laws that authorize grandparent visitation. However, visitation under these laws is not automatic. The US Supreme Court explained in *Troxel v. Granville* (2000) that overly broad grandparent visitation statutes must not infringe upon the liberty interests of fit parents, who have a constitutional, due process interest in rearing their children as they see fit. The court's ruling in *Troxel* means that states must give special consideration to the interests of fit parents, and grandparents may not be able to obtain visitation if fit parents object to such visitation.

Do stepparents ever have parental rights over a stepchild?

Only if they have agreed to assume certain parental obligations. Accepting legal responsibility for a stepchild usually gives a stepparent legal rights similar to parental rights. The extent of those rights would depend on the responsibilities assumed. A typical example of an assumed obligation might be an agreement to provide for a young stepson or stepdaughter.

Do former stepparents have any legal rights?

Sometimes. Courts occasionally grant visitation rights to former stepparents after determining that visitation would be in the child's best interests.

OTHER ISSUES RELATING TO DIVORCE

What's the difference between a divorce and a legal separation?

A divorce legally dissolves the marriage. A legal separation doesn't dissolve all marriage ties, but it does declare that the couple no longer live as husband and wife. It also declares that they no longer will be responsible for each other's debts.

What is "child snatching"?

Child snatching, sometimes called "child kidnapping," occurs when a noncustodial parent unlawfully takes a child from the custodial parent or from the custodial parent's home. Children are often snatched to exact a promise from the custodial parent to accept less child support or to pressure the custodial parent to change custody or visitation rights.

Child snatching is a crime. This means that a parent who is guilty of child snatching can be punished under state law. In addition, federal law requires state courts to enforce out-of-state custody orders. This means that if a child is taken across state lines in violation of a custody order, a state court must order the child returned to the custodial parent, regardless of how far away that parent happens to live. If a parent kidnaps or snatches a child and takes that child to another state, a federal law—known as the Parental Kidnapping Prevention Act (1980)—applies. This law provides a mechanism by which courts in different states can handle child custody disputes. Under the Parental Kidnapping Prevention Act, the home state of the child—where the child lived for the six months prior to the abduction—has jurisdiction over custody-related matters.

If a young person thinks his or her parents should get a divorce, what can he or she do?

From a legal standpoint, nothing. However, the child should consider discussing the family situation with a trusted relative or perhaps a guidance counselor or other adult, someone who plays a significant, caring role in the child's life.

FOR FURTHER READING

In General

Doskow, Emily. *Nolo's Essential Guide to Child Custody and Support*. 5th ed. Berkeley, Cal: NOLO, 2020.

Johnson, Linda Carlson. *Everything You Need to Know about Your Parents' Divorce*. Rev. ed. New York: Rosen Publishing Group, 1999.

McBride, Jean. *Talking to Children about Divorce: A Parent's Guide to Healthy Communication at Each Stage of Divorce*. San Antonio, TX: Althea Press, 2016.

Custody

Emery, Robert D. *Two Homes, One Childhood: A Parenting Plan to Last a Lifetime*. New York: Avery, 2016.

Harlow, Teresa. *Combative to Collaborative: The Co-parenting Code*. Amherst, NY: Promethean Publishing, 2021.

Hudson, David L., Jr. *Child Custody: Point/Counterpoint*. New York: Chelsea House, 2012.

Truly, Traci. *Grandparents' Rights*. 4th ed. Clearwater, FL: Sphinx Publishing, 2005.

OTHER INFORMATION SOURCES

Organizations

American Bar Association, Family Law Section, 321 N. Clark Street, Chicago, IL 60654. (312) 988-5603. E-mail: familylaw@abanet.org. Home page: www.abanet.org/family.

Children's Rights Council, 300 Eye Street NE, Ste. 401, Washington, DC 20002. (202) 547-6227. Home page: vix.com/crc/.

DadsDivorce.com, 10425 Old Olive Street Road, Ste. 7, Creve Coeur, MO 63141. (314) 983-0001. Home page: www.dadsdivorce.com.

Stepfamily Foundation, 334 Division Street, New York, NY 10023. (646) 789-2525. E-mail: staff@stepfamily.org. Home page: www.stepfamily.org.

Online Sources

Findlaw's Family Law Center: http://family.findlaw.com/

Report—*Rocking the Cradle: Ensuring the Rights of Parents with Disabilities and Their Children*: http://www.ncd.gov/publications/2012/Sep272012/

CHAPTER 8

Your Sexual Life

Do teens have a legal right to engage in all types of sexual activity?

No—the laws don't go that far. States legally regulate, or attempt to regulate, the sexual conduct of minors. Some forbid teens under a certain age to have sexual intercourse. Every state attempts to regulate teen sex through statutory rape laws, which are discussed later in this chapter. A law regulating teenage sex is intended to preserve community standards of morality.

BIRTH CONTROL

Are contraceptives legal?

Both nonprescription and prescription contraceptives are legal in the United States. At one time the laws of most states restricted the sale of contraceptives, although only Connecticut prohibited them altogether. These laws were challenged by individuals who wanted to use them and by doctors who wanted to prescribe them for their patients.

In 1965, the US Supreme Court ruled in *Griswold v. Connecticut* that states interfere with special privacy rights protected by the federal Constitution when they pass laws banning the sale or use of contraceptives. The court invalidated a Connecticut law that prohibited the dispensing of contraceptives to married persons, reasoning that the law intruded on the fundamental right of marital privacy. The Supreme Court later extended this reasoning by invalidating a ban on contraceptives to unmarried persons in *Eisenstadt v. Baird* (1972).

Can teens legally use contraceptives?

Yes. The early contraceptive cases dealt with the right of married couples to make decisions about childbearing, but later cases established that all sexually active people have this right.

Do teens have a right to obtain contraceptives without parental consent?

Teens don't need parental consent to purchase nonprescription contraceptives such as foams, jellies, sponges, and condoms, and stores don't need to notify a teen's parents about these purchases. But prescription contraceptives such as birth control pills, diaphragms, interuterine devices, cervical caps, and Norplant (a long-term contraceptive method) raise special legal issues.

As a rule, minors need parental consent for medical treatment, and this includes obtaining prescription drugs. Even so, in some states and the District of Columbia a minor is legally entitled to give consent for prescription contraceptives. In no state is parental consent explicitly required, although some states do specify an age above which parental consent is no longer needed.

See Table 8.1 for state-by-state information on these issues. If you have additional questions about contraception, call a confidential information source such as your local Planned Parenthood office or clinic. Planned Parenthood's national hotline number is (800) 541-7800.

Can a public school distribute condoms to minors without parental consent?

In some states courts have upheld condom distribution policies. The Massachusetts Supreme Judicial Court upheld a school's policy of allowing condoms to be available at school in *Curtis v. School Committee of Falmouth* (Mass. 1995). Some parents challenged the condom-availability policy, contending that it violated their parental rights to rear their children as they see fit and also their religious liberty rights. The state high court rejected these arguments, finding that the program did not impose a coercive burden on the objecting parents' rights. "There is no requirement that any student participate in the program," the court noted.

A federal district court in Pennsylvania ruled similarly in a challenge to a Philadelphia school district's policy of having condoms available for purchase for willing minors. The program at issue had an opt-out provision, which allowed students to sign a form saying they did not wish to participate in any condom distribution program.

Do teens have a legal right to obtain counseling and services from family planning agencies?

Yes. "Title X–funded clinics" make confidential family planning available to eligible persons at little or no cost. Title X–funded clinics provide their services regardless of age, marital, or residency status. They consider a teen's financial resources separate from the resources of the parents, so a young person can easily qualify.

TABLE 8.1: Minors' Access to Birth Control

State	*All Minors May Access Birth Control*	*No Explicit Policy*	*Certain Minors May Access Birth Control*
Alabama			Married minors, minors who are or have been pregnant, high school graduates, minors ages 14 and older
Alaska	X		
Arizona	X		
Arkansas	X		
California	X		
Colorado	X		
Connecticut			Married minors
Delaware			Minors ages 12 and older[a]
District of Columbia	X		
Florida			Minors requiring birth control for health reasons, married minors, minors who are or have been pregnant
Georgia	X		
Hawaii			Minors ages 14 and older[a]
Idaho	X		
Illinois			Minors requiring birth control for health reasons, married minors, minors who are or have been pregnant
Indiana			Married minors
Iowa	X		
Kansas			Mature minors
Kentucky	X[a]		
Louisiana			Married minors
Maine	X[a]		
Maryland	X[a]		
Massachusetts	X[b]		
Michigan			Married minors
Minnesota	X[a]		
Mississippi			Married minors, minor parents
Missouri			Married minors

(*Continued*)

TABLE 8.1: (Continued)

State	*All Minors May Access Birth Control*	*No Explicit Policy*	*Certain Minors May Access Birth Control*
Montana	X[a]		
Nebraska			Married minors
Nevada	X		
New Hampshire			Mature minors
New Jersey			Married minors, minors who are or have been pregnant
New Mexico	X		
New York	X[b]		
North Carolina	X		
North Dakota		X	
Ohio		X	
Oklahoma			Married minors, minors who are or have been pregnant[a]
Oregon	X[a]		
Pennsylvania	X		
Rhode Island		X	
South Carolina			Married minors, minors 16 years or older or mature minors
South Dakota			Married minors
Tennessee	X		
Texas			Married minors[c]
Utah			Married minors[c]
Vermont			Married minors
Virginia	X		
Washington	X		
West Virginia			Married minors, mature minors
Wisconsin		X	
Wyoming	X[b]		

[a]A physician may, but is not required to, inform the minor's parents.

[b]The state funds a statewide program that gives minors access to confidential contraceptive care.

[c]State funds may not be used to provide minors with confidential contraceptive services.

Source: Adapted from the Guttmacher Institute, "Minors' Access to Contraceptive Services," https://www.guttmacher.org/state-policy/explore/minors-access-contraceptive-services (accessed August 15, 2023).

Young women are especially dependent on Title X–funded clinics for contraceptives; four out of ten teens who are in need of birth control services turn to them. For a teen who wouldn't use birth control if she had to talk to a parent first, a confidential visit to a family planning clinic can help prevent a pregnancy.

Are the services of Title X–funded clinics always confidential?

Yes. Courts have overturned state laws requiring federally funded family planning clinics to notify a parent when a young woman receives a prescription for contraceptives. These clinics must maintain client confidentiality as a matter of law. Even so, a teen who goes to a family planning clinic should ask a staff person about its confidentiality policies.

For more information about Title X–funded clinics, see http://www.hhs.gov/opa/title-x-family-planning/.

Does a teen have a right to be sterilized without parental consent?

This depends on individual state laws. Few states actually have laws addressing this issue. When state law is silent, written consent would undoubtedly be required, even if state law expressly permits teens to obtain prescription contraceptives. In fact, the laws of many states *exclude* sterilization of a minor from the list of medical services that don't require parental consent.

In many states, parents can't sterilize a mentally competent minor over the minor's stated objection. But in any event, finding a physician willing to perform a sterilization on a minor would be extremely difficult.

See Chapter 10, "Your Right to Be Healthy and Safe from Abuse," for more about situations in which young people can arrange for their own medical care.

Would an older teen be entitled to federal funding for a sterilization?

No. Although public funds can be used to perform sterilizations on adults in some cases, none are available for persons under age twenty-one.

Does a young person have a right to sex education classes in public school?

Some states have laws that allow school districts to offer sex education classes. The laws vary in their reach and application. Many of the laws do not mandate sex education courses. Instead, they simply provide that a school district may provide such courses. For example, Illinois has a law that allows school districts to offer sex education courses. However, the law also provides that if such a course is offered, pupils can be excused from the course if there is a written objection from a parent or guardian. Mississippi has a law providing that if a sex education course is taught, abstinence must be stressed.

When sex education is included in the curriculum, parents sometimes argue that public schools violate their constitutional right to control their child's religious upbringing. Although parents have never won these cases in court, most states allow parents to stop a child from attending sex education classes if the requirements of the class can be fulfilled in some other meaningful way.

ABORTION RIGHTS

Are abortions legal?

Abortion laws vary dramatically from state to state in the aftermath of *Dobbs v. Jackson Women's Health Organization* (2022), a Supreme Court decision that struck down abortion rights at the federal level. Those federal rights had been in place since 1973, when the US Supreme Court ruled in *Roe v. Wade* that the decision to have an abortion is another type of private decision that the Constitution protects from excessive government interference. *Roe v. Wade* stated that before a fetus is able to survive outside the womb—before a fetus is "viable"—a woman has a constitutional right to choose an abortion. Viability is estimated to occur 12–13 weeks after conception.

Even when *Roe* was the federal law of the land, however, states had some power to pass laws restricting abortion in certain cases. With respect to the second twelve weeks of pregnancy—the second trimester—the court ruled that states may restrict abortions in cases in which the procedure is likely to endanger the woman's life or health. The court also ruled that states may legally forbid abortions in the third trimester.

In 1992, the US Supreme Court ruled in *Planned Parenthood v. Casey* that state laws restricting abortion were unconstitutional if they created an undue burden for women seeking an abortion. The undue burden standard means that the law must pose a significant obstacle to a woman seeking an abortion. Some states, interpreting their state constitutions, have applied a higher standard, subjecting abortion laws to more rigorous review.

However, the Supreme Court overruled both *Roe* and *Planned Parenthood* (1992) in *Dobbs*. In this decision, the court upheld a Mississippi law that imposed significant limitations on the right to obtain an abortion.

The court ruled that no fundamental right to an abortion existed under the US Constitution. The court explained that it was not ruling that abortion was legal or illegal—but rather that laws pertaining to the issue should be decided by state legislatures. According to the majority opinion penned by Justice Samuel Alito, "Our decision returns the issue of abortion to those legislative bodies, and it allows women on both sides of the abortion issue to seek to affect the legislative process by influencing public opinion, lobbying legislators, voting, and running for office."

In the wake of *Dobbs*, some state legislatures passed laws protecting a women's right to an abortion. Other states imposed more restrictions on abortions, either through new legislation or by defending old state-level abortion restrictions that were suddenly in effect again with the overturning of *Roe v. Wade*.

Thus, there are several states where abortion essentially has been criminalized. These states that have complete bans on abortion include Alabama, Arkansas, Oklahoma, Missouri, South Dakota, and West Virginia. Other states have more limited bans.

Does a teenager have a legal right to an abortion?

It depends upon individual state law in the wake of the Supreme Court's decision in *Dobbs*.

Can a teen legally obtain an abortion without parental consent?

It depends on individual state law. Most states require a minor to obtain parental consent for or give advance parental notice of an abortion. However, many of these states have an explicit judicial bypass provision that allows a judge to bypass parental consent for the minor's sake.

Eleven states—Connecticut, Hawaii, Maine, Montana, Nevada, New Jersey, New Mexico, New York, Oregon, Vermont, and Washington—and the District of Columbia do not require parental notification before a minor seeks an abortion.

In those states with a judicial bypass provision, specific court procedures must be followed. The minor and her assigned attorney or counselor must meet with a family court judge, who determines whether the minor understands the consequences of her decision as well as the alternatives to an abortion. Some factors that a judge would consider are the young woman's emotional and intellectual development, her outside interests, and her life experiences. If the judge believes that the minor is sufficiently mature to make her own decision, he or she will issue an order permitting parental consent to be bypassed. Once this happens, the minor can give the required medical consent on her own.

A confidential abortion is also possible in cases in which the judge *doesn't* believe the minor is mature enough to make an informed decision. In these situations the judge can order that parental notice be bypassed if a confidential abortion is clearly in the minor's best interests. It may be, for example, that the minor would face possible physical abuse if she raises the abortion issue with her parents. In such cases, the court would give the consent.

The bypass petition must move through the court swiftly. By virtue of this overall procedure, a young woman's constitutional right to privacy is protected. Her identity remains anonymous, and the court's involvement remains confidential.

Can a pregnant minor's parents legally force her to have an abortion if she doesn't want to?

No, and neither can the state.

Can a pregnant minor obtain an abortion without parental consent?

Not in most cases. Most states require parental involvement in a minor's decision to have an abortion. In a majority of these states, such a procedure requires the consent or notification of only one parent, usually 24 or 48 hours before the procedure. Some states, though, mandate the consent of both parents. Several states, however, permit grandparents or other adult relatives to grant consent in place of the minor's parents. Some states where abortion is legal also waive parental involvement requirements if there is a medical emergency or the young person is the victim of abuse or neglect.

If a teen can't afford an abortion, is she entitled to one at public expense?

Not in most cases, even in states where abortion remains legal. Federal legislation forbids the use of public money such as Medicaid funds for abortions except in situations of rape or incest, or if the mother's life is in danger. (Medicaid is a joint federal/state program, administered by each state, that provides health care to poor people.) Also, the Supreme Court has confirmed that neither the federal government nor the states are required to fund abortions, even if they fund pregnancy-related services. Critics argue that these laws impose a much greater burden on poor people.

SEXUALLY TRANSMITTED DISEASES (STDS)

Does a minor have a right to counseling and treatment without parental consent for STDs such as herpes, gonorrhea, syphilis, and HIV/AIDS?

Yes. Even though doctors usually are required by law to obtain parental consent before treating young people, every state makes an exception for STDs. Laws permitting minors to consent to treatment for STDs appear to cover treatment for HIV/AIDS. Even so, thirty-one states expressly authorize a minor to consent privately to HIV/AIDS treatment. Eighteen states provide that physicians may disclose to a minor's parents that he or she is receiving STD treatment. Minors can usually obtain these services at very low cost or no cost at Title X–funded clinics.

See Table 8.2 for the age at which minors may consent to STD services in each state.

RAPE

What is rape?

Rape occurs when a person is forced against his or her will to participate in sexual intercourse or other sexual acts involving penetration. Rape is the severest form of sexual assault.

Can a man also be raped?

Yes. A male or female can be raped, and a male or female can commit the offense of rape. The vast majority of rapists are male.

How pervasive is the crime of rape and/or sexual assault?

That is a difficult question to answer, because many rapes are not reported. The US Bureau of Justice Statistics reports that in 2021 there were 324,500 rape or sexual assault victimizations. In 2018, there were an even more alarming 734,000 reported rapes or sexual assaults. The Rape, Abuse, Incest National Network (RAINN) states on its Web site that there are more than 430,000 victims of sexual assault each year. RAINN also reports that "one in 9 girls and 1 in 20 boys under the age of 18 experience sexual abuse or assault."

TABLE 8.2: Minors' Access to STD Services

State	*Age at Which Minors May Consent to STD-Related Services*
Alabama	12 years[a]
Alaska	All ages
Arizona	All ages
Arkansas	All ages[a]
California	12 years
Colorado	All ages[b]
Connecticut	All ages[c]
Delaware	12 years[a]
District of Columbia	All ages
Florida	All ages
Georgia	All ages[a]
Hawaii	14 years[a]
Idaho	14 years
Illinois	12 years[a]
Indiana	All ages
Iowa	All ages[d]
Kansas	All ages[a]
Kentucky	All ages[a]
Louisiana	All ages[a]
Maine	All ages[a]
Maryland	All ages[a]
Massachusetts	All ages[e]
Michigan	All ages[a]
Minnesota	All ages[a]
Mississippi	All ages[f]
Missouri	All ages[a]
Montana	All ages[a]
Nebraska	All ages
Nevada	All ages
New Hampshire	14 years
New Jersey	All ages[a]

(Continued)

TABLE 8.2: (Continued)

State	*Age at Which Minors May Consent to STD-Related Services*
New Mexico	All ages[f]
New York	All ages[f]
North Carolina	All ages
North Dakota	14 years
Ohio	All ages[f]
Oklahoma	All ages[a]
Oregon	All ages
Pennsylvania	All ages
Rhode Island	All ages
South Carolina	16 years or mature minor
South Dakota	All ages
Tennessee	All ages
Texas	All ages[a]
Utah	All ages
Vermont	12 years[f]
Virginia	All ages
Washington	14 years
West Virginia	All ages
Wisconsin	All ages
Wyoming	All ages

[a]A physician may, but is not required to, inform parents of minor's consent to services.
[b]A physician may inform parents of minor's decision to consent to HIV/AIDS services if the minor is younger than sixteen.
[c]A physician must report a positive test result if the minor is younger than twelve.
[d]A parent must be notified of a positive HIV test result.
[e]A parent must be notified if the minor's health or life is at risk.
[f]Does not include right to consent to HIV/AIDS treatment.
Source: Adapted from the Guttmacher Institute, "Minors' Access to Contraceptive Services," https://www.guttmacher.org/state-policy/explore/minors-access-sti-services (accessed August 15, 2023).

Must a rape victim forcibly resist the aggressor for rape to occur?

No. Laws recognize that there a wide variety of circumstances—fear of severe physical violence, for example—under which rape victims might feel powerless to fight back.

What is "date rape"?

It is forced sexual activity that takes place in a social situation or between a dating couple. Date rape carries the same legal consequences as rape occurring in a nonsocial setting. Date rape is a significant problem at colleges and universities.

What is the difference between "simple rape" and "aggravated rape"?

Some state laws distinguish between "simple rape" and "aggravated rape." In simple rape there is no obvious injury and usually little evidence of a struggle. Simple rape can be more difficult to prove than aggravated rape, and fewer people are charged with it. Other states designate the crime as rape in the first degree and rape in the second degree.

What is statutory rape?

Statutory rape occurs when a man has sexual intercourse with a minor who is below a certain age. In every state a woman under that age is, by law, unable to legally consent to sex, even though she may have in fact consented, either expressly or by implication. If the young woman is below the legal age, the man is said to have committed a rape.

Statutory rape is also a crime. The age at which a minor can legally consent to sex is between fourteen and eighteen years, depending on the state. Because this type of rape is solely the creation of a state law or "statute," it is called "statutory" rape. In some states, a minor commits statutory rape only if he or she is at least three years older than the victim.

To be charged with statutory rape, does the man involved have to be over a certain age?

In many states, yes. It usually is between the ages of fifteen and eighteen, depending on state law. Usually, the male has to be a few years older than the female.

Does this mean that if a teenage couple has sex, the man can be charged with statutory rape?

In some states, yes.

Why isn't the woman also charged with statutory rape? Isn't the law unfair if it only punishes the male partner?

Statutory rape laws that punish only males aren't considered unfair and aren't unconstitutional. In *Michael M v. Superior Court of Sonoma County* (1981), the US Supreme Court ruled that California's law, which provided that only males could be convicted of statutory rape, did not violate the constitutional rights of young males. The court reasoned that young men and young women were in different situations in this context. The court explained: "We need not be medical doctors to discern that young men and young women are not similarly situated with respect to the problems and the risks of sexual intercourse. Only women may become pregnant, and they suffer disproportionately the profound physical, emotional, and psychological consequences of sexual activity."

Is it statutory rape for a woman over age eighteen to have sexual intercourse with a young man under, say, age fourteen?

In many states, yes, a female—like a male—can be charged with statutory rape (though note that many state laws do not use this term). Many state laws provide that a minor can be charged with a sexual assault, as long as the minor is more than two, three, or four years older than the younger party. Under many of these laws, the gender of the parties is irrelevant.

FOR FURTHER READING

Sex Issues and Sexual Rights

Lang, Jennifer. *Consent: The New Rules of Sex Education: Every Teen's Guide to Healthy Sexual Relationships*. San Antonio, Tex: Althea Press, 2018.

Wynne, Kathy. *Sex Education for Teens: Understanding Sex, Sexuality, and Relationships*. Pasadena, MD: Learn Inspire Press, 2022.

Pregnancy and Abortion

"After Roe Fell: Abortion Laws by State." *Center for Reproductive Rights*. https://reproductiverights.org/maps/abortion-laws-by-state/.

Hull, N. E. H. and Peter Charles Hoffer. *Roe v. Wade: The Abortion Rights Controversy in American History*. 2nd ed. Lawrence: University of Kansas Press, 2010.

Rosenblatt, Roger. *Life Itself: Abortion in the American Mind*. New York: Random House, 1992.

Ziegler, Mary. *After Roe: The Lost History of the Abortion Debate*. Cambridge, MA: Harvard University Press, 2015.

Rape and Date Rape

Anderson, Laurie Halse. *Speak*. New York: Farrar, Straus, & Giroux, 1999.

Brownmiller, Susan. *Against Our Will: Men, Women and Rape*. New York: Ballantine Publishers, 1993.

Koon-Magnin, Sarah. *Sexual Assault and Harassment in America: Examining the Facts*. Santa Barbara, CA: ABC-CLIO, 2022.

Levy, Barrie, et al. *When Dating Becomes Dangerous*. Center City, MN: Hazelden Press, 2013.

Scarce, Michael. *Male on Male Rape: The Hidden Toll of Stigma and Shame*. New York: Insight Books, 1997.

Vanasco, Jeannie. *Things We Didn't Talk About When I Was a Girl: A Memoir*. Portland, OR: Tin House Books. 2019.

Kraukauer, Jon. *Missoula: Rape and the Justice System in a College Town*. New York: Anchor, 2016.

Sexually Transmitted Diseases

Collins, Nicholas and Samuel G. Woods. *Frequently Asked Questions about STDS (Teen Life).* Buffalo, NY: Rosen Publishing Group, 2011.

Farber, Celia. *Serious Adverse Events: An Uncensored History of AIDS.* Chelsea, VT: Chelsea Green Publishing, 2023.

Pepin, Jacques. *The Origins of AIDS.* 2nd ed. Cambridge: Cambridge University Press, 2021.

Quinn, Paul. *Sexually Transmitted Diseases: Your Questions Answered.* Santa Barbara, CA: Greenwood Press, 2018.

OTHER INFORMATION SOURCES

Organizations

Guttmacher Institute, 125 Maiden Lane, New York, NY 10005. (212) 248-1111. E-mail: info@agi-usa.org. Home page: http://www.guttmacher.org/.

National Campaign to Prevent Teen and Unplanned Pregnancy (NCPTP), 1776 Massachusetts Ave. NW, Suite 200, Washington, DC 20036. (202) 478-8500. Home page: http://www.thenationalcampaign.org/.

National Organization on Adolescent Pregnancy, Parenting and Prevention (NOAPPP), 2401 Pennsylvania Avenue, Ste. 350, Washington, DC 20037. (202) 293-8370. E-mail: noappp@noappp.org. Home page: www.noappp.org.

Planned Parenthood Federation of America, 810 Seventh Avenue, New York, NY 10019. (212) 541-7800. E-mail: communications@ppfa.org. Home page: www.plannedparenthood.org.

Rape Abuse & Incest National Network (RAINN), 1220 L Street, Suite 505, Washington, DC 20005. (202) 544-3064 or 1-800-656 HOPE. E-mail: info@rainn.org. Home page: www.rainn.org.

Online Sources

Abortion Laws by State - Center for Reproductive Rights
Planned Parenthood for Teens: www.teenwire.com
The Safer Sex Page: www.safersex.org
Sex, Etc. (online magazine for teens): www.sexetc.org

Hotlines

AAA Abortion Helpline, (888) 41-WOMAN
Alcohol, Drug and Pregnancy Helpline, (800) 638-2229
America's Pregnancy Helpline, (888) 4-OPTIONS
Birthright, (800) 550-4900
Centers for Disease Control National AIDS Hotline, (800) 342-AIDS
Centers for Disease Control National STD Hotline, (800) 227-8922
Gay and Lesbian National Hotline, (888) THE-GLNH
National Teen AIDS Hotline, (800) 234-TEEN
Rape, Abuse, & Incest National Network (RAINN), (800) 656-HOPE

CHAPTER 9

Marrying and Having Children

PARENTAL CONSENT FOR MARRIAGE

At what age can a young person marry without parental consent?

At the age of majority, which in most states is age eighteen. The minimum age for marrying with parental consent is age sixteen in most states, although there are exceptions. For a marriage to be legal, both marriage partners must be old enough to marry or must have obtained the required consent. See Table 9.1 for ages at which minors can legally marry in the fifty states and the District of Columbia, and see Chapter 3, "At Home," for more about legal rights at the age of majority.

What happens if a minor marries without the required parental consent?

Some states say there is no marriage. Others take the position that the marriage can be set aside in court but is valid until this happens.

If teens who are too young to marry in their home state are married in a state where they are old enough to marry without parental consent, is the marriage legal?

The marriage is usually legal in the state where it was performed. As to the legality of the marriage at home, some states rely on the rule that if a marriage is legal where it was performed, it is legal everywhere. Others refuse to honor an out-of-state marriage that wouldn't have been legal if performed in-state.

TABLE 9.1: Marriage Laws by State

	Age of Consent to Marry	
State	*Age with Parental Consent*	*Age without Parental Consent*
Alabama	16[a]	18
Alaska	16[b]	18
Arizona	16[c]	18
Arkansas	Male, 17[b,d]/Female, 16[b,d]	18
California	No age limits	18
Colorado	16[b]	18
Connecticut	16[c]	18
Delaware	Male, 18[d]/Female, 16[d]	18
District of Columbia	16[a]	18
Florida	16[a,d]	18
Georgia	16[d,e]	18
Hawaii	15[e]	18
Idaho	16[b]	18
Illinois	16[f]	18
Indiana	17[d]	18
Iowa	16[e]	18
Kansas	16[c]	18
Kentucky	18[e]	18
Louisiana	18[b]	18
Maine	16[b]	18
Maryland	16[d,g]	18
Massachusetts	Male, 14[e]/Female, 12[e]	18
Michigan	16	18
Minnesota	16[e]	18
Mississippi	No age limits[e]	Male, 17/Female, 15
Missouri	15[h]	18
Montana	16[e]	18
Nebraska	17	19
Nevada	16[b]	18
New Hampshire	Male, 14[i]/Female, 13[i]	18
New Jersey	16[b,d]	18

TABLE 9.1: (Continued)

	Age of Consent to Marry	
State	*Age with Parental Consent*	*Age without Parental Consent*
New Mexico	16[d,h]	18
New York	16[i]	18
North Carolina	16[d]	18
North Dakota	16	18
Ohio	Male, 18[c]/Female, 16[b,d]	18
Oklahoma	16[b,d]	18
Oregon	17[j]	18
Pennsylvania	16[h]	18
Puerto Rico	Male, 18[b,d,h]/Female, 16[b,d,h]	Male, 21/Female, 21[d]
Rhode Island	Ma1e, 18[h]/Female, 16[h]	18
South Carolina	16[d]	18
South Dakota	16[d]	18
Tennessee	16[h]	18
Texas	16[e,i]	18
Utah	16[a]	18
Vermont	16[e]	18
Virginia	16[a,d]	18
Washington	17[h]	18
West Virginia	18[d]	18
Wisconsin	16	18
Wyoming	16[h]	18

[a]No parental consent required if previously married.
[b]Younger parties may marry with parental consent.
[c]Younger parties may marry with parental and judicial consent.
[d]Younger parties may obtain license in case of pregnancy or birth of child.
[e]Parental consent and/or permission of judge required.
[f]Judicial consent may be given when parents refuse to consent.
[g]If parties are at least sixteen years of age, proof of age and consent of parties in person are required. If a parent is ill, an affidavit by the incapacitated parent and a physician's affidavit required.
[h]Younger parties may obtain license in special circumstances.
[i]Below age of consent, parties need parental consent and permission of judge; no younger than fourteen for males and thirteen for females.
[j]If a party has no parent residing within the state, and one party has residence in the state for six months, no permission required.
Source: Adapted from the Legal Information Institute, https://www.law.cornell.edu/wex/table_marriage (accessed August 15, 2023).

In one case a fifteen-year-old New York woman married a twenty-year-old Virginia resident in Georgia. They separated a few years later. The woman sued to have the marriage set aside or "annulled" in New York. The court said the marriage was valid in Georgia, and it recognized the marriage under the laws of New York because it didn't involve polygamy (having more than one wife).

If a teen marriage is illegal, does it automatically become legal if the couple is still together when both partners have reached the age of majority?

In most states, yes.

OTHER TEEN MARRIAGE ISSUES

Does marriage emancipate a minor?

Yes. When minors are emancipated, their parents no longer have any legal power over them and are no longer required to support them. For more about emancipation, see Chapter 5, "On Your Own."

Are interracial marriages legal?

Yes. A law restricting marriage between members of different races would be in clear violation of the federal Constitution or state constitutions.

The US Supreme Court first ruled on this issue as late as 1967 in *Loving v. Virginia*. Two residents of Virginia, a black woman named Mildred Jeter and a white man named Richard Loving, were married in Washington, DC, in 1958. When they moved back to Virginia in the same year they were charged with violating Virginia's ban on interracial marriages. The couple pleaded guilty to the charges and were sentenced to one year in jail, although the judge suspended their sentences on the condition that they leave Virginia and not return for twenty-five years. Richard Loving appealed his conviction all the way to the US Supreme Court. At the time the Supreme Court heard the case, sixteen states banned interracial marriages. On appeal, the Supreme Court unanimously declared Virginia's ban on interracial marriages unconstitutional.

In his opinion for the court, Chief Justice Earl Warren held that the ban on interracial marriages violated both the due process and equal protection clauses of the Fourteenth Amendment. Warren reasoned that the law violated due process because the right to marry is a fundamental right. He also explained that the marriage ban violated the equal protection clause because Virginia's law was based on invidious racial discrimination. "There can be no doubt that restricting the freedom to marry solely because of racial classifications violates the central meaning of the Equal Protection Clause," Warren wrote.

Can a teen marry his or her cousin, assuming they both are of legal age?

It depends on individual states' laws. Nearly twenty states allow individuals, including teens who reach the age of majority, to marry first cousins. A few other states only allow first cousins to marry if the persons are more than sixty or sixty-five years old. Other states specifically forbid first cousins to marry at any age.

Can a married teen legally buy alcoholic beverages if the drinking age in a particular state is twenty-one?

No. State laws prohibiting the sale of alcoholic beverages to persons under age twenty-one apply to everyone.

Can a married couple be prohibited from obtaining public welfare benefits because they happen to be teens?

No, provided they are truly independent of their parents.

Can the parents of a married teen carry the teen on their car insurance policy?

Only if the auto that the teen drives is owned by the parents and is garaged at their residence. Insurance companies have special rules relating to coverage for married children of policyholders. A sales agent for the insurance company should be consulted when this issue arises.

THE RIGHTS OF TEENAGE PARENTS

Do teenage parents always have the right to make independent decisions about raising their children?

Yes, except when a family court decides that they really can't handle such decisions. The parent–child relationship is protected by the federal Constitution, and states may not excessively interfere with the way parents raise their children. This right extends to teenage parents and their offspring. For example, a state may not require a couple to abandon custody of a child just because one or both have not reached the age of majority.

As with adult parents, a child *can* be removed from a teenage parent's home if the child has been neglected, mistreated, abused, or abandoned, and *then* only after a full due process hearing. For more about these and related matters, including due process, see Chapter 10, "Your Right to Be Healthy and Safe from Abuse."

What legal responsibilities do teenagers have as parents?

The same responsibilities as adult parents. In every state, teenage parents must provide their offspring with adequate care, nurturing, education, and support. These responsibilities exist regardless of whether the child is born outside marriage, and they continue to exist until the child reaches the age of majority, even if a court forbids a parent to visit his or her child.

Can teenage parents consent to medical care for their child?

Yes, and furthermore, no state requires the involvement of a teen's parents in such matters.

Does a teen have legal rights with respect to a child born outside marriage?

Yes. The Constitution gives parents of all ages the right of custody over their minor children. This right always includes children born outside of marriage and children of teenage parents.

When the parents of a child born outside of marriage are involved in a dispute over child custody, will a family court always award custody to the mother?

No. Over the past few decades, most states have specifically moved away from a presumption that the child should remain with the mother. This is called either the "maternal preference" or "tender years presumption." Current law provides that a mother's right to custody of a child born outside of marriage is far from absolute—it will yield to the child's best interests.

As a practical matter, family courts are most likely to award custody to the parent who has been *caring* for the child, since that parent knows the child best. If the parents are unmarried teens, the mother almost always is the caregiver, because teenage fathers rarely live with their children. What this means is that unless a teenage father can convince a court that the mother can't take care of the child and that he can, the mother will usually be awarded custody.

Even so, a teenage father who wants to take day-to-day responsibility for his child can certainly seek to obtain custody. In a disputed case, if a family court determines that awarding custody to the father is in the child's best interests, it may make such an award, even if the parents have never lived as a couple under the same roof.

Can custody of a child ever be changed?

Family courts hesitate to modify custody arrangements once they have been established. To do so, the circumstances in the child's home must have changed dramatically, and the court must be convinced that a new home clearly would be in the child's best interests. The parent who petitions for a change in custody usually must show a material or substantial change in circumstances. If this can be shown, the court might award custody to the child's father, a grandparent, or another relative.

As discussed in Chapters 3 and 10, every state has the power to remove neglected, mistreated, or abandoned children from their homes, either temporarily or permanently. Matters such as these are handled in child protection proceedings in family court.

If a teenage mother has physical custody of a child born outside of marriage, is the father legally entitled to visit the child?

Yes, unless the family court believes that contact with the child isn't in the child's best interests. A teenage father has the right to be involved with his offspring unless he has been proved unfit or has forfeited his parental rights.

Can a teenage mother voluntarily place her child for adoption?

Yes. The consent of both parents is necessary in order to place a child for adoption, except in cases in which a parent's rights have already been terminated under state law. The consents must be in writing, and they can only be given after the birth of the child.

In a few states, such as Minnesota, if a birth parent is below age eighteen, his or her parents (or legal guardian) must also consent. However, the underage birth parent is entitled to the advice of an attorney, a member of the clergy, or a physician before executing the consent form.

Of course, if either parent's legal rights have already been terminated under state law, that parent's consent isn't required.

Can a teenage father stop the mother from placing their child for adoption?

The simple answer would be yes, because the father can withhold consent. But in fact, the answer is a bit more complicated. If the father can't be found or hasn't provided for the child financially, most states don't require his consent. Some require the father's consent only if his "paternity" has been established.

In an increasing number of states, a man who believes he may have fathered a certain child can establish his right to be notified of any and all adoption hearings relating to that child. He can, in other words, "register" for notice of the hearings—whether or not the birth mother has named him on the birth certificate as the child's father. The registration can occur any time prior to the birth of the child, but in most states, must occur no later than thirty days after the child's birth. If the birth mother decides to voluntarily relinquish her parental rights, the adoption agency and the family court must notify the registrant.

Some legal scholars believe that a state law that fails to require notification to the father is an unconstitutional denial of due process of law. For more about due process, see Chapter 2, "At School."

Can parental rights ever be terminated without a court hearing?

No. Terminating parental rights without a full due process hearing in family court would be a clear violation of the Constitution. Parents have procedural due process rights, which means that they have a right to notice of the termination process and a hearing at which they can contest the proceedings or present evidence on their behalf.

FINANCIAL HELP FOR YOUNG FAMILIES

Do teenage parents have the right to receive financial assistance at public expense?

Public financial assistance isn't a constitutional right. Even so, the federal government and state and local governments provide assistance to families in need. A family who meets the financial qualifications for assistance can't be turned down just because one or both parents are under age eighteen.

For many years the largest public assistance program for parents was Aid to Families with Dependent Children (AFDC). But Congress abolished AFDC in 1996 and replaced it with the Personal Responsibility and Work Opportunity Reconciliation Act of 1996. This legislation, popularly known as the "Welfare Reform Act," requires each state to establish a welfare plan meeting broad federal guidelines and gives each state a grant of money to assist in its implementation and operation. Like AFDC, the Welfare Reform Act assists needy families when one parent lives elsewhere or is incapacitated. It compensates families—very modestly—for the support that the missing or incapacitated parent would otherwise contribute.

The new program under the federal welfare law that replaced AFDC was the Temporary Assistance for Needy Families (TANF). Under this program, which began in July 1997, single parents with children can receive needed financial assistance for necessities. Under TANF, recipients must find a job within twenty-four months of receiving benefits under this program. Every state administers TANF programs a bit differently. To obtain public assistance, a minor with a child must live either at home or in an adult setting. Furthermore, the minor must go back to high school or attend a training program as soon as his or her child is twelve weeks old.

How does a family qualify for assistance under TANF?

The basic eligibility requirements carry over from AFDC. First, there must be a needy, dependent child in the house. A child is "needy" if the household's income and other resources are below a certain dollar amount. Second, one of the parents must have passed away, left home, or become incapacitated. If a family qualifies, it is almost automatically covered by Medicaid as well. (Medicaid is a joint federal/state program that provides medical care insurance coverage to low-income Americans.)

Persons on public assistance receive regular visits from an assigned caseworker. If the recipient refuses to allow the caseworker in the home, benefits can be terminated. Recipients must help caseworkers to establish the paternity of any child born outside of marriage and must cooperate to obtain support from the absent parent. Usually this means providing the other parent's name and address, unless giving such information would place the welfare recipient in obvious danger.

To find out where to apply for assistance under your state's TANF program, see http://www.acf.hhs.gov/programs/ofa/.

Can a minor qualify for food stamps?

If a teenage parent qualifies for public assistance because he or she has physical custody of a child, both parent and child will probably qualify for a federal or local food plan as well. By far the largest food plan is the federal food stamp program known as the Supplemental Nutrition Assistance Program, popularly referred to by its acronym SNAP. It is self-described as the "largest federal nutrition assistance program in the United States." In 2022, more than forty-one million individuals participated in SNAP.

Food stamps traditionally took the form of coupons. They were issued to the head of the household to purchase food items at grocery stores, but not in restaurants. These days many states are replacing the food coupons with electronic accounts. Instead of receiving a coupon book, a program participant receives a food stamp card worth a certain dollar amount. When the participant presents the card to the grocery store cashier, his or her account is electronically "debited" to reflect the value of the purchase.

Besides the food stamp program, a special federal program called the Special Supplemental Nutrition Program for Women, Infants, and Children (WIC) program, created in 1974, provides low-income pregnant women and their children with extra food such as eggs, milk, infant formula, fruit juice, cereal, and cheese. The WIC program covers needy children to age four. Also, nonprofit elementary and secondary schools and childcare institutions receive government funds to serve milk, well-balanced meals, and snacks to students and preschool children. For more information about the WIC program, see http://frac.org/federal-foodnutrition-programs/wic/.

FOR FURTHER READING

Couples

Garrett, Sarah. *So, You Think You're Ready to Date? A Guide to Teenage Dating*. Avondale, AZ: BookPatch LLC, 2020.

Hertz, Frederick and Emily Doskow. *Making It Legal: A Guide to Same Sex Marriage, Domestic Partnerships and Civil Unions*. 2nd ed. Berkeley, CA: Nolo Press, 2011.

Parenting

Zeiss. *Help! My Teen is Pregnant: A Survival Guide for Moms of Pregnant Teens*. New York: Morgan James Publishing, 2020.

Poverty

Desmond, Matthew. *Poverty, By America*. New York: Crown, 2023.

Elliott, Andrea. *Invisible Child: Poverty, Survival, & Hope in an American City*. New York: Random House, 2022.

Hershkoff, Helen and Stephen Loffredo. *The Rights of the Poor (ACLU)*. Carbondale: Southern Illinois University Press, 1997.

OTHER INFORMATION SOURCES

Organizations

Friends First, Box 356, Longmont, CO 80502. (800) 909-WAIT. E-mail: info@friendstirst.org. Home page: www.friendsfirst.org.

National Center for Fathering, Box 413888, Kansas City, MO 64141. (800) 593-DADS. E-mail: dads@fathers.com. Home page: www.fathers.com.

The National Parenting Center (TNPC), 22801 Ventura Boulevard, Ste. 110, Woodland Hills, CA 91367. (800) 753-6667. E-mail: ParentCtr@tnpc.com. Home page: www.the-parenting-center.com.

Online Sources

Food Research and Action Center: http://frac.org/federal-foodnutrition-programs/snapfood-stamps/
Office of Family Assistance: http://www.acf.hhs.gov/programs/ofa/help
Teen Advice Online: www.teenadviceonline.org

Hotline

Youth Crisis Hotline, (800) 448-4663

CHAPTER 10

Your Right to Be Healthy and Safe from Abuse

ABUSE AND NEGLECT

What is child abuse?

The definition varies from state to state. Some states define child abuse as a parent, custodian, or guardian engaging in conduct that leads to serious physical or mental harm or a substantial risk of physical or emotional harm to a child. The conduct can be performed by a parent or someone the parent allows to cause harm to the child. Alabama defines child abuse as "harm or threatened harm to a child's health or welfare by a person responsible for the child's health or welfare, which harm occurs or is threatened through nonaccidental physical or mental injury; sexual abuse."

A word of caution is appropriate, as the terminology varies quite widely in different states. Some states have a separate definition for "child neglect" that focuses on negligent conduct by a parent or guardian instead of intentional or reckless conduct that leads to harm to the child. Other states use the terms "abuse" and "neglect" as synonyms. For example, West Virginia law provides:

> "Child abuse and neglect" or "child abuse or neglect" means physical injury, mental or emotional injury, sexual abuse, sexual exploitation, sale or attempted sale or negligent treatment or maltreatment of a child by a parent, guardian or custodian who is responsible for the child's welfare, under circumstances which harm or threaten the health and welfare of the child.

Child abuse always includes child sexual molestation, though many states have separate definitions for "child sexual abuse."

By definition, how serious does the abuse actually have to be?

Serious physical injuries are certainly child abuse in every jurisdiction. Again, one needs to closely examine individual state law, but beatings, whippings, and severe spankings may constitute child abuse even if no cuts or bruises result.

Does this mean that a parent may not physically discipline a child?

No, not in many jurisdictions. In fact, some states specifically explain in their definitions of "abuse" that such abuse does not include normal spanking or paddling. For example, Oklahoma's law on child abuse provides: "nothing contained in the Oklahoma Children's Code shall prohibit any parent from using ordinary force as a means of discipline including, but not limited to, spanking, switching, or paddling."

How does child neglect differ from child abuse?

In many states, child neglect is defined somewhat less precisely than child abuse. Usually it is described as a lapse of care by a parent or other responsible person. Child neglect occurs when parents don't provide for a minor's basic survival needs. The most obvious example is the failure of a parent to provide a child with adequate food, clothing, shelter, or supervision.

The laws of many states limit state intervention in neglect cases to situations in which the parents are able to provide for a minor but refuse to do so. Certain states limit state action to situations in which the parents knowingly refuse to accept public assistance for a minor.

How does one report child abuse and child neglect cases?

The easiest way to report a suspected case is to call the police or the state or local child protection agency. There are also national child abuse hotlines. Groups and medical clinics such as Planned Parenthood can also be called. They have reporting information at their fingertips.

In addition, most communities have 24-hour child abuse and child neglect telephone hotlines (sometimes called "helplines"). The numbers to call are usually listed in the front of the local phone book. Calls to hotlines are always confidential.

If a young person is being abused by a parent, a housekeeper, a coworker, a date, a neighbor, a parent's boyfriend or girlfriend, a brother or sister—*anyone*—the young person or anyone else may report it. The abuser doesn't have to be a parent for the state to be concerned about stopping it and preventing it from happening again.

Can a minor report an abusing parent?

Anyone can make a report. For the sake of the victim, the abuser, and the abuser's family, all physical and sexual abuse cases should be reported, as should all neglect cases. The more detailed the report, the more quickly the child protection agency is likely to respond.

Are reports of abuse to child protection services offices confidential?

Always.

Can one parent report the other parent?

Yes.

If a person fails to report a case of child abuse or child neglect, has he or she broken the law?

In some situations, yes. In the past, only doctors and nurses were "mandatory reporters." But now the list includes teachers, psychologists, psychotherapists, dentists, and other healthcare providers, because these individuals are often the first to see evidence of the abuse. In most states, social workers, day-care employees, the police, and judges are also mandatory reporters, and in some states *everyone* is required to report. Even so, few individuals are ever prosecuted for failing to report a child abuse incident. This fact probably contributes to even greater underreporting.

Is a minor ever a mandatory reporter?

As a practical matter, no.

Can a person get in trouble for making a child abuse report if no abuse actually occurred?

Not usually—unless the caller made the report in bad faith or without a legitimate belief that abuse occurred. Every state provides legal immunity for mandatory reporters who make a child abuse report in good faith. This means that if a mandatory reporter makes a report of suspected abuse or neglect, and if the investigators finally determine that no abuse or neglect occurred, the reporter can't be taken to court for slander or libel. In many states this rule also applies to voluntary or "non-mandatory" reporters.

The questions and answers that follow assume that the suspected abuser is a parent. However, for a child protective agency to act, the abuser or neglectful person does not have to be a parent. He or she can be a teacher, housekeeper, relative, sibling, or any other person.

How does a child protection agency act on a report of abuse or neglect?

A "child protection team" of professionals goes to work. If the problem is in the home, the agency conducts a home investigation. At least one social worker will visit the child's residence, often unannounced. He or she will interview the parents, the child, other suspected abusers, and often neighbors and friends. Frequently the social worker will also interview the child's teachers and healthcare providers.

The child protection team might also include mental health experts, nurses, and attorneys.

If evidence of abuse or neglect turns up, the lawyer for the child protective agency may file a "petition" in state family court for authority to take custody of the minor or protect the minor in some other way. Filing a petition officially begins the case, which is a "civil action" as opposed to a "criminal action." In most states these cases are called "child protection proceedings."

For more about the difference between civil and criminal actions, see Chapter 17, "Taking Matters to Court."

Does the investigation procedure differ in an emergency situation?

Yes. If the young person appears to be in serious danger and there's no time for a home study or even a preliminary hearing in court, the child can be removed immediately. (This can also occur in cases of child abandonment.) But the family court must hold a hearing as soon as possible after the removal in order to decide exactly how to proceed. If it turns out that removing the child wasn't needed, the child must be returned home promptly.

Is a petition filed in family court after every investigation?

No. A petition won't be filed if the investigation doesn't reveal evidence of abuse or neglect. But even if such evidence exists, the agency may decide against filing a petition if the parents agree to participate in parenting classes, counseling, or some other suggested rehabilitation program. Meanwhile a social worker from the child protective agency will make periodic visits to the family to make certain the home situation is stable. If the parents don't make an effort to attend the special classes, counseling, or rehab program, the agency may decide to go ahead and file the petition.

Does the minor remain at home during the investigation?

It depends on the circumstances. If the abuse or neglect appears especially serious or if allowing the minor to stay home is likely to be a bad idea for some other reason, the judge may order the minor to stay with a relative or perhaps a family friend. Other possibilities are placing the minor in temporary foster care or with a volunteer family. (Foster care is discussed at the end of this chapter.)

What actually happens in a family court hearing?

Investigators, social workers, and medical witnesses present their evidence to the family court judge. These individuals may be cross-examined by the parents' attorney, who will attempt to protect their interests and their reputation as parents. Documents, medical records, and studies may be offered, and the judge often asks additional questions. Usually no one is in the courtroom except the judge, the witnesses, social workers, relatives, and persons with a stake in the outcome.

Will the minor testify at the hearing?

It depends upon his or her age and maturity, and upon the nature of the case. Small children seldom testify, but teens often do.

Although the minor is usually the key witness at an abuse or neglect hearing, minors often find court intimidating. There's never anything to be afraid of. But even so, many minors fear their testimony will infuriate their parents, and sometimes it does. For this reason, family court judges sometimes permit a minor's testimony to be taken outside the courtroom and away from the parents. Testimony might be videotaped or tape-recorded, or taken inside the judge's office. This presents interesting issues under the confrontation clause of the Sixth Amendment or confrontation clauses under state constitutions. Some defendants in these cases have contended that they have a right under such clauses to confront their accusers face-to-face. The courts generally have relaxed confrontation clause requirements when the victims are children.

Can a minor be required to testify?

Yes, if the judge determines that the minor is "competent" to do so. See Chapter 17, "Taking Matters to Court," for additional information about the testimony of minors.

Will the court always remove a minor from the home in a proven abuse or neglect situation?

No. If the problem isn't expected to continue and allowing the minor to stay at home appears to be the preferred arrangement, a family court won't authorize removal. Instead, a social worker will monitor the family and try to help them better understand their problems. In-home counseling often is an enormous help to troubled families.

If parents are suspected of abuse or neglect, will a lawyer be appointed to represent their interests if they can't afford one?

Yes, in both civil and criminal cases. Although parents don't have a constitutional right to a lawyer in child protection proceedings, most states now authorize court-appointed counsel to assist poor parents.

Is the minor entitled to a court-appointed lawyer as well?

Yes, although in some states the minor's representative doesn't have to be a licensed attorney. That layperson is often called a guardian *ad litem*.

In fact, a subtle difference exists between the roles of the lawyer and the guardian *ad litem*. A lawyer represents the minor; a guardian *ad litem* represents the best interests of the minor. Occasionally these positions conflict, such as in cases in which a minor with legal counsel insists on remaining with a parent in a troubled, unsafe home. When this occurs, the judge must decide what is best for the young person.

Will the minor's lawyer and the parents' lawyer always be different people?

Yes, because the parents' position in the case might be contrary to the child's. They might, for example, claim that neither has ever laid a hand on the child, despite the child's obvious cuts and bruises. For this reason, family courts almost always appoint a lawyer or guardian *ad litem* to represent the minor.

Who pays for the minor's lawyer?

Usually the state.

Does the family court go after the abuser?

No. A family court's basic purpose is to protect a minor from abuse or neglect. But as this is being arranged, the state prosecuting attorney may decide to charge the suspected party with criminal abuse or neglect, or perhaps even "battery" or attempted homicide. (Battery is any touching of another person without first obtaining the consent of the person who is legally allowed to give it.)

An important factor in the prosecutor's decision is this: he or she knows that *criminal* abuse and neglect are harder to prove than *civil* abuse and neglect. For a person to be convicted on criminal charges, the prosecutor must prove "beyond a reasonable doubt" that the person committed the act. But for a family court to intervene, the facts of the case only have to show it was "more likely than not" that abuse or neglect occurred. If the prosecutor doesn't believe the state's "burden of proof" can be met, he or she won't file criminal charges, and the case will only go to family court.

In addition, the criminal system can be slow to act. But civil or family courts are usually "at the ready" and are also more likely to help other family members.

Criminal abuse trials are discussed in detail in the next section.

SEXUAL ABUSE

How does the law define sexual abuse?

Sexual abuse is any forced or required sexual contact. The sexual contact includes any attempted or actual penetration of a minor's vagina or anus, and also oral sex. In addition, it includes an adult's handling of a minor's genitals or a request for a minor to handle an adult's genitals.

Sexual abuse doesn't have to involve actual physical contact. When no contact occurs, the abuse is sometimes called "child exploitation." It is sexual exploitation for a minor to be forced or required to look at an adult's genitals or forced or required to undress in front of another. It is also sexual abuse for an adult to require a minor to submit sexually to a third person. Sometimes child sexual abuse leads to other forms of abuse or exploitation such as child pornography.

Is sexual abuse always a crime?

Yes. Persons who sexually abuse or sexually molest minors or adults can be charged with criminal sexual abuse. This is a crime in every state. The penalties vary from state to state, but sexual abuse of a minor is a felony, with sentencing trends that often result in significant prison time for offenders.

Can a parent be criminally charged with child sexual abuse?

Anyone can be charged with child sexual abuse, including a parent.

If a parent is charged with suspected child sexual abuse, can the other parent also be charged?

In certain cases, yes. Usually it depends on whether the nonparticipating parent knew that the child was being sexually abused but didn't do anything to stop it.

What is "battered child syndrome"?

The US Department of Justice defines "battered child syndrome" as "the collection of injuries sustained by a child as a result of repeated mistreatment or beating." If a child has repeated injuries, there is a possibility that the child falls into this category.

These conditions exist when medical examinations establish that the minor has been either physically or sexually abused, but no clear link exists between an adult's misconduct and the minor's physical or psychological state. A parent or other adult can be charged with child abuse in connection with these conditions.

Proving these offenses requires the state prosecuting attorney to prove that only the person charged was undoubtedly responsible for the abuse. Often the syndrome isn't identified until the child has died or lapsed into a critical physical or psychological state.

The US Supreme Court approved the use of evidence that a child suffered from "battered child syndrome" in *Estelle v. McGuire* (1991), a case of infant death. The court held that the introduction of battered child syndrome evidence did violate the adult defendant's due process rights. "Maternal deprivation syndrome" is also a form of child abuse and involves a similar type of proof.

Can a teen be charged with criminal sexual abuse for having sex with another teen?

In many cases, yes. An obvious example of teen sexual abuse would be date rape. Another example is statutory rape, when an older teen has sex with a younger teen. For more about teens and sex, see Chapter 8, "Your Sexual Life."

How can a sexually abused minor obtain immediate help?

By contacting the state child protection agency or the police. Child sexual abuse is a form of child abuse, so the state child protective agency can always intervene. As in physical abuse and neglect cases, it can act in an emergency, then bring a child protection proceeding after intervening. At a later date the state prosecuting attorney will decide whether to criminally prosecute the suspected abuser.

What would a criminal abuse or neglect trial be like?

Prior to trial, the minor would be required to repeat the details of the incident to several different police officers, doctors, social workers, counselors, and the suspect's attorney. The trial would probably be open to the public. The minor might be required to take the stand, and there would be plenty of legal jargon used during the investigation and trial that the minor wouldn't comprehend.

No civil hearing or criminal trial on a physical or sexual abuse matter is pleasant for the individuals involved. The law can require or "subpoena" key persons to participate. Even so, the social workers, counselors, lawyers, and others involved are always extremely caring and supportive of the minor.

Are physical and sexual abuse tough to prove in court?

Not necessarily, but every case is different. Child abuse used to be difficult to prove because courts didn't trust the testimony of minors, even if the minor was a teen and the only witness to the abuse. But these days a minor's testimony is permitted and often required in both civil and criminal physical and sexual abuse cases, except when the minor is a young child.

A special issue in criminal sexual abuse cases is "hearsay," which is a person's statement about what someone else said. Hearsay statements usually aren't permitted in court to prove a point. In an abuse case, the rule against hearsay could prevent an individual such as a school nurse from stating what the minor confided about the sexual abuse. Instead, the court would require the minor to testify on his or her own. This can be a serious obstacle if the minor is afraid to testify.

The hearsay rule is often relaxed in child sexual abuse and rape cases, as well as in custody cases, but only if the minor's hearsay statements appear particularly reliable. Courts have treated "excited utterances" and "spontaneous declarations" of young people as reliable testimony on this theory.

Testimony by a minor in court is discussed earlier in this chapter and also in Chapter 17.

MEDICAL CARE

If parents don't provide a minor child with adequate medical care, what can happen?

The state child protection agency can intervene, because failing to provide medical care to a minor is a form of child neglect. The state can also intervene if parents remove their child from a doctor's care before treatment is complete.

Family courts consider both the seriousness of the problem and the risks and benefits of treatment in determining whether to order medical help. They also consider whether the child wants to go through with the procedure.

Does a minor's life need to be in danger before a family court will order treatment?

No, but sometimes it is difficult to predict whether treatment will actually be ordered.

Courts don't hesitate to issue orders for blood transfusions and other accepted procedures, despite parental objections. Vaccination cases fall into this category. In 1993, a Missouri court ordered the vaccination of a child (and also ruled that child neglect had occurred) after it found that the parents had knowingly failed to have him vaccinated during a measles outbreak. In that case the court ruled that the scientific basis for vaccinating children for measles was well established. It also ruled that the parents' opposition to vaccines was not based on their personal religious beliefs.

On the other hand, a Pennsylvania court earlier refused to order a spinal operation for a young boy because neither he nor his parents wanted to go through with it—even though his condition was quite serious. But in 1972 an Iowa court approved simple tonsillectomies for three siblings over the religious objections of the parents.

Can parents prevent a minor child from receiving medical treatment for religious reasons, even if the minor wants it?

Yes, but only if the refusal to obtain treatment doesn't seriously endanger the minor's health or otherwise amount to neglect. Cases like this raise a free exercise of religion right under the First Amendment, so courts usually hesitate to order treatment unless the minor's condition is very serious. Even if medical treatment is ordered, courts are reluctant to remove children from their homes or from the physical custody of their parents. But removal will be ordered if abuse, neglect, or abandonment is shown to exist.

In *Prince v. Massachusetts* (1944), the US Supreme Court held: "The right to practice religion freely does not include liberty to expose the community or the child to communicable disease or the latter to ill health or death." The reality is that in some cases adult parents have been criminally charged for failing to provide proper medical care to their children—even if they have sincere religious objections to such care. If the care is important and necessary enough, the state often may intervene to protect the child.

For more about First Amendment rights, including the First Amendment's free exercise clause, see Chapter 2, "At School."

Can a minor arrange for his or her own medical care?

As a rule, minors can't enter into agreements for medical care or provide consent for their own treatment. But two exceptions exist. First, a minor can legally consent to needed treatment if the parents refuse. Second, mature, married, pregnant, and "emancipated" minors and those who are parents or runaways can give consent to routine treatment. (Emancipation gives a minor most of the privileges and responsibilities of adulthood, as Chapter 5 explains.) In addition, most states have laws permitting minors to consent to confidential treatment for alcoholism, drug abuse, and STDs, including HIV/AIDS.

If a minor arranges for his or her own medical care, who is financially responsible?

Often the minor pays because he or she wants to keep the treatment confidential. Even so, medical "necessaries" are the legal responsibility of the parents even if they don't contract for them, and even if they don't have a close relationship with their minor child.

Wouldn't a doctor still hesitate to treat a minor absent parental consent?

In most cases, yes. Although the exceptions discussed earlier mean that a doctor can't be sued for battery if he or she treats a minor without parental consent, many won't take the risk.

What should a teen do if he or she needs medical care and the parents won't cooperate?

Call the state child protection agency or a teacher, minister, relative, or adult friend.

Can a minor sign up for publicly funded medical care such as Medicaid if he or she doesn't live at home?

In most states it depends on whether the minor is still under the control of his or her parents or is emancipated.

In a 1977 case, New York's highest court decided that because a teenage woman had emancipated herself, she could legally apply for publicly funded medical services. The young woman had left home to avoid her father's control. The state medical welfare agency argued that it shouldn't have to pay for her care because her father had enough income to support her and hadn't thrown her out of the house. The New York court ruled that the woman's "implied" emancipation relieved her father of his parental responsibilities. She was therefore entitled to public medical assistance.

OTHER ISSUES RELATING TO ABUSE AND NEGLECT

Can a minor be taken from the custody of a parent because the parent is "living with someone"?

Not for that reason alone. However, if the other person with whom the parent lives is a danger to the child, is an illegal drug user, or poses some other sort of problem, then the other parent could petition for a change in custody. Also, the state could intervene if the other person living in the home poses a real threat of physical harm to the child.

Can a minor be taken from the custody of his or her parents because their home is dirty and messy?

Again, not for that reason alone. A home that strikes someone as dirty or messy doesn't necessarily indicate that the parents are neglectful—some parents just place more importance on a clean house than others. However, a home that truly constitutes a health hazard could be the basis for neglect proceedings.

Can a minor be taken from the custody of his or her parents because one of them has been convicted of a crime?

The fact that a parent has been convicted of a serious crime can be grounds for child protection proceedings in some states. So can a parent's habitual drug or alcohol use.

Can a state take custody of a minor because a parent in the home is gay or lesbian?

No, just because a parent is lesbian or gay would not warrant the state taking custody of the child. Only if the gay or lesbian parent—just as with a heterosexual parent—harmed a child would the state intervene. To learn about situations in which parental rights can be terminated altogether, see Chapter 3, "At Home."

MENTAL HEALTH ISSUES

Can a teen see a psychiatrist or psychologist without parental consent?

Many states now permit minors to consent to confidential outpatient mental health treatment. For example, Washington State law provides that minors thirteen years of age or older may obtain mental health treatment without parental consent. California has an even more protective law for minors. Minors twelve years of age or older can seek mental health treatment. Under the California law, parents or guardians can only be informed of the minor's mental health treatment with the signature of the minor. See http://www.teenhealthlaw.org/fileadmin/teenhealth/teenhealthrights/ca/CaMCConfMentalHealthChart12-10.pdf for information on California's law.

It is very difficult for a young person to obtain mental health counseling without parental approval. Many public and private mental health agencies refuse to meet with a teen more than once without providing notice to a parent. Psychiatrists and psychologists in private practice rarely confront this issue, because teens usually can't afford to see them.

A local mental health association is the best place to contact for information about confidential mental health counseling and treatment.

Can parents admit a minor to a mental hospital without the minor's consent?

Parents have the legal power to consent to a minor's mental health treatment in a private hospital.

Can parents admit a minor child to a public mental hospital without a court hearing?

The US Supreme Court determined in *Parham v. J.R.* (1979) that a full due process hearing isn't required. The Supreme Court stated:

> We conclude that the risk of error inherent in the parental decision to have a child institutionalized for mental health care is sufficiently great that some kind of inquiry should be made by a "neutral factfinder" to determine whether the statutory requirements for admission are satisfied. That inquiry must carefully probe the child's background using all available sources, including, but not limited to, parents, schools, and other social agencies. Of course, the review must also include an interview with the child. It is necessary that the decision maker have the authority to refuse to admit any child who does not satisfy the medical standards for admission. Finally, it is necessary that the child's continuing need for commitment be reviewed periodically by a similarly independent procedure.

This procedure means that some review by a "neutral decision maker" must take place to determine whether admitting the minor is necessary or the parents are simply shoving a difficult minor aside. Usually these reviews are conducted by a doctor who hasn't treated the minor in the past.

For information about the meaning of due process, see Chapter 2, "At School."

FOSTER CARE

What is foster care?

This is a state-sponsored living arrangement for young people whose parents are unable to provide proper care and nurturing. In foster care, "foster parents" take minors into their homes and are responsible for their day-to-day care and supervision. Foster care is meant to last for a limited period, although sometimes foster care arrangements last many months, and sometimes years.

A foster child usually is placed in a foster home at the direction of a family court. However, parents can place a child in a foster home voluntarily. The state agency authorized to place children in foster care retains legal custody over the foster child, licenses foster homes, and supervises the foster parents.

Can a teen be a foster "child"?

Yes.

Why might a family court judge order a minor into foster care?

The reason might be that the parents have abused, neglected, or abandoned the child, or that one parent is in prison. It might be that the family is having severe financial difficulties or that a parent is experiencing poor health or emotional problems. There are dozens of reasons for placing young people in foster care.

Do minors in foster care have any legal rights?

Young people in foster homes always have the right to receive adequate care, including food, clothing, shelter, education, and medical treatment, all at state expense. In addition, foster children with special needs are legally entitled to receive special medical or psychiatric care and also rehabilitation training.

Foster children also have the right to be protected from abuse and neglect at the hands of their foster parents. If a young person is abused while in foster care, the state must remove the child. In most states a foster child (assisted by an adult) can go to court to recover money damages against the foster care agency for its failure to supervise the foster parents properly. For more about recovering damages in court, see Chapter 17, "Taking Matters to Court."

Do minors in need of foster care have a right to choose their foster parents?

No. The decision is made by the state foster care agency. But many agencies actively seek out relatives who might be willing to serve as foster parents.

Do the natural parents retain any authority over a child in foster care?

In most states, yes. Although the family court transfers legal custody to the foster care agency, it often permits the natural parents to continue to make major decisions relating to their child, including decisions about the child's medical care, schooling, and religion.

Do foster children have a legal right to see their natural parents while in foster care?

In most cases, yes, and the parents usually have a right to see their child. There is a strong belief that foster children need to maintain contact with their parents; as a result, foster care agencies now authorize regular visits by the parents, except in extreme cases.

Do foster children have a legal right to be reunited with their families after being in a foster home?

Yes. Federal law requires that states develop case plans to reunite foster children with their natural families as soon as possible, provided it is in the child's best interests. States must determine within eighteen months of placement whether the child should be returned home, placed for adoption, or put in a more permanent foster home. This law was passed after studies proved that children were remaining in foster care either too long or for no good reason.

Can foster parents legally prevent a foster child from being returned to his or her natural parents?

The laws of some states now permit foster parents to challenge a foster child's return to his or her natural parents. Usually the foster parents may object to a foster child's removal only if the child has been with them for a long time: 3–18 months, depending on the state.

Do foster parents have a legal right to adopt a foster child?

In many states, yes, but only if the parental rights of the natural parents have been terminated. Although foster parents used to be forbidden to adopt foster children, in recent years such adoptions have gained favor with legislatures, courts, and child protective agencies.

Can a minor adopt his or her foster parents?

No, but if foster parents want to adopt a foster child, many states require the child's consent to the adoption if the child has reached a certain age. The age of consent falls between ten and fourteen years, again depending on the state.

For a discussion of whether a minor can divorce his or her parents in favor of foster parents or others, see Chapter 7, "If Your Parents Divorce."

Do foster parents receive payment for taking a foster child?

In most cases, yes. The state makes regular payments to foster parents to assist with the cost of care.

Does the sexual orientation of a foster parent matter in child placement?

Again, the law varies from state to state. According to the Family Equality Council, as of 2014 six states specifically prohibit discrimination against prospective foster parents because of their sexual orientation: California, Massachusetts, New Jersey, Oregon, Rhode Island, and Wisconsin. Two states, Nebraska and Utah, explicitly restrict fostering by LGBT parents.

FOR FURTHER READING

In General

Goldentyer, Debra. *Family Violence*. Orlando, FL: Raintree/Steck Vaughn Company, 1995.
Hefner, Mary Edna, et al., eds. *The Battered Child*. Chicago, IL: University of Chicago Press, 1999.

Mariani, Cliff and Patricia Sokolich. *Domestic Violence Survival Guide*. Flushing, NY: Looseleaf Law Publications, 1996.
Marsh, Toni. *Juvenile Law*. Clifton, NY: Thomson Delmar Learning, 2007.
Morey, Ann-Janine. *What Happened to Christopher: An American Family's Story of Shaken Baby Syndrome*. Carbondale: Southern Illinois University Press, 1998.
Parton, Nigel. *Governing the Family: Child Care, Child Protection and the State*. New York: St. Martin's Press, 1991.

Legal Issues

Clement, Mary. *The Juvenile Justice System: Law and Process*. 2nd ed. Woburn, MA: Butterworth-Heinemann, 2001.
Guggenheim, Martin. *The Rights of Families: The Authoritative ACLU Guide to the Rights of Family Members Today*. Carbondale: Southern Illinois University Press, 1996.
Hubner, John and Jill Wolfron. *Somebody Else's Children: The Courts, the Kids, and the Struggle to Save America's Troubled Families*. New York: Crown Publishers, 1998.
Wallace, Harvey. *Family Violence: Legal, Medical, and Social Perspectives*. Needham Heights, MA: Allyn & Bacon, 1998.

Sexual Abuse

Dziech, Billie Wright, et al. *On Trial: America's Courts and Their Treatment of Sexually Abused Children*. Boston: Beacon Press, 1991.
Reinert, Dale Robert. *Sexual Abuse and Incest*. Springfield, NJ: Enslow Publishers, 1997.

Medical Care

Isler, Charlotte. *The Watts Teen Health Dictionary*. New York: Franklin Watts, 1996.

Mental Health Care

Cohen, Daniel and Susan Cohen. *Teenage Stress*. New York: Dell Publishing Company, 1992.
Newman, Susan. *Don't Be Sad: A Teenage Guide to Handling Stress, Anxiety, and Depression*. New York: Julian Messner, 1992.

Foster Care

Bartholet, Elizabeth. *Nobody's Children: Abuse and Neglect, Foster Drift, and the Adoption Alternative*. Boston: Beacon Press, 1999.
DeGarmo, John. *The Foster Parenting Manual: A Practical Guide to Creating a Loving, Safe and Stable Home*. London: Jessica Kingsley Publishing, 2013.
Falke, Joseph. *Living in a Foster Home*. New York: Crown Publishers, 1995.
Glatz, Janet Clayton. *Fostering or Adopting the Troubled Child: A Guide for Parents and Professionals*. Brunswick, ME: Audenreed Press, 1998.

OTHER INFORMATION SOURCES

Organizations

American Red Cross, 1621 North Kent Street, Arlington, VA 20009. (703) 248-4222. E-mail: info @usa.redcross.org. Home Page: www.redcross.org.

National Clearinghouse for Child Abuse and Neglect Information, 330 C Street SW, Washington, DC 20447. (800) 394-3366. E-mail: nccanch@calib.com. Home page: www.calib.com/nccanch.

National Foster Parent Association, 2021 E Hennepin Ave #320, Minneapolis, MN 55413-1769. 1-800-557-5238. E-mail: info@NFPAonline.com. Home page: http://nfpaonline.org/.

Rape Abuse & Incest National Network (RAINN), 635-B Pennsylvania Avenue SE, Washington, DC 20003. (800) 656-HOPE. E-mail: rainnmail@aol.com. Home page: www.rainn.org.

Online Sources

Child Abuse Prevention Network: www.child.comell.edu

Child Welfare Information Gateway: https://www.childwelfare.gov/

"Immunity for Reporters of Child Abuse and Neglect": https://www.childwelfare.gov/systemwide/laws_policies/statutes/immunity.pdf

US Department of Justice on battered child syndrome: https://www.ncjrs.gov/pdffiles1/ojjdp/161406.pdf

Hotlines

National Domestic Violence Hotline, (800) 799-SAFE, (800) 787-3224 (TTY)

Rape Abuse & Incest National Network (RAINN), (800) 656-HOPE 1-(800)-THERAPIST, www.1-800-therapist.com

CHAPTER 11

Alcohol and Drugs

THE LEGAL DRINKING AGE

At what age can young people legally buy alcoholic beverages?

The standard age is twenty-one (21). In 1984, the US Congress passed the National Minimum Drinking Age Act, which withheld federal funding to states that allowed those under twenty-one to purchase alcoholic beverages. Some states also have laws that specifically forbid those under twenty-one to purchase alcohol.

Businesses may not sell alcohol to underage persons; this is why teens and young adults often are "carded" when they attempt to buy it.

At what age can a person legally possess or consume alcohol?

The age is 21 - the same at which a person can legally buy it.

Does this mean that possessing alcohol when under the legal age is a crime?

Yes, although it is a misdemeanor. When a minor purchases, possesses, or consumes alcohol in most cases, he or she commits a delinquent act. In most states the case will go to juvenile court.

Are there any exceptions to this?

Yes, some states have laws that specifically provide an exception for minors' consumption of alcohol at religious services. For example, Illinois law provides: "No person, after purchasing or otherwise obtaining alcoholic liquor, shall sell, give, or deliver such alcoholic liquor to another person under the age of 21 years, except in the performance of a religious ceremony or service."

In other states, there may be an exception for minors who are given liquor by certain persons for medicinal purposes. For example, a Washington State law has an exception in its prohibition to furnishing alcohol to minors if "liquor [is] given for medicinal purposes to a person under the age of twenty-one years by a parent, guardian, physician, or dentist."

Procon.org provides a detailed review of all the state-level exceptions to the minimum legal drinking age of twenty-one, which is freely available online. See the "Online Sources" in the "Other Information Sources" section at the end of this chapter.

Can a minor legally drink alcohol at home?

In some states drinking at home isn't illegal if the minor has parental permission, although in recent years many states have repealed this twist in their drinking laws.

But even if young people can legally drink at home, they can't legally give alcohol to others. In other words, teens who can't legally buy alcohol can't have parties for other underage drinkers. In a 1989 New Jersey case, a nineteen-year-old, home from college for Christmas, threw a "kegger" at his parents' house when they weren't around. About 150 young people came. Many were sixteen or seventeen years old, and most of them were drinking when the police arrived. The underage host was charged with distributing alcohol to minors. If the host had been over age twenty-one, the charge would have been the same.

If a minor marries or is legally emancipated, is he or she still subject to state laws prohibiting persons under a particular age from purchasing and drinking alcohol?

Yes. Everyone is subject to state laws regulating the purchase and consumption of alcohol, regardless of marital or legal status.

If a minor is caught drinking under age or buying alcohol with false or altered ID, what can happen?

In most states the minor will be arrested, sent to juvenile court, and placed on probation.

Can minors work in bars?

Not usually. Most states prohibit minors from working in lounges, bars, night clubs, restaurants, and other establishments serving alcoholic beverages. However, some states and cities permit minors to bus tables in restaurants that serve alcohol.

DRINKING AND DRIVING

Is drunk driving a crime?

Yes, it is a crime. The police can arrest a person for committing the crime of DUI. This offense is also known as driving while intoxicated.

America's DUI statistics have improved in recent years. According to the National Highway Traffic Safety Administration, there were 1,249 fatalities of persons under age twenty-one killed in drunk driving accidents in 2011. This is down from 2,905 in 1991 and 5,125 in 1982. Even though there are fewer deaths, every day at least three people in the United States under age twenty-one die from drunk driving accidents.

Drunk driving arrests usually are "warrantless," because drunk drivers are an immediate danger to passengers, other drivers, and pedestrians. For more about arrests and warrants, see Chapter 12, "Teens and Crime."

On the other hand, the police don't arrest someone who commits a minor traffic offense such as exceeding the speed limit, parking illegally, or driving at night with one headlight. They simply issue a citation, which requires the offender to either pay a fine or appear in court.

How do the police know when a driver is intoxicated?

First, police officers are trained to recognize physical signs of inebriation in a driver or other individual. Among these indicators are slurred speech, alcohol breath, a flushed face, failing to comprehend the officer's questions, staggering when exiting a vehicle, and leaning on the vehicle for support.

Second, an officer can tell by the way a person drives that something isn't right. Intoxication is suggested when a driver swerves or weaves in and out of traffic, turns with an extra-wide radius, follows too closely, or fails to obey other basic rules of the road.

Other signals to an officer are when a driver stops unnecessarily, accelerates or decelerates too quickly, or drives without headlights at night.

Third, the police are able to put a DUI suspect through certain "field sobriety tests" after a stop. They might ask a suspect to attempt to walk steadily along a straight line, recite the ABCs, stand on one leg, or perform other basic actions requiring balance and coordination. A bad performance suggests intoxication and will usually result in the suspect's arrest.

Fourth, a driver is said to be intoxicated if his or her blood alcohol content, or BAC, is at or above 0.08 percent. A person with a BAC of 0.08 percent has 0.08 grams of alcohol per 100 milliliters of blood. A chemical test establishes an individual's BAC. In a "breathalyzer test" the DUI suspect is required to blow deeply into a breathalyzer machine or "drunkometer." Usually the test is administered at the police station, to both adults and teens.

It used to be that most states defined the level of intoxication at 0.10 percent. That has been lowered over the past decade or two to 0.08 percent. In every state a DUI suspect gives implied consent to be chemical tested. This includes minors. The suspect doesn't have the right to consult an attorney before taking a chemical test. If he or she requests one, the police won't wait for the attorney to appear before running the test.

Do states impose increased penalties if the person is heavily intoxicated?

Yes, nearly every state imposes increased penalties if the person is over a certain level of intoxication—beyond the normal offense level. For example, in many states if the offender's BAC is at 0.15 or 0.2, he or she will spend more time in jail and suffer more consequences.

Some states actually refer to the increased penalties under a "felony driving under the influence." This means that the driver will receive a felony if convicted, rather than a misdemeanor.

Is a minor always subject to the same BAC limit as an adult?

No. Many states have adopted "zero-tolerance" policies toward intoxicated teen drivers. Their legislatures have established lower BAC limits for persons under age twenty-one—usually 0.02 percent. Some states refer to this as a "driving while impaired" law. States with zero-tolerance policies report a significant decline in traffic fatalities among young drivers.

What is the purpose of a "penlight test" or "horizontal gaze nystagmus test" at the arrest scene?

This maneuver estimates the angle at which a DUI suspect's eye begins to jerk about or "oscillate." ("Nystagmus" is a medical term for eye oscillation.) To perform the test, the police officer requires the suspect to follow the beam from a penlight at close range, straight ahead, and then from right to left. If the suspect's eye begins to jerk before 45 degrees off the center, a BAC of over 0.05 percent is suggested. Although the results of this field test are usually inadmissible as evidence, the test is commonly used.

What happens if a DUI suspect refuses to take the field sobriety tests or the breathalyzer test?

With respect to the field sobriety tests, the police officer must determine whether to make an arrest—although probably his or her decision will already have been made, based on personally observing the suspect. Again, for further information about arrests and the probable cause requirement, see Chapter 12, "Teens and Crime."

A different rule applies with respect to the breathalyzer test and other chemical tests, such as blood or urine tests. In most states a DUI suspect's license or learner's permit is instantly suspended if the test is refused. Moreover, the suspension usually "sticks" regardless of whether the suspect is later found guilty. The length of the suspension can be up to twelve months.

Can a person be convicted of DUI if his or her BAC is less than 0.08 (or is less than the applicable limit)?

In most states, yes, assuming there is other reliable evidence of drunkenness such as slurred speech, stumbling, or alcohol breath.

Could a driver ever be sober, and thus innocent of a DUI offense, even though his or her BAC is above the legal limit?

In theory, perhaps, but seldom in reality. In recent years, forty-eight states have made driving with excess BAC a "per se" offense. This means that a driver with a BAC at or over the legal limit always breaks the law, no matter how well his or her body may tolerate alcohol.

Loosely translated from Latin, the term *per se* means "that's just the way it is."

Is alcoholic content the only substance that can be tested to see if someone is DUI?

No. Some state laws provide that a person is DUI if he or she has certain levels of THC, which stands for tetrahydrocannabinol. THC is a primary ingredient in marijuana. Most state laws prohibit a person from operating a motor vehicle under the influence of a variety of Schedule I drugs, including marijuana, cocaine, mescaline, opium derivatives, salts of such products, and a variety of other illegal drugs. Many laws are broad in prohibiting individuals from operating vehicles under the influence of such drugs. For example, Georgia law prohibits driving "under the influence of any drug to the extent that it is less safe for the person to drive."

If a minor is arrested for drunk driving, does the case go to adult court?

No, it goes to juvenile court.

If a minor accused of DUI can't afford a lawyer to fight the charge, will the court appoint one?

Yes, particularly if the offense is punishable by residential treatment. A DUI suspect should always be represented by an attorney.

Can a person be jailed for a DUI conviction?

Yes. This often happens to adults. In most states, however, an adult's first DUI conviction usually involves a stiff fine, a license suspension, mandatory attendance at a DUI rehabilitation course, and probation for a period of up to several years.

For a second offense, an adult will often go to jail. Furthermore, his or her vehicle may be impounded, a community service obligation may also be imposed, and attendance at a series of Alcoholics Anonymous meetings may be ordered. For a minor, the consequences are similar, although confinement in an institution is uncommon unless the minor is a "recidivist," a repeat offender.

Driving a moped and riding a bicycle while intoxicated are also punishable offenses. You can't legally ride a horse while intoxicated, either.

Is it against the law to have open alcoholic beverages in a car, even if none of the passengers is drinking or drunk?

Absolutely. These days just about everyone knows about statewide "open container" laws. For more information about open container laws, see https://alcoholpolicy.niaaa.nih.gov/Open_Containers_of_Alcohol_in_Motor_Vehicles.html.

Can the police stop cars at random to determine whether the driver is legally intoxicated?

Not usually. As a rule, a car stop is allowed only if the officer has a good reason to believe the driver is committing a traffic offense or some other criminal act. For example, a driver can only be pulled over if the officer sees the car speeding or drifting in and out of a lane of traffic. If the officer believes the driver is intoxicated after asking some questions, observing the driver's movements, and perhaps detecting alcohol on his or her breath, an arrest can be made on the theory of probable cause.

If an officer pulls a vehicle over at random and without the driver committing a driving offense, the officer arguably has violated the driver's Fourth Amendment rights. The Fourth Amendment prohibits government officials, including police officers, from engaging in "unreasonable searches and seizures."

Are drunk driving roadblocks legal?

It depends. The US Supreme Court ruled in *Michigan Department of State Police v. Sitz* (1990) that a Michigan system of sobriety checkpoints was not per se unconstitutional. Some state high courts have invalidated sobriety checkpoints under search and seizure provisions of their state constitutions. In many states, the legality of roadblocks or sobriety checkpoints depends on the specific way in which the roadblocks are administered. A key factor is whether the police officers are acting pursuant to specific guidelines or are exercising an excessive amount of discretion. In some states, if cars are stopped in a neutral, nondiscriminatory fashion, then the program will be held constitutional.

ILLEGAL DRUGS

Which drugs are illegal?

There are many illegal drugs. The Drug Enforcement Agency (DEA) groups illegal drugs into different categories, including narcotics, hallucinogens, stimulants, and depressants. Examples of narcotics are heroin and morphine. Examples of hallucinogens are ecstasy,

LSD, and marijuana. Examples of stimulants are cocaine and amphetamines. Examples of depressants are barbiturates and GHB. For more information, see the DEA's "Drug Fact Sheets" at http://www.justice.gov/dea/druginfo/factsheets.shtml.

The laws of each state list the drugs that are always illegal within its borders, regardless of whether the drug is possessed, purchased, or sold. Each state also lists the drugs that are illegal unless prescribed by a physician. In addition, federal law prohibits the possession, purchase, and sale of many types of drugs. State and federal laws usually refer to illegal drugs as "controlled substances"; the older term is "contraband."

Most states group drugs and narcotics into categories established under the federal Uniform Controlled Substances Act. They are categorized according to their potential for harm in contrast to their possible medical benefits. For example, "Schedule I" drugs have no beneficial medical use; they are always harmful. Heroin and LSD are Schedule I drugs. Schedule II drugs include cocaine, opium, and amphetamines. Because Schedule I drugs have no beneficial use, the penalty for possessing and selling any of them is the severest.

What are "bath salts"?

Bath salts are synthetic cathinones, designer drugs that look like white salt-like products. They are similar in effect to amphetamines and cocaine. One reason that bath salts are so popular among drug users is that they can be smoked, snorted, swallowed, or injected. They are dangerous. The US Department of Justice's National Drug Intelligence Center has dubbed bath salts "an emerging domestic threat." See http://www.justice.gov/archive/ndic/pubs44/44571/44571p.pdf.

Is the knowing possession of a controlled substance always a crime?

Yes. State and federal laws prohibit persons from "knowingly or intentionally" possessing illegal drugs. This may mean that being innocently in possession of a controlled substance usually won't be sufficient to support a criminal conviction. For example, if a person receives a package in the mail that contains drugs, the person can only be convicted of illegal possession if it is shown that he or she knew the drugs would be delivered and intended to take possession of them.

Of course, it isn't illegal for a person to possess certain drugs if they have been prescribed by a doctor for that same person's illness or injury.

Table 11.1 provides a rundown of medical and recreational marijuana laws by state.

Is purchasing a controlled substance a different offense from possessing a controlled substance?

Yes. A suspect can be charged with both acts in connection with a single incident.

Selling controlled substances and manufacturing them are also criminal acts. An adult who is convicted of either offense can receive a prison sentence of up to fifteen years and be fined as much as $25,000.

TABLE 11.1: Marijuana Laws by State

State	*Type Allowed*	*Age*
Alabama	Medical only	19
Alaska	Medical	None
	Recreational	21
Arizona	Medical	None
	Recreational	21
Arkansas	Medical	21
California	Medical	None
	Recreational	21
Colorado	Medical	18
	Recreational	21
Connecticut	Medical	18
	Recreational	21
Delaware	Medical	18
	Recreational	21
District of Columbia	Medical	Under 21 signed form from authorized practitioner
	Recreational	21
Florida	Medical	None
Georgia	Limited medical	None
Hawaii	Medical	None
Idaho	None	
Illinois	Medical	18
	Recreational	21
Indiana	Limited medical	None
Iowa	Limited medical	None
Kansas	Limited medical	None
Kentucky	Medical	18
Louisiana	Medical	21
Maine	Medical	none
	Recreational	21
Maryland	Medical	18 (under 18 may only obtain through caregiver)

TABLE 11.1: (Continued)

State	*Type Allowed*	*Age*
	Recreational	21
Massachusetts	Medical	None
	Recreational	21
Michigan	Medical	None
	Recreational	21
Minnesota	Medical	None
	Recreational	21
Mississippi	Medical	None
Missouri	Medical	18
	Recreational	21
Montana	Medical	18
	Recreational	21
Nebraska	None	
Nevada	Medical	None
	Recreational	21
New Hampshire	Medical	None
New Jersey	Medical	None
	Recreational	21
New Mexico	Medical	None
	Recreational	21
New York	Medical	None
	Recreational	21
North Carolina	Limited medical	None
North Dakota	Medical	19
Ohio	Medical	None
Oklahoma	Medical	None
Oregon	Medical	18
	Recreational	21
Pennsylvania	Medical	None
Rhode Island	Medical	None
	Recreational	21

(*Continued*)

TABLE 11.1: (Continued)

State	*Type Allowed*	*Age*
South Carolina	Limited medical	None
South Dakota	Medical	21
Tennessee	Limited medical	None
Texas	Limited medical	None
Utah	Medical	18
Vermont	Medical	None
	Recreational	21
Virginia	Medical	None
	Recreational	21
Washington	Medical	18
	Recreational	21
West Virginia	Medical	None
Wisconsin	Limited medical	None
Wyoming	Limited medical	None

Source: Adapted from IIHS, "Marijuana Laws," https://www.iihs.org/topics/alcohol-and-drugs/marijuana-laws-table (accessed August 15, 2023).

What is the difference between a possession charge and a distribution charge?

A possession charge usually does not carry the same heavy sentence as a distribution charge does. The idea is that a person possessing illegal drugs is not causing as much widespread harm as someone who is distributing the drugs to others. In many states the terms are "simple possession" and "possession with intent to distribute." Usually, if a teen has larger quantities of an illegal drug, he or she likely will face a distribution charge.

Is giving drugs to another person a criminal act?

Yes. The "sale" of a controlled substance includes giving a drug to someone. It's not necessary to receive something in exchange. This means that cash doesn't have to change hands for a drug sale to occur.

Can the police personally search a minor for drugs?

The police can search anyone who is under arrest. Once a person is under arrest, he or she can be searched for contraband, including weapons and drugs.

If a minor is arrested for a drug offense, does the case go to juvenile court?

In most cases, yes. If the minor's parents can't afford an attorney to represent their child, the minor has a right to be assigned one at public expense.

If the police find drugs on a minor, will the drugs always be used as evidence?

Not if the police search is illegal, in which case the drug evidence would be "suppressed." Without this evidence, a finding of delinquency probably wouldn't occur.

Rules relating to personal searches are discussed in Chapter 12.

How do juvenile courts handle drug cases?

Cases involving the possession, purchase, or sale of drugs are often easier to prove than other criminal offenses, because the "elements" of the offense are straightforward. As a result, guilty pleas are common in juvenile court, and formal hearings on drug charges are infrequent.

This makes a minor's sentencing the focus of the case. As explained in Chapter 12, juvenile delinquents are entitled to "treatment" after being convicted, because the legal philosophy behind juvenile courts is to rehabilitate rather than punish.

If a minor is found guilty of a drug offense, what is likely to happen next?

For a first offense, a minor will probably be required to attend rehabilitation classes and be subject to random drug testing. If and when the minor follows through with the program, the juvenile court will close the case. If the minor fails to complete it, the court won't hesitate to order detention, probation, or both, and the minor's driving privileges will almost certainly be suspended.

What is a juvenile drug court?

In many jurisdictions, the minor will be subject to a juvenile drug court. These courts, similar to adult drug courts, seek to provide immediate treatment to juvenile drug offenders and try to break the cycle of drug-related crime. One leading study of juvenile drug courts identified a key purpose of juvenile drug courts as to "provide immediate intervention, treatment, and structure in the lives of juveniles who use drugs through ongoing, active oversight and monitoring by the drug court judge." For more information about juvenile drug courts, see https://www.ncjrs.gov/pdffiles1/bja/197866.pdf.

In a drug-related offense, does a minor ever go to adult court?

Yes. If the offense involved a particularly large quantity of drugs, if the minor's "accomplices" were adults, or if the minor has been convicted of a drug offense in the past, in many states a juvenile will be waived into adult court, which will take jurisdiction.

When can school officials personally search a minor for drugs?

School officials generally can search a minor if they have a reasonable basis for conducting the search. Usually, school officials have authority to search teens' lockers and desks, because those are the property of the school. For more information on searches of teens and their property at school, see Chapter 2, "At School."

Can the police come onto school property to arrest a minor for possessing or selling drugs?

Yes, provided the police have "probable cause" for the arrest. Possessing or selling drugs on school grounds is a criminal act.

Drug possession on campus also violates school rules and usually results in long-term suspension or expulsion, whether or not the student is arrested. Most schools have "zero-tolerance" policies against drugs.

Important rules about school searches are discussed in Chapter 2.

Can a minor obtain drug treatment without parental consent?

In most states, yes. For more about situations in which a minor may legally consent to medical care, see Chapter 10, "Your Right to Be Healthy and Safe from Abuse."

FOR FURTHER READING

Alcohol

Cohen, Daniel and Susan Cohen. *A Six-Pack and a Fake ID: Teens Look at the Drinking Question*. New York: Dell Publishing Company, 1992.
Espejo, Roman. *Alcohol: Teen Rights and Freedoms*. Farmington Hills, MI: Greenhaven Publishing, 2012.
Grosshandler, Janet. *Coping with Drinking and Driving*. New York: Rosen Publishing Group, 1997.
Jacobs, James B. *Drunk Driving: An American Dilemma*. Chicago, IL: University of Chicago Press, 1989.
Land, Alan R. *Alcohol: Teenage Drinking*. Broomall, PA: Chelsea House Publishers, 1992.
Lewis, John F. *Drug and Alcohol Abuse in Schools: A Practical Guide for Administrators and Educators for Combatting Drug and Alcohol Abuse*. 2nd ed. Dayton, OH: Education Law Association, 1992.
Milhorn, Thomas, Jr. *Drug and Alcohol Abuse: The Authoritative Guide for Parents, Teachers, and Counselors*. New York: Plenum Publishing, 1994.

Drugs

Currie, Elliott. *Dope and Troubled Portraits of Delinquent Youths*. New York: Pantheon Books, 1992.
Grosshandler, Janet. *Drugs and Driving*. New York: Rosen Publishing Group, 1997.
Nelson, David. *Teen Drug Abuse*. Farmington Hills, MI: Greenhaven Press, 2010.
Schaler, Jeffrey A., ed. *Drugs: Should We Legalize, Decriminalize, or Deregulate?* Amherst, NY: Prometheus Books, 1998.
Scheier, Lawrence M. and William B. Hansen, eds. *Parenting and Teen Drug Use: The Most Recent Findings from Research, Prevention, and Treatment*. New York: Oxford University Press, 2014.
Taylor, Clark. *The House That Crack Built*. Chicago: Chronicle Books, 1992.

OTHER INFORMATION SOURCES

Organizations

Al-Anon & Al-Ateen, 1600 Corporate Landing Parkway, Virginia Beach, VA 23454. (888) 4AL-ANON. E-mail: SWO@al-anon.org. Home page: www.al-anon.alateen.org.

Cocaine Anonymous, Box 492000, Los Angeles, CA 90049-8000. (800) 347-8998. E-mail: cawso@ca.org. Home page: www.ca.org.

Mothers Against Drunk Driving (MADD), 511 E. John Carpenter Freeway, Suite 700, Irving, TX 75062. (877) ASK-MADD. E-mail: info@madd.org. Home page: www.madd.org.

Narcotics Anonymous, Box 9999, Van Nuys, CA 91409. (818) 773-9999. E-mail: info@na.org. Home page: www.na.org.

National Council on Alcoholism and Drug Dependence, 12 West Twenty-first Street, New York, NY 10010. (212) 645-1690. Hotline: (800) NCA-CALL. E-mail: national@ncadd.org. Home page: www.ncadd.org.

Students Against Driving Drunk, Inc. (SADD) (also, Students Against Destructive Decisions, Inc.), Box 800, Marlborough, MA 01752. (508) 481-3568. Home page: www.saddonline.com.

Online Sources

"Criminal Neglect: Substance Abuse, Juvenile Justice and The Children Left Behind": http://www.casacolumbia.org/addiction-research/reports/substance-abuse-juvenile-justive-children-left-behind

"Drug Offense Cases in Juvenile Courts 1985–2004": https://www.ncjrs.gov/pdffiles1/ojjdp/fs200803.pdf

"Eight Different Exceptions to the Minimum Legal Drinking Age (MLDA) of 21": http://drinkingage.procon.org/view.resource.php?resourceID=002591#chart2

Reclaiming Futures: http://www.reclaimingfutures.org/blog/

US Department of Justice on juvenile drug courts: https://www.ncjrs.gov/pdffiles1/bja/197866.pdf

CHAPTER 12

Teens and Crime

ARRESTS

What exactly is an arrest?

It is an action in which a police officer seizes a person or takes away that person's freedom in some significant way. A person can be arrested when an officer has a good reason to believe the person has committed a crime or is in the process of committing one.

A police officer doesn't have to say "you're under arrest" for an arrest to occur—a command such as "stand still" or "come along" usually is enough. A good test for an arrest is whether the suspect realizes or should realize that he or she isn't free to walk away. In the law this is referred to as the "free to leave" test.

If a person isn't sure whether he or she has been arrested, it is always appropriate to ask the officer, "Am I under arrest?"

Can minors be arrested?

Yes, although strictly speaking, minors aren't "arrested." They are "taken into custody." This distinction in the law emphasizes the fact that the juvenile court system exists to protect and rehabilitate minors rather than punish them. In this chapter, however, the terms "arrested" and "taken into custody" mean the same. "Minor" and "juvenile" also mean the same.

What are the two broad categories of offenses for which adults or minors can be arrested?

The two broad categories for which adults and minors can be arrested if they commit or are suspected of committing a crime are "felony" and "misdemeanor." Felonies are more serious than misdemeanors. Joyriding, for example, is a misdemeanor, but stealing a car without any intent to return it is a felony. As a rule, felonies are punishable by at least one year in prison, while misdemeanors are punishable by less than a year in prison.

Whom do the police represent?

Police officers represent the state or a political subdivision within a state, such as a city or county. States grant authority to their political subdivisions to enforce state laws and pass laws of their own. Police officers have the job of enforcing the law, and one of their most important enforcement tools is the power to arrest persons who commit crimes.

What makes a particular act a crime?

An act is a crime only if a public law says it is. If an act isn't prohibited by a federal, state, or local law, the police can't arrest someone for it, and the prosecuting attorney can't bring criminal charges against a person suspected of committing it.

Do the police have to be absolutely certain that a person committed a crime before he or she can be arrested?

No. To arrest an adult, a police officer only needs to have "probable cause" to believe that a crime was committed and that a particular individual committed it. This is a requirement based of the Fourth Amendment of the Constitution.

To understand probable cause, consider the following scenario. Two men are exchanging money on the street, and one has a brother who is a known drug dealer. With only this information, a police officer observing the transaction can't arrest either of them for attempting a drug deal. The evidence isn't sufficient to establish probable cause to conclude that the pair are trafficking in illegal substances—they could be exchanging money for a perfectly legal reason.

What is a warrant?

A warrant is a court order authorizing an arrest or a search by the police. Without a warrant, an arrest or search would be a violation of a citizen's privacy rights under the Fourth Amendment. "Warrantless" arrests and searches are legal only if they fall under one of the few exceptions to the Fourth Amendment's warrant rule. These exceptions include when a crime or contraband of a crime is in plain view ("plain view"), automobile searches, exigent (emergency-type) circumstances, hot pursuit, and search incident to a lawful arrest. Recall from Chapter 2 that searches of students at school also can be conducted without a warrant.

To obtain a search warrant from the court, a police officer must be able to detail, in writing, the person, place, or things to be searched. This is called the "particularity" requirement. The particularity requirement ensures that law enforcement officers don't have carte blanche to engage in roving, general warrant-type searches. One of the main reasons that the Fourth Amendment was added to the US Bill of Rights was to prohibit these general warrants, called writs of assistance. The officer's request to a "neutral and detached" magistrate or judge—usually a signed "affidavit"—must be based on probable cause that the item to be searched for is where the officer says it is.

However, an arrest warrant isn't needed if the officer believes he or she must detain the suspect on the spot. This exception to the warrant rule makes sense and is considered fair: if the officer needed to make a trip for a warrant, the suspect would undoubtedly vanish in the meantime.

Are innocent people arrested?

Yes, unfortunately this happens. When the police need to think fast, they sometimes make both reasonable and unreasonable mistakes.

If an arrest wasn't required, the officer may release the "arrestee" on the spot. Otherwise, the subject may be released at the station or upon his or her initial appearance in court.

Does probable cause apply when minors are arrested?

Yes. If, for example, a police officer observes a minor fumbling with a packet of white powder and overhears the minor tell a third person that it contains cocaine, the officer would have probable cause to believe a crime has occurred. The crime would be possession of a controlled substance.

If the officer observes the parties entering into negotiations for the sale and purchase of the cocaine, he or she now has probable cause to believe that the illegal sale of a controlled substance is occurring.

Can the police legally detain a person short of an arrest?

Yes. The police can make three kinds of "stops." The first is a basic type of police–citizen contact. It takes the form of a request for information or identification and allows a police officer to sniff out a potential problem. No force can be used, no weapons can be displayed, and the officer cannot legally restrict the subject's personal freedom in any major way.

The second type is a brief stop to investigate a suspicious situation and ask probing questions. Such a stop is called a "Terry stop," after the landmark Supreme Court case *Terry v. Ohio* (1968). For a Terry stop to be legal, the police officer must have "reasonable suspicion" to believe that a crime has been committed or is about to be committed. Reasonable suspicion requires less suspicion than probable cause. Reasonable suspicion is more than unparticularized suspicion, or a "hunch," but less suspicion than is required for probable cause.

The third type of stop is a full-scale arrest requiring probable cause. This also requires the arresting officer to give the suspect *Miranda* warnings, discussed in more detail in the next section.

THE *MIRANDA* WARNINGS

What happens when a person is arrested?

To begin with, a police officer confronts an individual and asks some questions about a particular incident. Then the officer will request the person's name and address and ask to see some identification. It is always best to cooperate on these preliminary matters.

If the officer has probable cause to believe the person being questioned has committed a crime, he or she will state that the suspect is under arrest and then recite the suspect's *Miranda* rights. That is, the officer will advise the suspect that

1. the suspect may legally refuse to answer any police questions,
2. the suspect may call a lawyer or be assigned one at public expense,
3. the suspect may stop answering police questions at any time or wait until a lawyer arrives before answering any additional questions, and
4. anything the suspect says may be used by the state prosecuting attorney to establish the suspect's guilt.

The US Supreme Court declared that officers must give these so-called warnings in *Miranda v. Arizona* (1966). A police officer's recitation of a suspect's *Miranda* rights is referred to all over the country as the *Miranda* warnings. The court issued its decision in *Miranda* over a concern that there were too many coerced confessions.

What is the constitutional basis for the *Miranda* decision?

Miranda flows from the privilege against self-incrimination found in the Fifth Amendment to the US Constitution, which provides: "No person . . . shall be compelled in any criminal case to be a witness against himself." The *Miranda* warnings encompass key procedural safeguards necessary to protect this important freedom from self-incrimination.

Are minors entitled to the *Miranda* warnings?

Yes. In fact, in many states the *Miranda* warnings must be given to an arrested minor, without exception, before any questions leading to a possible confession can be asked. *Miranda* warnings are required when a minor is subject to what is called "custodial interrogation." This means that the minor is in custody and faces police questioning. The US Supreme Court ruled in *J.D.B. v. North Carolina* (2011) that a minor's age is a relevant consideration in determining whether that minor feels he or she is in custody and not free to leave. The court explained that "a reasonable child subjected to police questioning will sometimes feel pressured to submit when a reasonable adult would feel free to go."

What happens if a police officer doesn't recite the *Miranda* warnings at the time of an arrest?

The law treats any statements made by the suspect as having been made in violation of his or her Fifth Amendment right to remain silent. The statements are deemed involuntary and are therefore illegal, even though the suspect may actually have made them willingly. When statements such as these are illegal under the law, they may not be used as evidence to convict a suspect of a crime. This rule of evidence is known as the "exclusionary rule."

What is the justification for the exclusionary rule?

A key justification for the exclusionary rule is that it is designed to deter police misconduct. It also supports the idea of judicial integrity. The US Supreme Court explained in *Mapp v. Ohio* (1961), a Fourth Amendment search-and-seizure case in which the court held that the exclusionary rule applied in state court prosecutions: "Nothing can destroy a government more quickly than its failure to observe its own laws, or worse, its disregard of the charter of its own existence."

What is the primary criticism of the exclusionary rule?

Justice Benjamin Cardozo, when he served as a judge in New York, famously remarked in *People v. Defore* (1926): "The criminal is to go free because the constable has blundered." Some critics contend that the exclusionary rule simply goes too far in allowing the suppression of evidence in cases involving people who actually committed the crimes for which they are arrested and charged.

Will the court overturn *Miranda*?

It is highly unlikely. Such an attempt was made in *Dickerson v. United States* (2000). However, Chief Justice William Rehnquist wrote in his majority opinion that *Miranda* was protected by the principle of stare decisis (Latin for "let the decision stand"). Rehnquist wrote: "*Miranda* has become embedded in routine police practice to the point where the warnings have become part of our national culture."

What happens if a suspect decides to confess to a crime after being "Mirandized"?

The confession can be used to convict. The suspect is presumed to have knowingly given up, or "waived," the right to remain silent.

Once a person waives the right to remain silent, can he or she withdraw the waiver and refuse to answer any more questions?

Yes. At any point, a criminal suspect may decide to quit talking—and may at that point also request a lawyer.

If a person receives the *Miranda* warnings and later confesses to a crime, will the confession always be treated as voluntary?

No. A court can also declare a confession illegal if it was given when the suspect was under too much pressure from the police during questioning, even if the *Miranda* warnings were recited.

Is a police officer required to recite the *Miranda* warnings in connection with casual questioning?

No. Neither probable cause nor reasonable suspicion is required for an officer to ask questions about a particular event, and the officer does not have to recite the *Miranda* warnings before asking them. (See the discussion about police stops in the "Searches and Seizures" section in this chapter.) But if probable cause develops during the questioning, the officer must recite the *Miranda* warnings before continuing.

WHEN MINORS ARE ARRESTED

What should a minor do if he or she is taken to the police station after an arrest?

First, if an officer again asks the minor to state his or her name and address, the minor should comply promptly. Second, the minor should ask to telephone a parent, guardian, or other adult.

Third, the minor should refrain from answering questions or volunteering information until an adult arrives, even if the minor fully understood the *Miranda* warnings. Police stations are particularly intimidating. For this reason, many states limit all police questioning of minors during a "custodial arrest" until a parent or other adult is on hand, especially if the police are likely to press for a confession.

Does a minor have a legal right to call his or her parents after being taken into custody?

Yes, although it's important to know that in some states the police aren't legally required to advise minors of this right.

Can a minor forfeit or "waive" his or her Fifth Amendment right to remain silent and proceed to talk?

Yes, but the law makes it difficult. If an adult waives the right to remain silent and then confesses to a crime, the waiver is presumed valid. But if a minor chooses to confess, the prosecuting attorney must prove that the minor's waiver was truly voluntary. This shifting of the "burden of proof" occurs because minors are considered particularly vulnerable to police pressure, especially at the police station, and therefore less likely to remain silent.

The legality of a minor's waiver depends on a variety of factors, including the minor's age, maturity, and past involvement with the police. It may also depend on whether the minor's parents or lawyer were present when the waiver and confession were made.

If a minor calls his or her parents but confesses before they arrive, is the confession valid?

It depends on whether the confession was the result of legal police questioning. Once a minor asks to talk to a parent, a lawyer, or another adult, the police must stop asking questions. If they continue and the minor confesses, the confession is treated as involuntary and is therefore illegal. But if, without additional questioning or pressure, the minor either spontaneously confesses or waives his or her right to remain silent and confesses "knowingly, voluntarily, and intelligently," the confession is probably legal.

It is always best to remain silent after a custodial arrest. Researchers note that *truly* knowing, voluntary, and intelligent waivers of Fifth Amendment rights by juveniles in custody, alone and without an attorney, are rare.

SEARCHES AND SEIZURES

Once the *Miranda* warnings are recited, are the police permitted to search their suspect?

Yes. The search is called a "search incident to an arrest." The police will always question their suspect both during and after a search incident to an arrest, unless the suspect has exercised his or her Fifth Amendment right to remain silent.

What are the main purposes of the search incident to a lawful arrest?

The main purposes behind the search incident to a lawful arrest are to protect officer safety and to secure contraband or evidence of a crime before it can be destroyed by the suspect.

Can a minor be searched?

Yes.

What is a search warrant? Does a search incident to an arrest require a search warrant?

A search warrant is a court order authorizing a search of a person, place (such as a bedroom or locker), or object (such as a purse or backpack). A request to the court for a search warrant must be based on "probable cause" that specific items actually will turn up and must clearly describe the person, place, or object to be searched. This is called the particularity requirement, mentioned earlier in this chapter.

Under the Constitution, every search requires a warrant. Warrantless searches are legal only if they fall under one of the few legal exceptions to the warrant requirement. One of these exceptions is the arrest warrant, discussed previously in this chapter. A search incident to an arrest can also be conducted without a warrant. Another type of warrantless search is one required in an emergency, such as a car search.

Are police searches ever illegal?

Yes. If a personal search, including a search incident to an arrest, is made without full probable cause, the search is illegal. It is again important to note that the "fruits" of an illegal search can't be used to convict a suspect in court.

Locker searches at school are governed by different, somewhat looser rules. For information about searches on school grounds, see Chapter 2, "At School."

Do special rules apply to car searches?

Yes. If a car is involved in an incident for which an arrest is made, certain areas of the car can be searched immediately and without a warrant. The police can search any bags and containers within the suspect's reach inside the car, including the glove compartment. The trunk usually can't be searched until the police obtain a warrant, although to prevent the contents of the trunk from being removed, they may seize or "impound" the car until a warrant is obtained.

What is a "stop-and-frisk" search?

A "stop-and-frisk", or a Terry stop, is a limited personal search that a police officer may conduct if he or she thinks a dangerous situation exists. The purpose of stop-and-frisks, or "pat-downs," is to search for weapons.

Reasonable cause to believe that danger is lurking, and not full probable cause, is needed for a stop-and-frisk. If the police detect a hard object such as a weapon during a stop-and-frisk, they can then arrest the suspect, recite the *Miranda* warnings, and proceed with a full personal search.

In 1993, the Supreme Court ruled in *Minnesota v. Dickerson* that if the police detect something that "feels like drugs" during a stop-and-frisk, they can make an arrest and then fully search their suspect. This case approved of the "plain feel" doctrine. The court explained that the "plain feel" concept was similar to the "plain view" doctrine, which allows police to seize evidence of contraband that is in plain view. However, the court invalidated the particular use of the "plain feel" search in *Minnesota v. Dickerson*, finding that the officer exceeded the lawful confines of the Terry stop rationale.

Why are stop-and-frisk policies controversial in some areas?

Stop-and-frisk practices are controversial in some areas, because critics contend that this proactive police tactic is used disproportionately against minorities. New York's aggressive stop-and-frisk policy has come under fire in recent years.

Can minors be subjected to stop-and-frisk searches?

Yes.

Can a minor consent to an otherwise unlawful personal search?

It depends. Like a minor's waiver of the right to remain silent, the legality of the consent depends on the minor's age, maturity, and past contacts with the police. Courts tend to rule that a minor can't legally consent to a search that would be illegal (because conducted without a warrant or conducted in connection with an unlawful arrest) except for the consent.

Do the police need a search warrant to enter a minor's home or bedroom to conduct a search?

Yes. Furthermore, an officer can seize additional criminal evidence once inside, but only if it is in "plain view." This is the "plain view exception" to the Fourth Amendment warrant rule. The rationale behind the plain view exception is that if items are in plain view, there is no real privacy interest to protect.

Consider the following example. A police officer obtains a warrant to search a minor's closet for illegal drugs. He notices drug paraphernalia on the minor's bed. He can seize these items also, without an additional search warrant.

Can parents consent to a warrantless police search of a teen's bedroom or car?

Courts in some states have ruled that parents legally control their minor children's property, so they have the power to forfeit a child's right to be free from warrantless searches. Other states take the position that parents who have no involvement in a suspected criminal act can't consent to a warrantless search of a child's private space.

In other states, whether a parent can legally consent to a warrantless search of a minor's room or other property depends on whether the minor should be able to expect an extra level of privacy with respect to the area to be searched. In these states, parents can lawfully permit the police to look at items on a child's desk or chest of drawers, but a closet or purse can't be searched without a warrant. If the police find illegal drugs inside a closet or purse, they can't be used as evidence against the minor.

INTAKE

What happens to a criminal suspect at the police station?

Unless the suspect has exercised his or her right to remain silent, the police will ask more questions. Their purpose will usually be to obtain a confession and discover the names of any accomplices.

The police have the power to detain a suspect even if they don't yet have enough evidence for criminal charges. When they do have sufficient evidence, they will "book" the suspect. (Sometimes the police let suspects go in simple misdemeanor cases, especially if the "misdemeanant" didn't injure anyone.)

If the police book a minor, will the case always end up in juvenile court?

No. After booking, the police and one or more juvenile probation officers (and possibly a social worker) meet to discuss how the case should be handled. This stage is called "intake." States have laws that set the parameters of the intake process. The intake participants may decide to place the minor on probation, send the minor to counseling, dismiss the case altogether, or determine that the minor should be charged with a delinquent act.

Intake officials consider many factors in deciding how to handle a case, including the seriousness of the offense and the minor's age, school record, home life, and previous delinquent acts. "Attitude" is also a consideration. A young person's attitude is usually conveyed by his or her actions or language at intake, but it can also be shown by clothing, tattoos (especially if they are supposedly "gang tattoos"), and even hairstyle.

Does the minor participate in the intake meeting?

Yes. Intake officials always interview the minor, although the minor does have the right to remain silent. The parents also participate.

Can a minor be represented by a lawyer at intake?

In many cases the minor won't yet have a lawyer. But in any event, a lawyer normally doesn't participate because the purpose of intake is to decide whether to handle the minor's case outside juvenile court, without judges and lawyers. But a lawyer can always advise what kinds of information the minor should reveal at intake and what to keep quiet about.

What is diversion?

This is a special way of handling a minor's case outside the juvenile court system. Under a diversion program, intake officials may decide to "divert" a minor to a private agency that arranges for special services such as counseling, rehabilitation, or foster care. The agency might also assist the minor in finding a job or adjusting better at home or in school.

Diversion programs operate with the consent of the juvenile court, the prosecuting attorney, and the court's probation officials. Their success depends on the minor's voluntary participation, because the agencies coordinating them don't have any real enforcement power. This sometimes reduces their success.

Teens should note that in some states diversion may not be an option if they commit certain more serious crimes. Attorneys likely will argue for diversion when it is available.

What are juvenile drug courts?

Juvenile drug courts present a diversion option for the juvenile justice system that focuses more on treatment than prosecution. The minor goes into treatment to battle the addiction rather than being placed in a prison-type environment that does not treat the underlying causes.

If the intake officials determine that a minor should be charged with a delinquent act, when are formal charges made?

At the minor's "advisory hearing," which is usually the minor's first encounter with the juvenile court judge. At this hearing, which is short, the judge states the charges, explains that the minor has the right to a lawyer, and asks the minor how he or she wants to plead. In addition, a trial date is set.

In some states the advisory hearing is called the "initial appearance."

Does a minor have a right to a lawyer in juvenile court?

Yes, at every stage—and the court is legally required to advise the minor of this fact. If the parents can't afford a lawyer, the state will provide one at public expense.

Is a minor always free to plead not guilty?

Yes. A plea of not guilty means there will be a trial, or "formal hearing."

Is a minor always free to plead guilty?

Yes. In fact, a minor's lawyer often recommends that he or she do so in return for a lighter sentence. But a juvenile court won't accept a guilty plea unless the minor fully understands its consequences, including the fact that there won't be a formal hearing to present evidence.

Guilty pleas are common in juvenile court.

PRETRIAL DETENTION

If a minor isn't diverted out of juvenile court at intake, is detention next?

It can be, although "pretrial detention" is the exception rather than the rule. Usually the police release the minor to a parent or relative pending the formal hearing. But if the minor is dangerous, likely to leave the state, or in need of special protection from his or her family, a judge may order detention. Pretrial detention may be in a juvenile facility, a foster home, or shelter care.

In most states a minor can't be held in pretrial detention for more than 72 hours without a detention hearing, and in some states the time limit is 24 hours. Detention without an immediate hearing often occurs if the minor is picked up over the weekend. The hearing usually takes place at the same time as the advisory hearing.

Detention of juveniles prior to the formal hearing is one of the thorniest issues in juvenile law. Critics argue that the juvenile is being punished before the court determines guilt or innocence. Their point is worth considering.

Is there a minimum age for pretrial detention?

Detention below a specified age is prohibited in about fifteen states. The minimum age varies: from New York, which prohibits detention below age ten, to Illinois, which prohibits detention below age sixteen.

Can a minor be represented by a lawyer at his or her pretrial detention hearing?

Yes. The constitutional right to be represented by a lawyer in criminal cases applies to minors in all juvenile court hearings.

Does a minor have any legal rights while in detention?

Yes. The juvenile "detainee" has a right to be free of all special restrictions—except, of course, the right to leave. This means he or she has a right to adequate clothing, bedding, sanitary conditions, educational facilities, and medical care, and also access to a library.

Is a detention facility the same as a jail?

No. Only adults go to jail. Minors cannot legally be incarcerated with adults. Physical and sexual abuse of juveniles illegally detained in adult jails isn't uncommon.

In a 1974 Kentucky case, a sixteen-year-old was taken into custody for a curfew violation. The police refused to allow him to call his parents, and he was immediately detained in an adult jail, although under Kentucky law he should have been released. The boy remained in jail for five days.

A federal appeals court stepped in, ruling that by refusing to permit the boy to call a parent and by keeping him in an adult jail before trial, the police inflicted "cruel and unusual punishment" on him in violation of the Constitution.

JUVENILE COURT HEARINGS

What types of cases do juvenile courts handle?

They handle criminal offenses committed by minors. In every state these offenses are called "delinquent acts." Sometimes juvenile court is referred to as family court or children's court.

Juvenile court is always separate from adult court. A minor's age at the time of his or her offense determines which court receives the case. In most states the age limit is eighteen, although in some states, including New York, juvenile court jurisdiction only extends to minors through age sixteen.

What is a "juvenile delinquent"?

A juvenile delinquent is a young person, usually under age eighteen, who is proved to have broken a criminal law.

In some states a minor who is charged with murder, rape, kidnapping, or other serious crime can be tried in adult court. If convicted of one of these offenses in adult court, the minor will be a "criminal" rather than a "juvenile delinquent."

How does a minor's case actually get to the juvenile court judge?

If the juvenile court's intake process doesn't divert the minor out of the system, the prosecuting attorney files a "petition" against the minor. This formal document describes the specific charges against the juvenile and the facts supporting them.

How does a minor discover the contents of the petition?

The minor and his or her parents are entitled to a copy of it. In some states if the petition doesn't clearly spell out the possible consequences of a finding of guilt, a juvenile court conviction on the charges can be "reversed."

If a minor doesn't plead guilty to a delinquency charge, can he or she present witnesses and evidence at the formal hearing?

Yes, usually through his or her lawyer. These are constitutional rights, guaranteed by the due process clause of the Fourteenth Amendment. Minors also have the constitutional right to question or "cross-examine" those who testify against them. The US Supreme Court established that juveniles have these fundamental constitutional rights in *In re Gault* (1967), writing: "Under our Constitution, the condition of being a boy does not justify a kangaroo court."

What happened in the *Gault* case?

Arizona authorities charged fifteen-year-old minor Gerald Gault as a delinquent for allegedly making an obscene phone call to a woman. Gault was technically on juvenile probation for the being in the presence of another minor who had taken a lady's purse. At his "hearing," the juvenile judge declared Gerald delinquent and ordered him to the care of the State Industrial School until he was twenty-one years of age.

The US Supreme Court found that Arizona's juvenile court proceedings did not comport with due process, a concept that the court venerated in its opinion. The court explained: "Due process of law is the primary and indispensable foundation of individual freedom. It is the basic and essential term in the social compact which defines the rights of the individual and delimits the powers which the state may exercise."

The court identified the following constitutional rights which also apply to juveniles:

Notice of Charges

Right to Counsel

Confrontation

Self-Incrimination

Cross-Examination

Appellate Review and Transcript of Proceedings

The court found that the proceedings in Gerald Gault's case were glaringly unconstitutional. For example, Gerald and his parents were not given an attorney or even given proper notice of the charges facing their son. The court found that the procedures taken in Gerald Gault's case resembled more a "kangaroo court" than a court of law.

Why did the court in *Gault* emphasize the right to counsel?

In his majority opinion, Justice Abe Fortas explained that juveniles need the expertise of an attorney to deal with the situations they are facing. He explained: "The juvenile needs the assistance of counsel to cope with problems of law, to make skilled inquiry into the facts, to insist upon regularity of the proceedings, and to ascertain whether he has a defense and to prepare and submit it." The child "requires the guiding hand of counsel at every step in the proceedings against him."

For more about court procedure, including cross-examination, see Chapter 17, "Taking Matters to Court."

Can a juvenile suspect handle his or her formal hearing without a lawyer?

Yes, but as in waiving the right to remain silent, the minor must have a keen understanding of the consequences of waiving the right to a lawyer. For a juvenile court judge to accept such a waiver, the minor must fully comprehend the charges and also the possible punishment. In addition, he or she must understand that a lawyer will be assigned free of charge if his or her parents can't afford one. Finally, the minor must understand the difficulties involved in going ahead without a lawyer, especially the challenges involved in presenting evidence.

Some juvenile courts prohibit a minor from waiving the right to a lawyer unless one has already been involved in the case and has explained to the minor the consequences of the waiver.

Do minors have a right to a jury at a formal hearing?

Not usually. Under the Constitution, the right to a jury trial applies only to adults. But some states, including Alaska, Colorado, Michigan, Texas, Wyoming, and New Mexico, do allow jury trials in juvenile court.

Can a minor choose to remain silent during the formal hearing?

Yes. Minors can't be required to testify against themselves.

Can a minor insist on taking the stand in his or her own defense?

No one can prevent a minor from testifying. But taking the stand can hurt rather than help a minor's case, since it gives the prosecuting attorney a chance to cross-examine. In other words, it gives the state an opportunity to probe the minor about his or her earlier "direct" testimony. The perils of cross-examination are the reason lawyers often advise both criminal defendants and minors charged with delinquent acts not to testify at all.

Can a minor be convicted in juvenile court on a confession alone?

It depends on the state. In most, a minor's out-of-court confession is insufficient to convict unless it is supported by additional "hard" evidence, because a minor is considered more likely than an adult to give a false confession. In some states, a minor's confession is sufficient if supported by the testimony of another person involved in the crime. In others, even an accomplice's testimony isn't enough to convict. Rather, the confession must be supported by the testimony of an independent, innocent witness.

What must the state prove in order to convict a minor of a delinquent act?

It must prove the minor's guilt "beyond a reasonable doubt." This is the state's burden of proof.

Proving guilt beyond a reasonable doubt is the burden of proof required in all criminal cases, including juvenile court cases. This is a higher burden than in a noncriminal or "civil" case—which means that convicting a minor in a juvenile court trial can sometimes be difficult. For more about burden of proof, see Chapter 17, "Taking Matters to Court."

What happens if the minor is found guilty?

He or she is then considered a juvenile delinquent. At that point the judge has a right to sentence the minor.

The term "disposition" is used instead of "sentence" in juvenile court. A judge's disposition may include community service, restitution for property damage, probation, treatment such as counseling or therapy, or participation in a chemical dependency program. Dispositions and disposition hearings are discussed later in this chapter.

Can a minor claim insanity as a defense to a delinquent act?

In some states, yes. In others, the insanity defense has no bearing on whether the minor is guilty of a delinquent act; it is only important in deciding how to handle the minor's case after the court has declared the minor a delinquent.

Proving the insanity defense is complicated and difficult. To establish insanity under the Constitution, it must be shown that the offender was insane when the offense was committed and couldn't have understood the nature of the act because of the insanity. In cases in which the offender actually understood what he or she was doing, it must be shown that insanity prevented the defendant from realizing the act was wrong.

Can a minor appeal a juvenile court conviction?

There is no federal constitutional right to appeal any court decision. However, state constitutions or state laws guarantee this right to both adults and minors.

If a minor has the right to appeal a determination of delinquency, does the minor have the right to a lawyer free of charge for the appeal?

Yes.

MINORS IN ADULT COURT

Can a minor be tried as an adult?

Yes. Every state permits minors above a certain age to be tried in adult court for a handful of serious offenses. In Connecticut, for example, a minor can be transferred to adult court if he or she is charged with murder, rape, or another serious felony *and* has committed a serious felony in the past. To try a minor as an adult in Illinois, the minor must be at least age thirteen, the offense must be very serious, and the juvenile court judge must have determined that it wouldn't be in the best interests of either the minor or the community to try the case in juvenile court.

In most states a minor can be transferred to adult court between the ages of fourteen and sixteen, provided the minor has committed an offense such as murder or attempted murder, aggravated robbery, arson, burglary, and sometimes possession of explosives or killing by auto if under the influence of drugs. (The types of offense vary from state to state.) Some states set the age at sixteen for any crime and age fourteen for a short list of particularly serious crimes. A few permit transfer to adult court for certain offenses regardless of age.

To determine the circumstances under which a minor in a given state can be tried as an adult, check the state's criminal laws at any public library. A reference librarian can provide needed assistance. For more about how to find the law, see Chapter 18, "How to Find the Law."

Who finally decides if a minor should be tried as an adult?

Usually a juvenile court judge does, although in some states an adult court judge decides.

The laws in this area are changing. In response to the growing number of minors committing serious crimes such as murder, some states have revoked the power of the juvenile court to decide the transfer issue. This means that with respect to certain serious offenses, either the case goes directly to adult court or the *prosecutor* decides which court will hear it. When juvenile cases go to adult court, punishment replaces treatment as the driving force behind the case, as the next section explains.

But in fact minors are sometimes better off being tried as adults. Certain protections apply in adult court that don't apply in juvenile court, including stricter rules of evidence. Furthermore, because criminal juries are more sympathetic to young criminals, they are often less likely to convict. They know a conviction means the minor may end up in a hopeless prison situation for many years.

What factors are important in determining whether a minor actually goes to adult court?

In addition to the nature of the offense and the age requirement, important factors are the maturity of the minor, whether he or she has previously committed serious offenses, the amount of evidence supporting the charges, whether any accomplices are adults, and whether the minor is likely to respond to discipline or treatment from the juvenile court.

If the prosecuting attorney wants a transfer to adult court, is the minor entitled to a hearing on the issue?

Yes—due process of law requires it.

If the prosecuting attorney seeks an adult court trial, he or she must establish the factors described. But if state law requires that cases involving particularly serious offenses *originate* in adult court, the burden is on the minor's attorney to prove to the adult court judge that adult court is inappropriate—that juvenile court is the best "forum" for the case. In other words, the burden of proof shifts to the minor's attorney.

If a minor is tried in adult court, will he or she go to an adult prison if sentenced to a prison term?

In most circumstances, yes.

Adult prisons aren't safe places for minors. Research indicates that minors in adult institutions are much more likely to face sexual assault, beatings by correctional officers, or other physical attacks.

Can a minor be sentenced to death in adult court?

No, the US Supreme Court ruled in *Roper v. Simmons* (2005) that minors cannot be subject to the death penalty. The court reasoned that executing a person who committed murder while a juvenile violates the Eighth Amendment, which prohibits the imposition of "cruel and unusual punishment." The court focused on three key differences between minors and adults. First, minors lack maturity and have less sense of responsibility than adults. Second, minors are more vulnerable to peer pressure and have less control over their own environment. Third, minors' characters are not as fully developed as those of adults.

The court in *Roper* overruled its 1989 decision in *Stanford v. Kentucky*, which had upheld the death penalty for older minors who commit murder. Previously, in *Thompson v. Oklahoma* (1988), the court had rejected the death penalty for a fifteen-year-old. When the court invalidated the death penalty for minors in *Roper*, it also focused on the fact that the trend in more states had moved in the direction of no death penalty for juveniles. The court also relied in part on international law; nearly all countries in the world had abolished the death penalty for juvenile offenders.

Can a minor receive a sentence of life in prison without the possibility of parole for a nonhomicide crime?

No, the US Supreme Court ruled in *Graham v. Florida* (2012) that minors who are convicted of crimes short of homicide may not be sentenced to life without the possibility of parole (LWOP). The court reasoned that for a young person, a sentence of life in prison without the possibility of parole was akin to a death sentence. The court focused on the differences between minors and adults that it had articulated in the *Roper* decision. "Life without parole is an especially harsh punishment for a juvenile," the court wrote. "Under this sentence a juvenile offender will on average serve more years and a greater percentage of his life in prison than an adult offender."

Can a state automatically impose life in prison without the possibility of parole on every minor convicted of murder?

No, the US Supreme Court ruled in *Miller v. Alabama* (2012) that state laws from Arkansas and Alabama that automatically imposed the sentence of LWOP on minors convicted of homicide violated the Eighth Amendment prohibition against cruel and unusual punishment. The court ruled that "a judge or jury must have the opportunity to consider mitigating circumstances before imposing the harshest possible penalty for juveniles."

Does the ruling in *Miller* provide relief to juveniles who were sentenced automatically to life sentences before the court decided *Miller*?

Yes, the US Supreme Court ruled in *Montgomery v. Louisiana* (2015) that the *Miller* decision was so important that it should be applied retroactively—to cover those juvenile defendants who received life sentences before the court decided the *Miller* decision.

Henry Montgomery was seventeen years old when he shot and killed a Louisiana deputy sheriff in East Baton Rouge, Louisiana. He was tried for the death penalty and convicted. However, the Louisiana Supreme Court ruled that he did not receive a fair trial and he was retried. In 1970, he was convicted of "guilty without capital punishment." State law at the time required Montgomery to receive a life sentence.

The US Supreme Court determined that its Miller decision had created a new "substantive rule of constitutional law" that must be applied retroactively. Thus, Henry Montgomery would have the ability to argue that his original, automatic life sentence was unconstitutional under *Miller v. Alabama* (2012).

In November 2021, Henry Montgomery walked out of Louisiana prison a free man after serving fifty-seven (57) years.

SENTENCING

How are juvenile delinquents sentenced?

Sentencing occurs by the juvenile court judge at a "disposition hearing."

Juvenile court dispositions have historically focused on rehabilitation and treatment rather than punishment, and this distinguishes them from sentencing in adult court. In every state the juvenile court's stated goal is to act "in the best interests of the child" and to correct the underlying reasons for the delinquency.

When is the disposition hearing?

Usually within two months of the formal hearing. This time lapse occurs because a court worker must gather together the juvenile's school, medical, work, and other records. Based on this information and also the court record, the court worker tailors a "social history report." The judge's decision rests heavily on the findings and recommendations in this key document. Psychological testing or counseling may also occur.

Where does the delinquent stay in the meantime?

Usually at home, although if the minor needs special supervision, the court can order secure detention or place the minor in a foster home.

Is the minor entitled to have a lawyer at the disposition hearing?

In most states, yes. But in fact the prosecuting attorney, the minor's attorney, and a social worker often work out the specific terms of the disposition, and the judge simply reviews it and agrees. This means the disposition hearing may be quite short.

What type of treatment or rehabilitation might a delinquent receive?

Because the judge must order the least restrictive alternative, in-home detention and probation are common for lesser offenses. For more serious cases, the delinquent is placed in a foster home, a supervised group home, or a nonsecure treatment facility. A nonsecure treatment facility is somewhat like a group home: an institutional setting without the regimentation of a secure institution.

Sometimes secure treatment facilities for delinquents are called "training schools," "industrial schools," or "juvenile correction facilities." These days, many aren't unlike prisons. School instruction is given in them, however, and delinquents who are sentenced to them have a right to be personally safe.

When a minor is institutionalized, an important goal is to reunite the minor with his or her family as soon as possible.

Can a minor be required to pay a fine or perform community service for a delinquent act?

Yes, and the juvenile court can also require a minor to repair property he or she has damaged. This is called "restitution." Some of these measures are part of today's more punishment-oriented approach to treating juvenile delinquents and are also part of the growing concern for the rights of crime victims.

However, a minor can't be convicted in juvenile court just because he or she can't pay a fine. In a recent case a minor who stole a baseball cap, a knife, and a wrench was convicted in juvenile court of petty theft. The judge would have dropped the case if the youth had been able to come up with $62.50 to pay restitution. The appeals court set aside the boy's sentence, ruling that a minor can't be convicted simply because he or she is poor, or "indigent."

Does a delinquent ever leave court without receiving any form of treatment or punishment?

Yes, if the judge believes this course of action is appropriate.

PROBATION

What is probation?

This is a type of disposition in which the delinquent stays under court supervision but isn't sent to an institution or foster home. In fact, because the judge is required to order the "least restrictive alternative," a delinquent on probation usually stays at home or with a relative.

Probation always restricts the delinquent's personal freedom. Contacts with a probation officer take place on a regular basis, by phone and in person. There may be a strict curfew. The delinquent may have to maintain good grades in school and must remain a law-abiding citizen. If the offense involved a car, a driver's license may be suspended. In addition, the delinquent may be required to enroll in a local treatment program for drugs, alcohol, or a behavioral problem.

Also, the juvenile court may prohibit the delinquent from possessing weapons; associating with gang members; and wearing gang clothing, tattoos, and symbols. It can also forbid a delinquent to associate with persons not approved by a parent or probation officer.

Can minors challenge these probation conditions?

Yes, minors can challenge the constitutionality of these probation conditions, although most of them are upheld by the appellate courts that hear such challenges. However, sometimes a probation condition is too vague or too broad. For example, a California appeals court struck down an Internet-use condition imposed on a juvenile that prohibited him from any "use of" or "access to" an Internet-enabled computer. The appeals court pointed out in *In re Victor L.* (2010) that such a restriction was too broad because it "could ensnare a minor on a claimed probation violation even if he were engaged in completely innocent and legitimate use of a computer for scholarly or job-related purposes, and even if he were supervised by an adult during such use."

Can parents be involved in the probation process?

Yes, hopefully parents can and will be involved in the probation process. The modern trend is to directly involve the parents in the probation process. For example, a parent may be required to attend and complete patenting classes. If the parent doesn't bother to take the classes, the juvenile court can hold the parent "in contempt." This means the court may order the parent, under threat of a heavy fine or other punishment, to complete the classes by a certain date.

How long does probation last?

It varies, but many states limit it to two years. In certain states probation can't extend into a delinquent's majority (usually age eighteen), but in others it can extend up to age twenty-one.

If a juvenile delinquent violates the terms of his or her probation, is there a right to a hearing before probation is revoked?

Yes. Adults have been granted this right by the Supreme Court, and in most states it has been extended to minors. The reasoning of the courts is that juvenile defendants, like adult defendants, have basic due process rights at such proceedings. Juvenile delinquents don't have a constitutional right to an attorney at a probation revocation hearing, but again, certain states have made this guarantee.

What must the state prove to revoke probation?

It must prove that the delinquent violated at least one condition of the judge's probation order and that no good reason existed for the violation.

What happens if the judge revokes probation?

He or she has the power to send the delinquent to a treatment facility, group home, or foster home, or to simply place the minor back on probation.

TREATMENT IN AN INSTITUTION

Does an institutionalized delinquent always have a right to treatment?

In theory, yes. As a matter of constitutional law, a delinquent in a treatment facility is entitled to counseling, educational and social services, and treatment for special medical problems. The form of treatment might be classes to correct a behavioral or emotional problem, a learning disability, or a physical impairment.

But as a practical matter, sending a delinquent to secure treatment is often intended as a type of "shock therapy" or "juvenile boot camp." Few would deny that these facilities are dismal. Usually they are overcrowded and understaffed, and the employees rarely have much expertise in counseling or vocational training. Treatment and rehabilitation take a second seat to everyday control and discipline.

How long does institutional treatment last?

In most states the judge works with official "length of stay guidelines." This means that the judge's order for treatment will be within a recommended minimum and maximum time period, in light of the particular offense. The delinquent's case is reviewed once he or she has completed the minimum length of stay. If at this point the supervising agency doesn't believe the delinquent is rehabilitated or otherwise ready to leave, more time may be ordered.

Note, however, a modern trend toward institutionalizing delinquents for a minimum number of months for particularly serious offenses, regardless of how much treatment or rehabilitation they need. This is called "specific sentencing" and is another example of today's more punishment-oriented approach to treating delinquents.

In New York, for example, minors age fourteen and fifteen who have committed serious felonies against elderly victims may be held for six months to one year in a secured facility and kept another six months to one year in residential treatment.

Can the juvenile court give a longer sentence than an adult court could give for exactly the same offense?

In most states, yes. A delinquent can be kept in a treatment facility until the agency supervising the treatment believes the delinquent is ready to leave.

If equal or better treatment can be obtained for the delinquent outside a treatment facility, is he or she entitled to it?

In many states, yes, because most states require their juvenile courts to consider the least restrictive alternative to institutional treatment.

In a 1987 Nevada case, an appeals court set aside a thirteen-year-old girl's sentence to one year in a treatment facility after she struck a schoolmate. The young woman had never been in juvenile court before, and her church had even suggested its counseling program to the court for her probation. A higher court set aside the girl's sentence, ruling that probation is always proper unless it is against the best interests of either the minor or the state.

Most states will not provide a lawyer to assist a minor in challenging a sentence to a treatment facility.

Are personnel in treatment facilities prohibited from using corporal punishment?

The Constitution prohibits punishment that is excessive to the point of being cruel and unusual, so corporal punishment would appear to be unconstitutional in a juvenile treatment setting. Beatings, solitary confinement for an extended length of time, and the use of unnecessary psychiatric medications have been declared forms of cruel and unusual punishment.

Is a juvenile delinquent a criminal? Does a juvenile delinquent have a "record"?

The answer to both questions is no. A delinquent isn't a criminal because a conviction in juvenile court isn't a criminal conviction.

Are juvenile court records confidential?

Yes. Most states have laws that specifically ensure the confidentiality of juvenile court records. The purpose of keeping juvenile court records confidential is to promote the rehabilitation of young people. Confidentiality keeps the records out of the hands of school officials, government agencies, future employers, and the general public.

Inactive juvenile court files are either sealed, stamped "confidential," or destroyed. If a file is sealed, a judge's written order is required to open it. States that don't destroy juvenile court records usually permit limited inspection of them by the minor, probation officers, any agency caring for the minor, and persons doing scholarly research.

Some states have laws requiring a delinquent's court file to be destroyed or permanently sealed after the delinquent reaches age twenty-three or after a specified number of years from the date of the conviction. On the other hand, police records relating to a delinquent's actions (such as arrests) are never confidential.

In states in which juvenile court records are confidential, can a delinquent deny that he or she has a record?

Yes. The delinquent can legally deny that delinquency proceedings ever took place.

If a minor is a witness in an adult criminal trial, can he or she be required to answer questions about past juvenile court convictions?

Yes. Minors can be cross-examined about past delinquent acts as a way to test their credibility as witnesses, particularly if their delinquent acts were both serious and recent.

Can juvenile court records be used against a former delinquent who is on trial in an adult criminal case?

In most states an adult can't be cross-examined about previous delinquent acts. The reason is that delinquent acts aren't considered crimes and should therefore be off-limits. However, many states permit judges to review juvenile records to help in determining what sentence to give a convicted adult.

Can a judge legally exclude the press or public from a juvenile court hearing?

State courts are inconsistent on this issue. However, for the sake of privacy and fairness, most states exclude the press in at least some circumstances. In 1995, a federal appeals court in Massachusetts agreed that a formal hearing relating to juveniles charged with hate crimes was properly closed to the press. Similar orders have been issued in other jurisdictions.

Whether the media are allowed in the courtroom, if at all, depends on a number of factors. These include the nature of the offense, the surrounding circumstances, the juvenile's age, whether his or her name will be used in the newspaper (especially if the juvenile is quite young), and whether the press has already covered the case to excess.

Can the press be prosecuted for publishing the name of a young person charged with a delinquent act?

It is very unlikely. The US Supreme Court has held that the First Amendment provides a great deal of authority to media entities that publish truthful information that was lawfully obtained. States violate the First Amendment if they pass laws prohibiting the media from publishing information about trials, whether or not a minor is being tried.

If such laws could legally be enforced, newspapers could be prosecuted for publishing truthful information.

In *Smith v. Daily Mail Publishing Co.* (1979), two West Virginia newspapers reported the identity of a high school student who was charged with murdering a classmate. The newspapers were prosecuted under a state law prohibiting the print media from publishing the name of any delinquent without prior authorization from the juvenile court. The Supreme Court overturned the conviction, ruling that laws prohibiting the media from printing truthful information about delinquents that the media lawfully obtained violate the First Amendment. The court established the so-called *Daily Mail* principle: "State action to punish the publication of truthful information seldom can satisfy constitutional standards."

Is there any middle ground for the state when an older juvenile or young adult commits a crime?

Yes, some states have so-called youthful offender adjudications who in a few states can apply to those who are facing criminal charges when they are 16–21 years of age. These youthful offender laws are a hybrid between juvenile and adult criminal legal systems. If faced with a crime, your attorney should check to see if the corresponding state has a youthful offender law.

FOR FURTHER READING

In General

Bergmanm, Paul and Sara J. Berman-Bennett. *The Criminal Law Handbook*. Berkeley, CA: Nolo Press, 1997.
Bernard, Thomas J. and Megan C. Kurlychek. *The Cycle of Juvenile Justice*. New York: Oxford University Press, 2010.
Boland, Mary L. *Crime Victim's Guide to Justice*. Naperville, IL: Sourcebooks, 1997.
Drinan, Cara H. *The War on Kids: How American Juvenile Justice Lost Its Way*. Oxford: Oxford University Press, 2017.
Feld, Barry C. *The Evolution of the Juvenile Court: Race, Politics, and the Criminalizing of Juvenile Justice*. New York: New York University Press, 2019.
Gardner, Martin T. *Understanding Juvenile Law*. 3rd ed. San Francisco: Matthew Bender Publishing, 2009.
Heilbroner, David. *Rough Justice: Days and Nights of a Young D.A.* New York: Random House, 1990.
Lewis, Anthony. *Gideon's Trumpet*. New York: Vintage Books, 1989.
Sheidlin, Judy. *Don't Pee on My Leg and Tell Me It's Raining: America's Toughest Family Court Judge Speaks Out*. New York: HarperCollins, 1997.

Suspects' Rights/The Miranda Warnings

Feld, Barry C. *Justice for Children: The Right to Counsel and the Juvenile Courts*. Boston: Northeastern University Press, 1993.
Wice, Paul B. *Miranda v. Arizona: Suspects' Rights: You Have the Right to Remain Silent*. New York: Franklin Watts, 1996.

Searches and Seizures

Rossow, Lawrence F. and Jacqueline A. Stefkovich. *Search and Seizure in the Public Schools*. 2nd ed. Dayton, OH: Education Law Association, 1996,

Vile, John R. and David L. Hudson Jr., eds. *The Encyclopedia of the Fourth Amendment*. Thousand Oaks, CA: SAGE Publications, 2012.

Wetterer, Charles M. *The Fourth Amendment: Search and Seizure*. Springfield, NJ: Enslow Publishers, 1998.

Probation

Hammer, Hy. *Probation Officer, Parole Officer*. 5th ed. Foster City, CA: IDG Books Worldwide, 1996.

Jacobs, Mark D. *Screwing the System and Making It Work: Juvenile Justice in the No-Fault Society*. Chicago, IL: University of Chicago Press, 1990.

Sentencing/Death Penalty

Breyer, Stephen and John Bessler. *Against the Death Penalty*. Washington, DC: Brookings Institution Press, 2016.

Hudson, David L. Jr. *Capital Punishment: A Documentary and Reference Guide*. New York: Bloomsbury Publishing, 2023.

Mello, Michael. *Against the Death Penalty: The Relentless Dissents of Justices Brennan and Marshall*. Boston: Northeastern University Press, 1996.

Mello, Michael A. and David Von Drehle. *Dead Wrong: A Death Row Lawyer Speaks Out against Capital Punishment*. Madison: University of Wisconsin Press, 1999.

OTHER INFORMATION SOURCES

Organizations

American Bar Association, 321 N. Clark Street, Chicago, IL 60654. Online contact page: http://www.americanbar.org/about_the_aba/contact.html. Home page: www.americanbar.org.

American Civil Liberties Union, 125 Broad Street, New York, NY 10004. (212) 549-2500. E-mail: aclu@aclu.org. Home page: www.aclu.org.

Center on Juvenile and Criminal Justice, 1622 Folsom Street, San Francisco, CA 94103. (415) 621-5661. E-mail: info@cjcj.org. Home page: www.cjcj.org.

National Center for Youth Law, 114 Sansome Street, Ste. 900, San Francisco, CA 94104. (415) 543-3307. E-mail: info@youthlaw.org. Home page: www.youthlaw.org.

National Council of Juvenile and Family Court Judges, P.O. Box 8970, Reno, NV 89507. (775) 784-6012. E-mail: staff@ncjfcj.org. Home page: http://www.ncjfcj.org/.

Teens, Crime, and the Community, 1600 K Street NW, Ste. 602, Washington, DC 20006. (202) 293-0088. Home page: www.nationaltcc.org.

The Urban Institute, 2100 M Street NW, Washington, DC 20037. (202) 833-7200. E-mail: webmaster@ui.urban.org. Home page: www.urban.org.

Online Sources

Information on juvenile drug courts: http://www.ncjfcj.org/our-work/juvenile-drug-courts

Office of Juvenile Justice and Delinquency Prevention: http://www.ojjdp.gov/

US Department of Justice's publication on juvenile drug courts: https://www.ncjrs.gov/pdffiles1/bja/197866.pdf

CHAPTER 13

Equal Protection and Employment Discrimination

RACE DISCRIMINATION

No state shall make or enforce any law which shall . . . deny to any person within its jurisdiction the equal protection of the laws.

—The equal protection clause of the Fourteenth Amendment, US Constitution

What is the equal protection clause?

The equal protection clause is part of section one of the Fourteenth Amendment that provides that the government generally must treat similarly situated people the same. In other words, the Equal Protection Clause is the part of the Constitution designed to breathe a measure of equality into the US Constitution.

The Equal Protection Clause provides that no state shall "deny to any person within its jurisdiction the equal protection of the laws." This means that the government generally must treat similarly situated people the same and not discriminate on prohibited bases, such as race. The equal protection clause only limits government employers, not private employers. However, there are a host of laws, or statutes, that also prohibit race discrimination by public and private employers.

What are some examples of illegal race discrimination that have occurred in the past?

Following are some decisions in which the US Supreme Court has struck down race discrimination:

1. In *Strauder v. West Virginia* (1879), it struck down a state law excluding African Americans from serving on juries.
2. In *Yick Wo v. Hopkins* (1886), it found illegal discrimination when each of two hundred Chinese applicants was denied a permit to operate a laundry in San Francisco, even though almost every non-Chinese applicant was granted one.
3. In *Buchanan v. Warley* (1917), it struck down a St. Louis city law prohibiting blacks from living on any city block if at least 50 percent of the residents on the block were white.
4. In *Missouri ex rel. Gaines v. Canada* (1938), it struck down a scheme in which Missouri provided a state-funded law school for whites but paid for blacks to go to law school out-of-state.
5. In *Brown v. Board of Education* (1954), it unanimously rejected the "separate but equal doctrine" in public education. In this decision it ruled that placing black children in separate schools or classes within a school system deprived all children—blacks as well as whites—of an equal education.

All the above cases were about violations of the equal protection clause. In each a racial minority was illegally denied the "equal protection of the laws."

Brown v. Board of Education is a landmark case, in which the court rejected the idea that separate facilities based on race were constitutional as long as they were roughly equal. The court determined that this "separate but equal" doctrine had no place in education. The decision is important in part because shortly after it was handed down, the modern civil rights movement began to reshape America's thinking on countless issues relating to race and other personal rights. The nation was ready. Many believe that the feminist and gay and lesbian rights movements, and even the environmental movement, were modeled after the civil rights movement of the 1950s and 1960s, inspired by the *Brown* decision.

Why did it take so long for many Southern cities and counties to desegregate their schools?

The Supreme Court ruled in *Brown* that segregated schools violated the Equal Protection Clause. However, the court did not determine how that should be done. The court heard *Brown v. Board of Education II* in 1955 and ordered that officials desegregate schools "with all deliberate speed."

Unfortunately, many in the South focused more on the adjective "deliberate" rather than the noun "speed." In other words, there was massive resistance to the *Brown* decision in parts of the South. However, justice eventually prevailed and the schools were forced to integrate.

How did the Supreme Court's rejection of "separate but equal" in *Brown v. Board of Education* affect other racial segregation laws?

After *Brown*, the Supreme Court struck down state laws authorizing the separation of races in public parks, restaurants, and bathrooms; at golf courses, beaches, and airports; and in public transportation. The decision also ushered in a period during the 1960s when the federal government passed a series of laws designed to prohibit racial and other forms of discrimination, including the federal Equal Pay Act of 1963, the Voting Rights Act of 1965, the Civil Rights Act of 1967, the ADEA of 1967, and the Fair Housing Act (FHA) of 1968. The *Brown* decision reached every comer of American life. Now, no law or public policy can treat people differently simply because of race or nationality. A white person can't be prohibited from marrying a black person, and the armed services are fully integrated. America's second black justice now sits on the Supreme Court. In 2008, Barack Obama was elected, the first black president of the United States.

Is it ever legal to have discriminatory laws?

Yes. State and city governments pass them all the time.

Government has the power to treat different categories of people differently. That's what many laws do, so it is true to say that laws can legally discriminate.

For example, a city can legally require all its homeowners to pay a property tax to finance its public schools even though certain homeowners don't have children. Such a law would discriminate against childless homeowners. It would be legal, however, because laws that discriminate for reasons other than race, gender, nationality, religion, age, or disability only have to be reasonable. A law to raise money for schools would clearly be that.

But a law that discriminates on the basis of race, gender, nationality, religion, or disability must be much more than reasonable. The purpose of such a law must be extremely important, and the law must *precisely* fit the government's purpose. Laws that discriminate on the basis of nationality or race never pass this test.[1]

Can private persons or private businesses discriminate on the basis of race?

If an individual or business is engaged in a government-related function, even remotely, any type of race-based discrimination is prohibited. Furthermore, states, counties, cities, and Congress have passed laws prohibiting discrimination by private individuals and private businesses in situations that the Constitution may not cover. Clear examples are state and local laws requiring restaurants to seat blacks and other minorities and laws prohibiting private clubs from excluding minorities under their membership policies.

How does student busing relate to race discrimination?

Busing is state-sponsored "desegregation." Busing white children to predominantly black schools and black students to predominantly white schools is a state-sponsored way of correcting racial imbalances and racial injustice.

Busing has almost always been court-ordered, and the practice has always been controversial. These days it is under heavy attack in legislatures, in the courts, and in academia. Busing is criticized as both ineffective and disruptive of the learning process. In many areas, it has been curtailed or ended.

Is "reverse discrimination" against white people illegal?

It can be, because it is another form of race discrimination. The US Supreme Court explained in *Regents of the University of California v. Bakke* (1978) that a white applicant to medical school suffered an equal protection violation when he was denied admission. Here the Supreme Court ruled that public schools could not set aside a specific quota or number of seats for racial minorities because of general societal discrimination and discrimination in the past.

The *Bakke* case involved a medical school admissions program that set aside sixteen of hundred seats for racial and ethnic minorities. One applicant, Alan Bakke, was denied a seat in the freshman class even though he had a better academic record than the average student admitted under the minority program. He was white.

The Supreme Court ruled that the admissions program illegally discriminated against whites and in favor of minorities. The school's interest in having a diverse student body with a variety of races and backgrounds—a compelling interest that the court praised—didn't justify the existence of the set-aside program. *Bakke* was admitted because the school's set-aside program amounted to a form of discrimination.

What can governments legally do to remedy discrimination that has occurred in the past?

They can, for example, establish "affirmative action programs," which endeavor to admit or hire a certain percentage of minorities. Under these programs, minorities who are admitted or hired must be at least as qualified as nonminorities who are turned down. However, the use of exact numerical quotas has vanished since the *Bakke* decision.

For more about affirmative action and reverse discrimination, see Chapter 4, "On the Job."

Are affirmative action programs treated with more leniency than other forms of race discrimination?

No, the US Supreme Court has made clear that all forms of racial discrimination—whether hostile or benign discrimination—are evaluated under a legal test known as "strict scrutiny." Under this high form of judicial review, race-based classifications are rarely, if ever, justified. The government must show a compelling, or very strong, interest in a very narrowly drafted way.

Is race discrimination in employment illegal?

Yes. Race discrimination in employment is prohibited by federal and state laws. The primary federal antidiscrimination law is Title VII of the Civil Rights Act of 1964. It applies to employers with fifteen or more employees. Title VII prohibits discrimination in employment on the basis of race, color, religion, sex, or national origin. Many state laws also prohibit similar types of race discrimination in employment. Many of these laws apply to smaller employers. For example, the Tennessee Human Rights Act applies to employers who have eight or more employees. Unlike the ADEA, there is no age requirement in Title VII. This means that employers should not discriminate against any employees on the basis of race.

Does Title VII apply to protect all races?

Yes. Even though Title VII was enacted during the civil rights movement in the 1960s in the wake of rampant discrimination against African Americans, the law protects members of all races. The US Supreme Court clarified that Title VII protects individuals of all races in *McDonald v. Santa Fe Trail Transportation Co.* (1976).

Is it employment discrimination if a worker hears racial slurs?

It depends on the frequency of the comments and who utters them. Title VII does protect workers from racially hostile workplace environments. However, to constitute a racially hostile workplace, the harassment must be severe and pervasive. It must be bad enough for the harassment to affect the employee on the job and become an abusive environment. In some cases, a court might determine that there was more a "stray comment" than severe and pervasive harassment. It also matters who is uttering the slur. It is worse for an employer if a supervisor utters racial slurs to an employee than if a co-employee does it. If a co-employee does it, an employer often can try to protect itself by taking immediate, corrective action against the offending co-employee.

However, the utterance of racial slurs is always probative evidence in an employment discrimination suit. If there is enough of that type of boorish and racial conduct, an employer may be liable for a racially hostile workplace.

SEX DISCRIMINATION

Are the constitutional standards the same for race discrimination and sex discrimination?

No. Under equal protection law, race-based classifications are subjected to the highest form of judicial review, known as strict scrutiny. Gender-based classifications are subjected to a lower form of judicial review, known as intermediate scrutiny. Some scholars have argued that gender discrimination ought to be treated the same as race discrimination. But at least so far, race-based classifications are viewed with even more suspicion and scrutiny than gender-based classifications.

Is sex discrimination legal?

It used to be legal, across the board. In *Goesaert v. Cleary* (1948), the US Supreme Court upheld a Michigan state law prohibiting any woman from obtaining a bartender's license unless she was the wife or daughter of a man who already had one. This is just one example of past state-sponsored gender discrimination; literally hundreds of instances occurred nationwide.

Laws authorizing or permitting sex discrimination began to fall in the 1970s based on equal protection challenges. In *Stanton v. Stanton* (1975), the US Supreme Court ruled unconstitutional a Utah law placing the age of majority at twenty-one for males but age eighteen for females. Utah reasoned that parents should have to support their sons through their college years because a man's education is so important—but because women marry younger, parents should only have to support their daughters to age eighteen. Similar laws have been struck down.

The Supreme Court has ruled against gender discrimination in other types of cases. Here is a sampling:

1. In *Craig v. Boren* (1976), it ruled that Oklahoma couldn't set the legal age for males to buy 3.2 percent beer at age twenty-one but set it at age eighteen for females (3.2 percent beer has less alcohol content than regular beer).
2. In *Caban v. Mohammed* (1979), it struck down a New York law requiring the consent of a child's natural or "birth" mother, but not the birth father, to place a child born outside marriage for adoption.
3. In *Kirchberg v. Feenstra* (1981), it struck down a state law enabling a husband to dispose of property jointly owned with his wife without the wife's consent.

What are some examples of lawful sex or gender discrimination?

For years it was determined that women could legally be kept out of combat. However, in 2013, the Pentagon changed that policy and determined that by 2016 women had to be allowed into combat. In 2014, the Marines announced an experimental project of having women in combat.

One example of permissible gender discrimination concerns topless nudity. Men normally can walk around without a shirt, but women can be cited for exposing their breasts in public. Public nudity laws generally have been upheld in constitutional challenges.

Can public high schools legally put men and women on separate high school sports teams?

Sometimes, although it usually depends on whether the sport is a contact sport. For more about gender rules in high school athletic programs, see Chapter 2, "At School."

Can a business fire a woman because she becomes pregnant?

No. Congress passed an amendment to Title VII known as the PDA, which prohibits discrimination against women simply because they are pregnant. Furthermore, under a 1993 federal law known as the FMLA, full-time women employees can now take unpaid pregnancy leave from certain jobs without fear of job loss or demotion. For more about gender issues at work, see Chapter 4, "On the Job."

AGE DISCRIMINATION

Is age discrimination against minors legal?

In many situations, yes. Society lawfully discriminates against minors on the basis of age every day and in dozens of situations. Young people can't legally drive, vote, go to school, drink, buy tobacco, marry, or hold certain jobs until they reach a certain age. In criminal matters, they don't have the range of constitutional due process rights in juvenile court that exists for adults in adult court.

Discrimination on the basis of minority or "nonage" is in many ways the opposite side of teen rights.

The federal ADEA prohibits age discrimination in employment, but only with respect to persons forty years of age and older. But when federal and state age discrimination laws do apply, they prohibit employers from discriminating because of age with respect to pay, conditions of employment, promotions, and fringe benefits. Age discrimination is often called "ageism." Most state laws are modeled after the ADEA and only prohibit discrimination against those who are forty years of age or older. However, New Jersey's age discrimination law also prohibits discriminating against younger workers. However, even New Jersey's expansive concept of age discrimination does not prohibit an employer from refusing to hire someone who is under eighteen years of age.

For more about laws relating to age discrimination in the workplace, see Chapter 4, "On the Job."

NOTE

1 In fact, on one occasion the Supreme Court *did* uphold a law that discriminated on the basis of a racial class. In *Korematsu v. United States* (1944), it let stand a federal law authorizing the creation of relocation or "internment" camps to hold Japanese Americans during the Second World War. This decision still disturbs the national conscience.

FOR FURTHER READING

In General

Alexander, Michelle. *The New Jim Crow: Mass Incarceration in the Age of Colorblindness.* 10th anniversary ed. New York: The New Press, 2020.

Cordova, Teresa, ed. *Chicana Voices: Intersections of Class, Race, and Gender.* Austin: University of Texas Press, 1993.

Duvall, Lynn. *Respecting Our Differences: A Guide to Getting Along in a Changing World.* Minneapolis, MN: Free Spirit Press, 1994.

Hudson, David L. Jr. *Equal Protection: Documents Decoded.* Santa Barbara, CA: Holtzbrinck, 2018.

Kendi, Ibram X. *Stamped from the Beginning: The Definitive History of Racist Ideas in America.* New York: Bold Type Books, 2023.

McGee, Heather. *The Sum of Us: What Racism Costs Everyone and How We Can Prosper Together.* London: One World, 2022.

Rothstein, Richard. *The Color of Law: A Forgotten History of How Our Government Segregated America*. New York: Norton, 2018.
Williams, Juan. *Eyes on the Prize: America's Civil Rights Years, 1954–1965*. New York: Penguin Putnam, 1987.
Wolfson Nicholas. *Hate Speech, Sex Speech, Free Speech*. Westport, CT: Praeger Publishers, 1997.

Race-Based Discrimination

Angelou, Maya. *I Know Why the Caged Bird Sings*. New York: Random House, 1970.
Anson, Robert Sam. *Best Intentions: The Education and Death of Edmund Perry*. New York: Random House, 1987.
Brown, Claude. *Manchild in the Promised Land*. New York: Macmillan, 1990.
Cleaver, Eldridge. *Soul on Ice*. New York: McGraw-Hill, 1968.
McDonald, Laughlin, et al. *The Rights of Racial Minorities (ACLU)*. New York: Puffin Books, 1998.
Parks, Rosa and Jim Hoskins. *Rosa Parks: My Story*. New York: Dial Press, 1993.
Schwartz, Bernard. *Swann's Way: The School Busing Case and the Supreme Court*. New York: Oxford University Press, 1986.
Steele, Shelby. *The Content of Our Character: A New Vision of Race in America*. New York: Harper Perennial Library, 1991.
Steele, Shelby. *A Dream Deferred: The Second Betrayal of Black Freedom in America*. New York: HarperCollins, 1998.
Wormser, Richard. *The Rise and Fall of Jim Crow: The African-American Struggle Against Discrimination, 1865–1954*. New York: Franklin Watts, 1999.

Affirmative Action

Ball, Howard. *The Bakke Case: Race, Education & Affirmative Action*. Lawrence: University of Kansas Press, 2000.
Caplan, Lincoln. *Up Against the Law: Affirmative Action and the Supreme Court*. New York: Twentieth Century Fund, 1997.
Curry, George E. *The Affirmative Action Debate*. New York: Addison-Wesley Publishing Company, 1996.
Jencks, Christopher. *The Black-White Test Score Gap*. Washington, DC: Brookings Institute, 1998.
Urofsky, Melvin I. *Affirmative Action on Trial: Sex Discrimination in Johnson v. Santa Clara*. Lawrence: University of Kansas Press, 1997.

Sex-Based Discrimination

Cassell, Justine and Henry Jenkins, eds. *From Barbie to Mortal Kombat*. Cambridge, MA: MIT Press, 1998.
Cochran, Augustus B. *Sexual Harassment and the Law: The Mechelle Vinson Case*. Lawrence: University of Kansas Press, 2004.
Gay, Kathlyn. *Rights and Respect: What You Need to Know about Gender Bias and Sexual Harassment*. Brookfield, CT: Millbrook Press, 1995.
Hauser, Barbara. *The Women's Legal Guide: A Comprehensive Guide to Legal Issues Affecting Every Woman*. Golden, CO: Fulcrum Publishing, 1996.
Hopkins, Ann Branigar. *So Ordered: Making Partner the Hard Way*. Amherst: University of Massachusetts Press, 1996.
Landau, Elaine. *Sexual Harassment and Teens: A Program for Positive Change*. Minneapolis, MN: Free Spirit Publishing, 1992.
Sack, Steven Michael. *The Working Woman's Legal Survival Guide*. New York: Prentice Hall, 1998.

Other Minorities

Dietrich, Lisa C. *Chicana Adolescents: Bitches, 'Ho's, and Schoolgirls*. Westport, CT: Praeger Publishers, 1998.
Haines, David W. and Karen E. Rosenblum, eds. *Illegal Immigration in America: A Reference Handbook*. Westport, CT: Greenwood Press, 1997.
Houston, Jeanne Wakatsuki. *Farewell to Manzanar: A True Story of Japanese American Experience during and after the World War II Internment*. New York: Bantam Books, 1983.
Mirande, Alfredo. *Gringo Justice*. South Bend, IN: University of Notre Dame Press, 1990.
Pevar, Stephen L. *The Rights of American Indians and Their Tribes (ACLU)*. New York: Puffin Books, 1997.
Rodriguez, Roberto. *Justice: A Question of Race*. Tempe, AZ: Bilingual Press, 1997.
Utter, Jack. *American Indians: Answers to Today's Questions*. Lake Ann, MI: National Woodlands Publishing Co., 1993.

OTHER INFORMATION SOURCES

Organizations

American Civil Liberties Union, 125 Broad Street, New York, NY 10004. (212) 549-2500. E-mail: aclu@aclu.org. Home page: www.aclu.org.
National Association for the Advancement of Colored People (NAACP), 1025 Vermont Avenue NW, Ste. 1120, Washington, DC 20005. (202) 638-2269. Home page: www.naacp.org.
National Council of La Raza, 1119 Nineteenth Street NW, Ste. 1000, Washington, DC 20038. Home page: www.nclr.org.
National Organization for Women (NOW), 733 Fifteenth Street NW, 2nd Floor, Washington, DC 20005. (202) 628-8NOW. E-mail: now@now.org. Home page: www.now.org.
Native American Rights Fund, 1506 Broadway, Denver, CO 80303. (303) 447-8760. E-mail: pereira@narf.org. Home page: www.narf.org.

Online Source

US Department of Justice—Civil Rights Division: www.usdoj.gov

CHAPTER 14

Gay and Lesbian Teens

IS IT LEGAL?

Are same-sex sodomy laws valid?

No. In a landmark decision the US Supreme Court ruled in *Lawrence v. Texas* (2003) that the due process clause of the Fourteenth Amendment protected the private sexual acts of consenting adults in the privacy of their own home. The court invalidated a Texas law that criminalized acts of sodomy between persons of the same sex.

The court overruled its decision in *Bowers v. Hardwick* (1986), in which the court had upheld a Georgia sodomy law from a constitutional challenge by a gay man. In *Lawrence*, Justice Anthony Kennedy wrote that *Bowers* "demeans the lives of homosexual persons." Kennedy explained: "The State cannot demean their existence or control their destiny by making their private sexual conduct a crime. Their right to liberty under the Due Process Clause gives them the full right to engage in their conduct without intervention of the government."

Justice Kennedy did note that "[t]he present case does not involve minors" as opposed to consenting adults.

If homosexual conduct between consenting adults isn't illegal under the laws of a certain state, would the same conduct be legal between consenting teens?

It depends on individual state laws. *Lawrence v. Texas* stands for the principle that gays and lesbians should be treated the same as heterosexuals in the area of private, consensual sex. However, there is a passage in *Lawrence* in which the court wrote that the case does not involve minors. For example, the North Carolina Supreme Court ruled that a fourteen-year-old male juvenile could be charged under a state "crimes against nature" law for committing sex acts with his twelve-year-old girlfriend. While this case involved two heterosexual minors, two gay minors presumably could be punished as well. Furthermore, gay and heterosexual minors can be punished for committing lewd and lascivious acts with much younger minors. If a juvenile is convicted of such an offense, that juvenile will have to register as a sex offender.

Can a person who has homosexual relations be convicted of statutory rape?

Generally, in most states, the offense of statutory rape applies when the "victim" is not an adult and the older person is either an adult or a minor who is several years older than the "victim."

In some states, heterosexual minors can obtain the benefit of a "Romeo and Juliet" statute, which allows a heterosexual minor to avoid prosecution or receive a reduced penalty if he has sexual relations with a younger minor. In some states, LGTB youth do not receive the benefit of such a defense. The result has been that in some areas of the country LGBT youth have been disproportionately punished for sexual conduct in comparison to heterosexual youth.

As discussed in Chapter 8, statutory rape occurs when an adult has sex with a minor. It doesn't matter that both parties may have privately agreed to engage in sex. In most states only the older sex partner can be charged, because the younger party is the victim.

FAMILY MATTERS

Can parents forbid a minor child to engage in homosexual acts?

Yes, consistent with their right to raise and discipline their children. However, a rule forbidding a minor child to engage in sex, whether the child is gay, lesbian, or straight, isn't always the easiest rule for parents to enforce.

For more about teen and parental rights at home, see Chapter 3, "At Home."

Can parents throw a minor out of the house because he or she is gay or lesbian?

No. Parents are responsible for the care and nurturing of their minor children, regardless of a child's sexual orientation or sexual activities. According to a 2010 report by the Center for American Progress (http://cdn.americanprogress.org/wp-content/uploads/issues/2010/06/pdf/lgbtyouthhomelessness.pdf), there are anywhere from 1.6 to 2.8 million young people from ages twelve to twenty-four who are homeless. The report estimates that at least 20 percent of those individuals are gay, lesbian, or transgendered youth.

Can parents emancipate a minor just because he or she is gay, lesbian, or bisexual?

No, that wouldn't be a sufficient reason. To be emancipated, the minor must be financially independent and able to live safely and in good health on his or her own. For more about emancipation, see Chapter 5, "On Your Own."

Can two persons of the same sex legally marry?

Yes, the US Supreme Court ruled that state laws banning same-sex marriage violated both the Equal Protection and Due Process Clauses of the First Amendment in *Obergefell v. Hodges* (2015). Justice Anthony Kennedy, in his majority opinion, wrote that "the nature of injustice is that we may not always see it in our own times." He added that "[e]xcluding same-sex couples from marriage thus conflicts with a central premise of the right to marry."

Can a parent who is lesbian or gay obtain custody of a minor child in a divorce?

Yes, lesbian and gay parents can obtain custody of a child in a divorce. As discussed in Chapter 7, the basis for awarding custody is the best interests of the child. Some state laws specifically prohibit considering sexual orientation as a factor in child custody disputes.

After divorcing, can a gay or lesbian parent be denied the right to visit his or her child?

Not because of being gay or lesbian. In order for a court to deny visitation to a gay or lesbian parent, the straight parent would have to persuade the court that such visits would for some proven reason be against the child's best interests. Visitation might be denied, for example, if the homosexual parent and his or her same-sex partner had a habit of using drugs or engaging in some other conduct that would cause substantial harm to the child.

AT SCHOOL

Can school administrators prevent a gay and lesbian club or support group from meeting on public school property?

No. A federal law known as the Equal Access Act of 1984 prohibits public high school administrators from discriminating against gay and lesbian student clubs. These clubs may only prohibit lesbian and gay rights clubs from meeting at school if clear evidence shows that the meetings would cause a substantial disruption of school activities. US Secretary of Education Arne Duncan stated in 2011: "Schools must treat all student-initiated clubs equally, including those of LGBT students."

Massachusetts was the first state to officially ban discrimination against gays and lesbians in public schools. Other states have followed suit. The first gay student group for high schoolers was recognized in 1973; the first gay high school was founded in Boston in 1982. For more about the constitutional right of free assembly, see Chapter 2, "At School."

If school officials can't prevent gay and lesbian teens from organizing at school, what types of school facilities can the club use?

The same facilities that other clubs use, such as meeting rooms, school supplies, access to bulletin boards, and other school benefits and services.

Can schools make gay and lesbian teens stay away from each other at a public school?

No. That would be a clear violation of the constitutional right of free assembly.

In *Fricke v. Lynch* (1980), a federal district court in Rhode Island ruled that a public high school couldn't prohibit a male student from taking another male to the senior prom. However, the court based its decision on the First Amendment right of free speech and not the right of free assembly; it ruled that taking a gay man to the prom was a form of symbolic speech. In *McMillen v. Itawamba County School District* (2010), a federal district court in Mississippi reached a similar result, ruling that school officials violated Constance McMillen's right to take another female student to the prom. The school had canceled the prom after McMillen's request to take another female student to the event.

For more about symbolic speech under the First Amendment, see Chapter 2, "At School."

Can schools forbid gay and lesbian teens to display intimate feelings of affection at school?

Yes. It is clearly within the authority of schools to prohibit all students from kissing, embracing, and caressing on school grounds.

What can be done if gay and lesbian teens are harassed by other students at school?

The incident should be reported to school authorities. This type of conduct would violate a school's antibullying policy. If the problem persists, or if this solution is unwise or even foolish, the best thing to do is discuss the matter with a lawyer associated with a gay or lesbian rights club or a community legal services organization. Legal services attorneys charge little or nothing and are legally required to keep such matters in confidence. The same approach should be followed if a gay or lesbian teen is harassed by a teacher.

Educators, parents, and others should take note that much of this increased harassment takes place online. A 2013 study by the Gay Lesbian Straight Education Network (GLSEN) found that gay and lesbian teens experience online bullying and harassment at a rate much higher than do heterosexual students.

IN PUBLIC

Can a person be discriminated against at work because he or she is gay or lesbian?

Many federal laws protect racial and ethnic minorities, women, people with disabilities, and the elderly from employment discrimination, but not gays and lesbians. However, the federal government is prohibited from firing or demoting a government employee simply because of sexual orientation. A gay or lesbian worker can only be dismissed from federal government work due to sexual orientation if his or her sex-related conduct is inappropriate in light of the job.

The laws of California, Massachusetts, Minnesota, New Jersey, and other states forbid discrimination at work on the basis of sexual orientation. In addition, many communities have laws forbidding such discrimination in restaurants and sports clubs, and with respect to membership in business and professional organizations.

Moreover, many businesses have nondiscrimination policies for gay and lesbian workers. More than half of the Fortune 1000 companies now have such policies.

Can a landlord legally refuse to rent to a gay or lesbian person or to a gay or lesbian couple?

It depends on whether there is a state or local law that forbids discrimination in housing on these grounds. The federal FHA prohibits discrimination in housing on the basis of race, color, national origin, religion, sex, disability, and familial status. However, it does not prohibit discrimination on the basis of sexual orientation. Thus, protection for gays and lesbians must come from a state or local law. If a nondiscrimination law applies, a landlord may not ask a prospective tenant anything about his or her intimate life. In the absence of a nondiscrimination law, however, a landlord may legally seek out such information and may refuse to rent to anyone—for almost any reason.

The laws of California, Connecticut, Minnesota, and many other states prohibit this type of discrimination, as do the laws of the District of Columbia and many other cities.

Can gays and lesbians join the US armed forces?

Yes, gays and lesbians can join the US armed forces. In 2010, the US Congress passed the "Don't Ask, Don't Tell" Repeal Act, which ended the military's previous policy of "don't ask, don't tell." President Barack Obama signed the measure into law, saying: "For we are not a nation that says, 'don't ask, don't tell.' We are a nation that says, 'Out of many, we are one.'" This law repealed the military's previous policy, adopted in 1993, under which recruits could not be asked about sexual orientation or be questioned about past sexual conduct. However, if a member of the military engaged in gay sex acts or even indicated he or she was homosexual, that person could be dismissed from the service.

FOR FURTHER READING

Bausum, Ann. *Stonewall; Breaking Out in the Fight for Gay Rights*. New York: Speak, 2016.
Cenziper, Debbie and Jim Obergefell. *Love Wins: The Lovers and Lawyers Who Fought the Landmark Case for Marriage Equality*. New York: William Morrow, 2017.
Curry, Hayden, et al. *A Legal Guide for Lesbian and Gay Couples*. 12th ed. Berkeley, CA: Nolo Press, 2004.
Faderman, Lillian. *The Gay Revolution: Story of the Struggle*. New York: Simon & Schuster, 2016.
Flook, Maria. *My Sister Life: The Story of My Sister's Disappearance*. New York: Random House, 1999.
Garretson, Jeremiah. *The Path to Gay Rights: How Activism and Coming Out Changed Public Opinion*. New York: New York University Press, 2018.
Louganis, Greg. *Breaking the Surface*. New York: Random House, 1995.
Mcllhaney, Marion. *Sex: What You Don't Know Can Kill You*. Grand Rapids, MI: Baker Book House, 1997.
Monette, Paul. *Borrowed Time*. New York: Avon Books, 1990.
National Museum and Archive of Lesbian and Gay History. *The Gay Almanac*. New York: Berkley Books, 1996.
Newton, David E. *LGBT Youth Issues Today: A Reference Handbook*. Santa Barbara: ABC-CLIO, 2014.
Savage, Dan and Terry Miller, eds. *It Gets Better: Coming Out, Overcoming Bullying and Creating a Life Worth Living*. New York: Penguin, 2011.
Scarce, Michael. *Smearing the Queer: Medical Bias in the Health Care of Gay Men*. New York: Harrington Park Press, 1999.
Scholinski, Daphne. *The Last Time I Wore a Dress*. New York: Putnam Publishing Group, 1997.
Silver, Diane. *The New Civil War: The Lesbian and Gay Struggle for Civil Rights*. New York: Franklin Watts, 1997.
Young, Perry Dean and Martin Duberman. *Lesbians and Gays and Sports*. Broomall, PA: Chelsea House Publishing, 1994.

OTHER INFORMATION SOURCES

Organizations

American Civil Liberties Union Gay and Lesbian Rights/AIDS Civil Liberties Project, 125 Broad Street, New York, NY 10004. (212) 549-2500. E-mail: aclu@aclu.org. Home page: www.aclu.org.

Lambda Legal Defense and Education Fund, 120 Wall Street, New York, NY 10005. (212) 809-8585. E-mail: lambdalegal@lambdalegal.org. Home page: www.lambdalegal.org.

National Gay and Lesbian Task Force, 1700 Kalorama Road NW, Washington, DC 20009. (202) 332-6483. (202) 332-6219 (TTY). E-mail: ngltf@ngltf.org. Home page: www.ngltf.org.

!OutProud! The National Coalition for Gay, Lesbian, Bisexual & Transgender Youth, 369 Third Street, Ste. B-362, San Rafael, CA 94901. E-mail: info@out proud.org. Home page: www.outproud.org.

Parents and Friends of Lesbians and Gays (PFLAG), 1101 Fourteenth Street NW, Washington, DC 20005. (202) 638-4200. E-mail: info@pflag.org. Home page: www.pflag.org.

Online Sources

ACLU map of nondiscrimination laws by state: https://www.aclu.org/maps/non-discrimination-laws-state-state-information-map

"An Estimate of Housing Discrimination Against Same-Sex Couples": http://www.huduser.org/Publications/pdf/Hsg_Disc_against_SameSexCpls_v3.pdf

GayLawNet: E-mail, dba@labyrinth.net.au. Home page: www.labyrinth.net.au -Growing Up LGBT in America at http://www.hrc.org/youth?gclid=CLLx6Ozol70CFa47Ogod0iAAgg

GLSEN study on online harassment of gays, "Out Online: The Experiences of Lesbian Gay Bisexual Transgender Youth on the Internet": http://glsen.org/sites/default/files/Out%20Online%20FINAL.pdf

Hotlines

CDC National AIDS Hotline, (800) 342-AIDS, (800) AIDS-TTY (TTY)

Gay and Lesbian National Hotline, (888) THE-GLNH

CHAPTER 15

Property Rights and Crimes against Property

EARNINGS

Are minors legally entitled to keep their personal earnings?

Not necessarily. Because parents are entitled to their children's services, they actually have a legal right to their children's income. This issue is discussed at length in Chapter 3.

Do minors legally own the property that their parents provide for them, such as clothes, books, bicycles, electronic equipment, and cars?

Not usually. Although parents "give" such property to their children in a definite sense, courts say the parents are the owners. This is because parents have the right to reclaim the property if it is stolen, and they have "standing" to bring a court case against someone if the property is damaged or destroyed.

WHAT CAN A MINOR OWN?

Can teens legally own property?

Yes, despite the fact that they might not have a legal claim to their earnings. They can purchase property, inherit it, and receive it by gift. Property actually and legally owned by a minor belongs to the minor exclusively, although a minor can also own property "jointly" with someone else. (When a person owns property jointly, at one owner's death all the property passes to the other joint owner.)

Can a minor have a bank account?

In most states a minor can establish a bank account and make withdrawals without parental consent. But a parent can serve as a "custodian" for a minor's account. This means a parent's name can appear on the account along with the minor's, as a sort of money manager. The parent can make deposits and sign for withdrawals, but only for the minor's benefit.

In addition, federal law permits parents to serve as custodians for property they give to a child directly, except when the property is real estate. (The parent would serve under the authority of the federal Uniform Transfers to Minors Act of 1986.) Except for custodial accounts, parents don't have the automatic right to manage their children's property simply because of their adult or parental status.

Can a minor legally sell property?

Minors do have the power to "transfer title" to property. But in many states if a minor sells property—if a minor sells a large item such as a house or business—the minor may later revoke the sale unless his or her "property guardian" obtained court approval for the transaction.

What is a property guardian's job?

A property guardian is appointed by a court to manage a minor's "estate" and serves until discharged. The guardian must manage the estate with a high degree of care and regularly report or "account" to the court about the estate's status and value. Some transactions that property guardians enter into, such as selling land and purchasing large investments, must be preapproved by the court.

Property guardians are sometimes called "conservators" or "guardians of the estate." As a practical matter, courts only appoint property guardians if the amount of property owned by the minor is worth more than a few thousand dollars. A property guardian is paid from the property being managed (subject to court approval) unless the guardian agrees to do the job for free.

In fact, one or both parents usually are the ones who serve, but a relative, friend, or bank could be appointed instead. (This often happens when a minor inherits property from a deceased parent.) Guardians are also appointed to manage property for adults who, because of illness or old age, are incapable of managing money or property on their own.

Does this mean a minor can't legally sell or trade personal items to friends or even strangers?

No. Such transactions are really too small to involve a court or guardian.

Do parents have a legal right to use property inherited by a child?

Only if the property was inherited by the child and the parents jointly. Parents are powerless to dispose of a minor's interest in property unless they are the minor's custodian or court-appointed property guardian.

Can a minor require a property guardian to enter into a particular transaction?

No. The property guardian manages the property independently.

Can a minor have a property guardian dismissed?

In certain circumstances. Some states provide that minors age fourteen years or older may nominate their own property guardian, although the court must approve the choice. In most states a minor is free to choose a new property guardian at age fourteen, again subject to court approval.

Might a minor have a legal guardian as well as a property guardian?

Yes, and they can be the same person. For more about legal guardians, see Chapter 3, "At Home."

Can a minor retrieve his or her estate from the guardian at the age of majority?

Usually. The court revokes the guardianship at that point unless it believes a good reason exists to keep it in place, such as a person's physical or mental disability.

Can a minor legally give property away?

Yes, but like a minor's sale of property, the gift can be revoked. Again, this only applies to large gifts of property—not birthday presents and such.

WHEN PARENTS DIE

If a parent dies, who inherits his or her property?

It depends on whether the parent died leaving a valid will. Persons above the age of majority may legally decide how their property is to pass at death, and wills are the normal way of directing who gets what. Married people often leave their entire estate to a surviving spouse, although they aren't legally required to. If the "decedent" is a child's second parent to die, the estate often passes to the child and his or her brothers and sisters. This would happen regardless of whether the children are minors.

What happens if a parent dies without a valid will?

The property passes "intestate," which means it passes according to the state's inheritance laws. Under most state "intestacy" laws, if a parent is survived by a spouse and children, the spouse is entitled to one-third to one-half of the decedent's estate, and the children are entitled to the rest. If there is no surviving spouse, the children share the estate equally. Contrary to popular belief, if someone dies intestate, his or her property isn't forfeited to the government.

Do the courts get involved in the distribution of decedents' estates?

In most cases, yes—particularly when the estate is large.

"Probate" is the legal process for determining the validity of a decedent's will (when one exists), collecting the decedent's property, paying all debts, and distributing the estate to the proper persons. Most states have separate probate courts that supervise the orderly administration of decedents' estates, whether or not the person died with a will.

Can a spouse or child be disinherited?

Yes, but only under a will and not under the laws of intestacy. In some states, if a spouse attempts to disinherit a spouse in a will, the spouse inherits the amount he or she would have inherited had the decedent died intestate.

Can adopted children inherit from their adoptive parents?

Yes. Children of adoptive parents have the same legal rights as children who are related to their parents by blood. In many states adopted children may also inherit from the parents, aunts and uncles, and other relatives of their adoptive parents.

Can adopted children inherit from their natural parents?

In most states an adopted child may not inherit from a natural or "birth" parent if the birth parent dies intestate. This is because the relationship between child and parent no longer exists under the law. But nothing legally prevents a birth parent from leaving property by will to a child who has since been adopted.

Can children born outside of marriage inherit from their parents?

In years past, children born outside of marriage couldn't inherit from their natural *fathers*. Today they may inherit from both parents. To inherit under state intestacy laws, however, the identity of the father may have to be legally established in a "paternity" proceeding in court.

In some states an "illegitimate" child can inherit from his or her father only if the father's identity is established before he dies. Paternity can also be established if the child's parents marry one another or if the father legally declares the child to be his own.

Are stepchildren entitled to inherit from their stepparents?

Only under a will. Intestacy laws don't apply to the relationship of stepparent and stepchild.

If a minor inherits property, can he or she sell it, spend it—do anything with it whatsoever?

No. Again, because minors are legally incapable of managing their own property (except bank accounts), a probate court often will appoint a property guardian to handle their financial affairs. In an inheritance situation, property guardians often are nominated in the decedent's will.

Property guardianships can be complicated and inconvenient, particularly if the minor owns or inherits substantial property. For this reason, parents often create "trusts" during their lifetime to manage property that their children stand to inherit. In a trust, money or property is set aside by one or both parents before death. After they die, a "trustee" manages it for the minor and distributes it when the minor becomes an adult. The property never needs to pass through a probate court proceeding.

Although trusts are easy to establish, less costly than guardianships, and subject to little court supervision, a lawyer should draft the trust document. In addition, the trustee should contact a lawyer if problems arise with the trust's management.

WHEN MINORS DIE

Can a minor write a valid will?

No. Only adults can make legally binding wills.

If a person dies before reaching the age of majority, who inherits his or her property?

Because a minor is too young to leave property by will, it must pass intestate, which again means that state law dictates who inherits it. Usually the minor's parents (or the surviving parent) inherit the property. If neither is living, the minor's brothers and sisters inherit it in equal shares.

THE PROPERTY OF OTHERS

Is shoplifting the same as theft? What kind of punishment can a minor receive for shoplifting?

Shoplifting is a form of "larceny," the official term for theft. From a legal standpoint, shoplifting is taking property displayed for sale without paying for it. The mere act of concealing store property inside a coat or purse is shoplifting; this means the shoplifter doesn't have to leave the store to commit the offense.

Teens who are caught shoplifting go to juvenile court. But whether or not the teen is convicted, and regardless of whether the court orders probation, the shoplifter is usually required to return the property or make restitution for it.

Is robbery the same as larceny?

Robbery is larceny accompanied by the use of force and is a more serious crime than simple larceny.

Do teens who steal and rob always go to juvenile court?

Usually, although a teen minor can be tried in adult court in some states if charged with "aggravated robbery," which is robbery using a deadly weapon, and for other serious crimes such as arson, kidnapping, rape, murder, and attempted murder. In most states, if the teen is fourteen years of age or older and faces the serious charge of armed robbery, the teen can be transferred into adult criminal court.

Chapter 12, "Teens and Crime," provides important information about how courts handle young offenders.

TRESPASSING AND PROPERTY DAMAGE

If a store manager asks a teen to leave the business premises, can the teen legally refuse? If the teen refuses, is he or she a trespasser?

A store manager can legally request any customer to leave, but only if the reason for wanting the customer out isn't based on race, color, gender, nationality, religion, or disability. If the customer refuses, he or she becomes a trespasser and can be arrested.

So trespassing is against the law?

Yes; it is a misdemeanor. A person can be a trespasser if he or she refuses to leave after being asked to, and also if the person wasn't legally on the property in the first place.

If a person causes damage to property or vandalizes it while trespassing, what can the owner do?

Recover money against the trespasser as compensation for the damages, because the property damage is a civil "tort." For more about torts and recovering money in court actions, see Chapter 17, "Taking Matters to Court."

Legally, what can happen when a minor damages property?

He or she can be sent to juvenile court. Minors can land in juvenile court for throwing rocks through windows, drawing on street signs, defacing bridges and buses, driving across lawns, and breaking through gates and fences. See Chapter 12, "Teens and Crime."

Is spray-painting, or "tagging," graffiti on walls and buildings illegal?

Defacing property owned by the government (such as a city or state) or a private property owner is a crime. Most state codes specifically identify the act of placing graffiti on the property of another as vandalism. Defacing the property of another is not only a crime, but also can give rise to a civil cause of action against the teen who committed the act of vandalism. Some juveniles have even been charged with felonies for particularly egregious acts of graffiti-based vandalism.

Some laws give judges the power to impose various sorts of additional requirements on convicted vandalizers. For example, California law specifically provides that if a minor is convicted of vandalism by tagging graffiti on the property of another, the court may order the minor or his or her parents or guardians to "keep the damaged property or another specified property in the community free of graffiti for up to one year."

Can parents be forced to reimburse a property owner for damage caused by their minor children?

In many cases, yes. They can be held liable in court for the torts of their children, particularly if the parents should have been supervising the child when the damage occurred. There is a specific tort, called "negligent supervision," that can apply to parents under these circumstances. This rule applies to legal guardians as well.

FOR FURTHER READING

Castleman, Craig. *Getting Up: Subway Graffiti in New York*. Cambridge, MA: MIT Press, 1984.

Clifford, Denis. *Quick and Legal Will Book*. Updated ed. Berkeley, CA: Nolo Press, 2023.

Dickens, Charles. *Bleak House*. New York: Everyman's Library, 1991.

Editors of Nolo. *Neighbor Law: Fences, Trees, Boundaries, and Noise*. 3rd ed. Berkeley, CA: Nolo Press, 2023.

Fick, Barbara J. *The American Bar Association Guide to Wills and Estates*. 4th ed. New York: Random House Reference, 2013.

Leonard, Robin and Ralph Warner. *Legal Forms for Personal Use: Delegating Authority to Care for Children, Pets and Property*. Berkeley, CA: Nolo Press, 1998. Nolo eForm Kit at www.nolo.com.

Pollot, Mark F. *Grand Theft and Petty Larceny: Property Rights in America*. San Francisco: Pacific Research Institute for Public Policy, 1992.

OTHER INFORMATION SOURCES

Organization

National Guardianship Association, 1604 North Country Club Road, Tucson, AZ 85716. (520) 881-6561. Home page: www.guardianship.org.

Online Sources

Art Crimes (graffiti preservation): E-mail, winsom@graffiti.org. Home page: www.graffiti.org
Juvenile Crime, Graffiti and Gang Violence Task Force: http://www.myharlingen.us/users/0001/docs/JuvenileCrimeGraffiti_GangViolence.pdf

Hotline

Shoplifters Anonymous, (800) 848-9595

CHAPTER 16

Entering into Contracts

THE BASICS

What is a contract?

It is an agreement in which one party promises to do something in exchange for another party's promise to do something in return. If one party performs but the other doesn't, the first party can take the second party to court for "breach of contract."

People make contracts all the time, and many are so simple that people don't realize that they have entered into them. A customer contracts with a grocery store when the customer brings his or her selections to the checkout. The nature of their contract is simply this: the store will permit the customer to take the items away if the customer pays the amount shown on the register.

Consider another basic contract. When a person buys an airline ticket, the airline is contracting to take the person to a particular destination. The contract actually is written out; the printed information on the front and back of the plane ticket are the contract terms.

A sophisticated type of contract would be a contract for the sale of land or a contract to buy a car.

Do certain types of contracts have to be in writing?

Yes. By law, contracts that can't be performed in less than one year and contracts for the sale of land must be written. But contracts that don't have to be in writing often are anyway. Written contracts give the parties a permanent and reliable record of their agreement. Sometimes state laws require various types of contracts to be in writing.

How are contracts enforced if one party refuses to perform?

The party who wants the contract performed often takes the other party to court for "breach of contract." If that party loses money as a result of the other's failure to perform, the court can award money or "damages" to the injured party.

Breach of contract actions in civil court are explained in Chapter 17.

Do minors have a legal right to enter into contracts?

Yes, minors can enter into contracts. However, in most jurisdictions a minor may "disaffirm" a contract because of his or her age. This means that contracts entered into by minors are "voidable." The idea behind this is the "infancy doctrine," which is based on the legal system wanting to protect minors from adults who may take advantage of them.

There are exceptions to the application of the "infancy" doctrine. One is called the "benefit rule"; it has been applied in cases in which a minor contracts to purchase a product, such as a vehicle, uses the vehicle, and then seeks a full refund. The "benefit rule" provides that the contracting minor is not entitled to full recovery of the purchase price, because the minor should not be compensated when the minor received a benefit from using the product. As one court explained: "The infancy defense may not be used inequitably to retain the benefits of a contract while reneging on the obligations attached to that benefit."

If a minor enters into a contract, does an adult have to cosign it or agree to be jointly responsible in order for it to be enforceable?

No, but an adult can certainly agree to do so. Cosigning a contract or agreeing to be jointly responsible means the adult can be required to perform the entire contract (such as paying all the money owed), not just half of it.

DISAFFIRMING CONTRACTS

Why can minors disaffirm contracts?

The reason given is to protect minors against businesspeople who try to take unfair advantage of them in the marketplace. This is based on the "infancy" doctrine explained above. Many people think the rule allowing minors to disaffirm contracts is outdated and actually unfair, for two reasons. First, it can be a hardship on the adults who contract with minors evenhandedly and in good faith. Some states, including California, have passed specific laws that govern minors who are entertainers and limit their ability to disaffirm contracts. Second, most minors are at home in the marketplace and are usually smart about how it operates.

The rule that minors can avoid contracts doesn't mean, for example, that a minor can agree to buy a computer, take it home, use it, then refuse to pay for it. It simply means a minor can agree to buy a computer, take it home, then back out of the contract and return it even if the seller doesn't have a return policy. It means the seller must refund the amount paid—although in many states the seller can reduce the refund by the value of any wear and tear.

If the computer has been damaged, many states now require the minor to pay the difference between the original price and its current value. This is called "restitution." Even so, the minor can disaffirm the contract, but an adult can't.

Can a minor disaffirm a contract for a car?

It depends on the state. In many, minors can't disaffirm contracts for cars, motorcycles, car insurance, or school loans. Furthermore, minors can't back out of contracts once they reach age sixteen in California and a number of other states.

Can an adult disaffirm a contract with a minor?

No, an adult cannot disaffirm a contract with a minor if the minor wants to keep it in force. The contract is "binding" on the adult but not the minor, and the minor can require the adult to complete it.

If an adult agrees to be jointly responsible with a minor on a contract, can the adult disaffirm the contract as well?

No. The adult may be required to perform the contract fully or pay contract "damages."

NECESSITIES

Are there any types of contracts that can't be disaffirmed by minors?

Yes. Contracts for "necessities" such as food, clothing, lodging, and medical care can't be disaffirmed, assuming the minor is still dependent on his or her parents. Both the minor and the parents can be legally required to pay the entire bill. This is sometimes referred to as the "mature minor" exception. And as stated above, sometimes insurance contracts, school loan agreements, and contracts for certain professional services aren't voidable. For more about emancipation, see Chapter 5, "On Your Own."

A proper education often is considered a "necessity," although what constitutes a "proper" education will vary from family to family.

If a minor misrepresents his or her age in order to enter into a contract, can the minor later disaffirm it?

In many states, no. Certain states also prohibit minors from avoiding their contract obligations if they engage in business as an adult.

Does a minor's voidable contract ever become "nonvoidable"?

Yes, a voidable contract cannot be voided once the minor reaches the age of majority.

FOR FURTHER READING

American Bar Association, The American. *The American Bar Association Guide to Consumer Law: Everything You Need to Know about Buying, Selling, Contracts, and Guarantees*. New York: Times Books, 1997.

Burnham, Scott J. *Contract Law for Dummies*. New York: John Wiley & Sons, 2011.

Smith, Wesley J. *The Smart Consumer: A Legal Guide to Your Rights in the Marketplace*. Washington, DC: HALT: Americans for Legal Reform, 1998.

Ulmer, Mari Privette. *Sign Here: How to Understand Any Contract Before You Sign*. 2nd ed. Angel Fire, NM: Intrigue Press, 1998.

OTHER INFORMATION SOURCES

Organization

Public Citizen, 1600 Twentieth Street NW, Washington, DC 20009. (202) 588-1000. E-mail: pcmail@citizen.org. Home page: www.citizen.org.

Online Source

Insurance Information Institute: www.iii.org

CHAPTER 17

Taking Matters to Court

THE VOCABULARY OF A LAWSUIT

What is a lawsuit?

It is a process in which a "plaintiff" takes a "defendant" to court to satisfy a wrong the plaintiff believes the defendant caused. The plaintiff is the party who files the lawsuit, and the defendant is the party being sued.

Parties don't have to be individuals; they can be businesses, cities, states, the federal government, or even a foreign country. A lawsuit begins when the plaintiff files a document called a "complaint." This is the initial charging document by which a legal action is commenced.

A plaintiff's injuries—physical, emotional, or otherwise—are called "damages." When a plaintiff's relief takes the form of money, the monetary award is called "compensation."

Cases are "civil" in nature when a plaintiff seeks to protect a personal or private right, such as personal or real property. Cases are "criminal" in nature when a public entity such as a state or city seeks to protect rights embodied in its public laws.

This chapter is about *civil* cases. For more about the criminal justice system and what happens when young people commit criminal acts, see Chapter 12, "Teens and Crime."

What are the basic types of monetary damages?

There are three basic types of monetary damages in the civil system: compensatory, punitive, and nominal. Compensatory damages are designed to compensate the plaintiff for the harm that he or she has suffered. This includes "pain and suffering" damages, which can vary dramatically. Punitive damages are designed to punish the defendant or the wrongdoer. Punitive damages awards generally apply only when the defendant has acted very recklessly or egregiously. They are controversial and have been the subject of a movement known as "tort reform." Nominal damages refer to damages in name only. These apply when a plaintiff has technically suffered a legal wrong but has not suffered any harm of any consequence.

WHY PEOPLE GO TO COURT

What types of wrongs can a plaintiff seek to recover for?

There are literally dozens of types, but the two main categories are "tort" and "breach of contract."

Most tort and breach of contract cases aren't based on laws, or statutes, passed by legislative bodies. They are based on decisions handed down by the courts through the years. These collections of judicial opinions are referred to as case law or "the common law." There are exceptions, as many tort and contract actions are specifically governed by statutes. For example, in tort law, many states have specific laws dealing with products liability actions or medical malpractice claims. In contract law, most states have adopted a version of the so-called Uniform Commercial Code.

What is a tort?

A tort is a civil cause of action in which the defendant has violated a duty or engaged in socially unreasonable conduct that harms the plaintiff. The word "tort" comes from the Latin word *tortus*, or twisted. The person who commits a tort is called a "tortfeasor."

What are the three main categories of torts?

Intentional torts, torts of negligence, and strict liability torts. Intentional torts refer to actions by a defendant who intends to achieve a certain result or acts with substantial certainty that his or her conduct will cause harm. Common intentional torts against a person include assault, battery, false imprisonment, and intentional infliction of emotional distress.

For example, let's say that a woman is very upset that her boyfriend has cheated on her. She punches her boyfriend in the face. This woman has committed the intentional torts of assault and battery.

On the other hand, consider this example. A man is driving too fast and crashes into another vehicle on the road. The driver owes a duty to other drivers on the road to drive in a reasonable manner. The driver did not intend to hit another car, but he was at fault, or negligent in the way he drove the car. This is an example of a tort of negligence.

Strict liability torts apply when a defendant is liable to a plaintiff even when the defendant did not act intending to cause harm or wasn't even specifically at fault. Strict liability applies to some products liability actions, when a defective product causes harm to someone or a defendant transports highly dangerous materials and those materials harm someone else. When strict liability applies, a defendant is liable even if he or she did not intend for a bad thing to happen or is even at fault.

How does a plaintiff show that someone was negligent?

There are several basic elements to a negligence claim. The plaintiff must show a duty of care that the defendant breached the duty of care, causation, and damages. When a person operates an automobile, that person owes a duty to everyone else on or near the roadway to operate that vehicle reasonably. If a defendant texts on his phone and swerves into another lane, that individual has breached a duty. The defendant's poor driving was both the actual cause of the plaintiff's harm and also the legal, or proximate, cause of the plaintiff's harm. In addition, the plaintiff will have suffered damages from the accident.

What are other examples of negligence cases?

Some of the more common are auto accidents, slips and falls, acts of professional negligence (medical malpractice, legal malpractice, accountant malpractice), negligent supervision, negligent retention, and the negligent failure to provide adequate security to patrons or customers. There are many different types of negligence cases. Negligence cases comprise the largest percentage of tort cases.

Is a tort a crime?

A tort is a separate action than a crime, but the same conduct can constitute both a tort and a crime. The primary purpose of tort law is compensation. The plaintiff is seeking damages for the harm he or she has suffered. If the act is also a crime—if the act violates a public law—the state's attorney can prosecute for it. In other words, the state (or one of its legal subdivisions, such as a county) can bring a separate case or "charge" against the defendant. This happens frequently.

What are some examples of torts that are also crimes?

Vandalism is one example. Damaging another's property is against the law even if the damage isn't major. It is also a tort, so the property owner can bring a civil action against the vandal.

Another example is battery. A person who physically strikes and assaults another person can be sued civilly for the tort of battery. But, the person also can be persecuted criminally for the attack.

What is breach of contract?

A breach of contract occurs when a party to an agreement fails to perform according to its terms, thereby causing loss to the other party to the agreement. For example, a person breaches a contract if he or she agrees to sell a motorcycle, accepts full payment from the buyer, but then refuses to deliver it. Here the buyer is the potential plaintiff and the seller is the potential defendant.

For more about contracts, see Chapter 16, "Entering into Contracts."

What are some other examples of breach of contract?

Common examples are failing to pay rent or make a mortgage payment, failing to pay a credit card debt, failing to make prompt delivery of an order of manufactured products, and failing to complete construction of a building on schedule.

What forms of relief can courts award in civil actions?

Money is the most common form of relief in both tort and contract cases. But courts can also issue "injunctions," which either order a defendant to stop doing something that causes constant harm to the plaintiff or order the defendant to specifically perform an action.

MINORS AS PLAINTIFFS

Can a minor be a plaintiff?

Yes. A minor can be a plaintiff or a defendant and can sue or be sued for almost all the same reasons as an adult.

But minors lack the legal capacity to file lawsuits on their own, and for this reason an adult files on the minor's behalf. This long-standing rule is meant to protect minors from their own lack of knowledge of the court system and the world at large. The adult representative might be the minor's parent, guardian, or so-called next friend, an individual appointed by the judge to protect the minor's interests.

A teen, for example, could sue a negligent driver for injuries and car damages resulting from an accident. The teen would sue through a parent or next friend. A young person could also be a plaintiff in a lawsuit resulting from another person's carelessness at school or work.

It would be difficult for a minor to sue on his or her own for another basic reason. Hiring a lawyer can be an expensive proposition. Payments to lawyers are discussed later in this chapter.

Can a minor sue his or her parents?

For certain wrongdoings, yes. In the United States, the first lawsuit by a child against a parent took place in 1891. As a result of this case, states rushed to pass laws to protect parents against lawsuits by their children. In 1905, a Washington court went so far as to prohibit a civil lawsuit by a fifteen-year-old who had been raped by a parent—it refused to hear the lawsuit out of concern for family harmony!

Today almost every state permits minors to sue their parents for certain torts. The most common is a suit for personal injuries resulting from a parent's negligent driving. (The child's representative in this type of suit is often an insurance company.) Also, almost every state permits minors to sue one or both parents for personal injuries *intentionally inflicted.* A few permit children to sue for emotional injury caused by bad parenting, but these cases are almost impossible to win.

Can a minor sue an aunt, uncle, grandparent, or other relative?

Yes. These individuals have the same status as unrelated persons.

If a minor's parent is killed by a third party, can the minor sue the killer for money?

Most states have "wrongful death" statutes, which permit certain survivors to sue a person who negligently causes a family member's death. Those who can sue usually are the decedent's spouse and minor children. It doesn't matter whether the death was deliberate or accidental.

Some states limit damages in wrongful death cases to the loss of the deceased parent's services at home and the value of his or her future earnings. This means a dependent child might be able to recover for the estimated dollar value of a deceased mother's or father's services as a parent.

Many states also permit survivors to recover damages for mental anguish endured as a result of a wrongful death. When a court permits recovery for mental anguish, the jury is asked to place a dollar value on the survivors' emotional pain and suffering.

MINORS AS DEFENDANTS

Can a minor be a defendant?

A minor over a certain age can be sued for torts and sometimes for breach of contract. In many jurisdictions, a minor under the age of seven cannot be sued. However, older minors can be.

Minors who commit torts usually are held to a lower "standard of care" than adults. What this means is that instead of measuring a minor's actions against the level of care of a reasonable adult, courts hold them to a degree of care that a young person of the same age and maturity would be expected to exercise.

Most acts by teens are measured against a standard of care very close to that of adults.

How does a minor go about defending a case?

Again, the minor has an adult representative, who assists the attorney. The representative must act in the minor's best interests and isn't required to take orders from the minor.

Who pays the damages when a jury decides a minor committed a tort?

In theory, the minor. But minors usually don't have much money—in legal jargon, they are "judgment proof." For this reason, parents often are jointly responsible for the torts of their minor children, particularly in cases in which the minor wasn't properly supervised when the tort occurred.

For example, if a parent left a handgun where anyone could reach it, and a minor child managed to wound or even kill someone, the minor and the parents could be sued jointly. They would be "codefendants." The minor could be sued for negligence, and the parents could be sued for negligent supervision. This type of case is definitely on the increase.

LAWYERS

How important is a lawyer?

In most civil cases and certainly in all felony criminal cases, a lawyer is critical. Anyone who wants to file a lawsuit in other than a small claims court should consider talking to a lawyer first. A lawyer can determine whether a person has a valid legal claim in tort or contract, whether the person has a decent chance of winning, and whether the estimated damages are worth the effort and expense of going to court.

What if a person doesn't have the money to pay for a lawyer?

The US Supreme Court ruled in *Gideon v. Wainwright* (1963) that a criminal defendant in state court facing felony charges is entitled to a lawyer even if he or she cannot afford one. The case involved Clarence Earl Gideon, who allegedly stole money from a pool hall. At that time the state of Florida would not provide Mr. Gideon, who was indigent, with an attorney. He appealed all the way to the US Supreme Court, which ruled in his favor. The court reasoned that attorneys in criminal cases were "necessities, not luxuries." The court's decision in *Gideon v. Wainwright* led to the adoption of public defender systems around the country.

Does a person need a lawyer to go to court?

No. Individuals can file lawsuits and go to court without legal representation. When a person represents himself or herself, he is known as a pro se litigant. For better or worse, this happens all the time. Even so, court is exceedingly complex—it befuddles most nonlawyers (and even many lawyers). As a rule, the more complex the case, the more important it is to have legal representation.

Would a lawyer talk privately to a teen about a case the minor wants to file?

A lawyer would undoubtedly urge a minor to bring a parent or other adult along, even for a first office meeting. In addition, a lawyer's availability might depend on whether the minor has any money. Many attorneys do not charge for an initial consultation, but any further representation can be quite expensive. Most attorneys charge by the hour, and an hourly rate of $250 isn't at all unusual.

Are lawyers always paid by the hour?

No. Their fees depend on the type of case. For tort actions, the plaintiff's lawyer usually charges a "contingency fee," which means his or her pay is a percentage of the amount recovered from the defendant. Under contingency fee arrangements, the lawyer doesn't get paid *unless* and *until* the *plaintiff* collects.

A contingency fee is usually one-third of the amount recovered. If the plaintiff loses and the case is appealed, the percentage goes up. In addition to the contingency fee, the plaintiff usually pays filing fees and other standard court charges regardless of the outcome of the case. Some states have laws that regulate contingency fees.

In tort actions the *defendant*'s lawyer is paid by the hour.

What if my lawyer does a lousy job?

You always have the ability to fire a lawyer and hire another lawyer. You can also file a complaint against a lawyer with the professional responsibility organization that governs lawyers in your state. For example, a person can file a complaint about their lawyer if the lawyer fails to return their phone calls, neglects to show up to court, or generally does not do her job during the case.

SMALL CLAIMS COURT

What is small claims court?

It is a court that only hears cases in which the damage claim doesn't exceed a certain dollar amount. The limit varies state by state, ranging from $3,000 up to $25,000. In many states it is either $5,000 or $10,000. Claims for unpaid bills or minor property damage often end up before a small claims court judge.

Small claims courts have different names in different states. In some states they are called "courts of common pleas." In other states, they are called "general session courts." Again, the legal system in the United States is complicated mainly because state laws and courts are not all the same. But, these courts are in the nature of "people's courts," because the parties rarely use lawyers. Sometimes state law prohibits parties in small claims court from having legal representation at all.

Can a minor take a case to small claims court?

Only if state law permits minors to file lawsuits. Minors lack the legal capacity to file most civil suits on their own.

BRINGING A LAWSUIT

How does a plaintiff begin a civil case?

By filing a "complaint," which is a court document in which a plaintiff explains his or her legal claims against a defendant and requests a specific type of relief. As a rule, the plaintiff must always set forth enough factual information in the complaint to put the defendant on notice of the substance of the claim. If there isn't enough information given, the defendant can ask the judge to dismiss the case. The defendant would file what is known as a motion to dismiss for failure to state a claim.

Most courts charge a filing fee to open a case, and the amount depends on the state and also the type of court. The filing fee can be excused if the plaintiff can't afford it.

What if I am sued merely for exercising my right to free speech?

If you are sued merely for exercising your right to free speech, then you may have been "SLAPPed" or the victim of what is called a "Strategic Lawsuit Against Public Participation." Many states have so-called anti-SLAPP laws that allow individuals to file an expedited or early motion to dismiss to try to get rid of this SLAPP suit.

For example, let's say that a citizen activist complains about the abuses to the environment caused by a large development company. The company, in an attempt to shut up the citizen, files a lawsuit for defamation or libel. This is likely a SLAPP suit. Hopefully, you can get a lawyer to file a special motion to dismiss to protect you from this SLAPP suit.

Can a plaintiff file in any court?

No. Courts have the legal power or "jurisdiction" to hear certain types of cases but not others. A court's jurisdiction depends on several factors, including the residence of the parties, the subject of the case, the damages in dispute, and the legal concepts upon which the plaintiff's claims are based.

There are federal, state, city, municipal, traffic, and tax courts. To find out the appropriate court for a particular case, ask the chief clerk of court at any state or county court.

What is the difference between state courts and federal courts?

Basically, their respective jurisdictional powers. Federal courts, which are present in every state, have jurisdiction over cases in which

- the US government is a party;
- there is an issue concerning the federal Constitution or a federal statute;
- the dispute involves more than $50,000 and is between two states, a state and citizens of another state, or citizens of different states; or
- the defendant is charged with a federal crime.

State courts usually deal with civil controversies between a state's residents and property owners, and civil and criminal matters based on state law. County courts and small claims courts are part of the state court system.

How are federal courts organized?

The federal courts are organized generally in a three-tiered system of trial courts, intermediate appellate courts, and a final appellate court. The trial courts in the federal system are the federal district courts. There are ninety-four different federal judicial districts in the United States.

The intermediate appellate courts are the US Circuit Courts of Appeal. There are thirteen different circuit courts: First Circuit through the Eleventh Circuit, the D.C. Circuit, and the Federal Circuit. Each circuit court has jurisdiction over federal cases brought in federal district courts in that jurisdiction. For example, the Sixth Circuit has control over federal cases that are brought in Tennessee, Kentucky, Ohio, and Michigan. To take another example, the Eleventh Circuit has jurisdiction over federal cases brought in Alabama, Georgia, and Florida.

The final appellate court in the federal court system is the US Supreme Court. It is sometimes called "the Court of Last Resort."

How are state courts organized?

It varies from state to state. Some states have a two-tiered court system, others have a three-tiered court system, and some even have a four-tiered system. Most state court systems have a three-tiered system similar to the federal court system of (1) trial courts, (2) intermediate appellate courts, and (3) final appellate courts. For example, in the Tennessee state court system, the trial courts are the circuit and chancery courts, the intermediate appellate courts are the Tennessee Court of Appeals and the Tennessee Court of Criminal Appeals, and the final appellate court is the Tennessee Supreme Court.

Can there be more than one plaintiff in a case?

Yes, there can be multiple plaintiffs and multiple defendants. In fact, sometimes a plaintiff may pursue a "class action" lawsuit, which seeks to add in many people who are in a similar situation to the plaintiff. There are special rules of procedure dealing with class action suits.

How does a person find out that he or she is a defendant in a lawsuit?

The person receives a "summons," which proclaims that a case naming that person as a defendant has been filed. The law allows the defendant a reasonable time, 20–30 days in most states, to prepare and file his or her "answer."

What should the defendant's answer contain?

It must admit or deny the statements in the complaint, and it may also state why the defendant believes he or she didn't do anything wrong and shouldn't be found responsible. In a nutshell, the answer is the defendant's "defense" to a complaint.

What happens if the defendant doesn't answer?

A "default judgment" can be entered for the plaintiff. This basically means the plaintiff wins. At that point the plaintiff must present evidence to the judge concerning the damages he or she claims to have suffered. Once the judge calculates the damages (plus lawyer's fees), the plaintiff has an enforceable "judgment" against the defendant in a particular dollar amount.

If the defendant answers, will the case always go to trial?

No. Most lawsuits settle before trial. In the long run, settling a case is almost always less expensive than going to trial, especially if one party's position is weak.

PREPARING A CIVIL CASE

If the parties don't settle their dispute, what happens between the date the answer is filed and the first day of trial?

The parties conduct "discovery," which is the overall process by which they learn more about one another's positions. Common tools of discovery include interrogatories, depositions, requests for production of documents, and requests for admission. Interrogatories are written questions sent by one party to the other. Depositions are the oral testimony of a party or witness taken down outside the courtroom, usually in the office of an attorney.

Why don't the parties wait until trial to learn more about each other's case?

Because today's court rules encourage parties to share as much as possible about one another's claims and defenses and settle as many issues as they can out of court. Judges only want to hear issues that the parties can't resolve on their own. This philosophy encourages better use of the court's time and, because the lawyer's fees mount up fast once a case goes to trial, always saves money.

Can the defendant ask to see documents in the plaintiff's possession that are likely to damage the plaintiff's case?

Yes, and the plaintiff can obtain damaging documents from the defendant. Prior to trial, a party must produce copies of any documents relating to the case that the other party requests.

Are documents in one party's control ever considered confidential?

Yes. Such items are called "privileged" communications, and they don't have to be turned over to the opposing party. They are protected because they occur in relationships in which honesty and trust are of critical importance. A privileged communication usually takes the form of a personal letter or memorandum, or a medical report.

The attorney–client relationship is a type of privileged relationship, which is why it is called the "attorney–client privilege." A party who claims this privilege may refuse to produce material generated during the course of the relationship, and his or her lawyer *must* refuse. Other examples of privileged relationships are the relationship of husband and wife, the doctor–patient relationship, and the priest–confessor relationship.

Can a party force a person to testify?

Yes. The party would do so by asking the court to "subpoena" the person. A subpoena is a court order directing a particular person to appear as a witness. Often a party requests a subpoena if there is reason to believe the witness won't show up. If the witness ignores the subpoena, the judge declares him or her to be "in contempt of court." If the witness still won't appear, he or she can be fined or even jailed.

TRIALS

How does a trial begin?

Each party presents its "opening statement," which explains what each will attempt to prove during the trial.

What happens after the opening statements?

Each of the plaintiff's witnesses takes the stand and testifies. The plaintiff's lawyer conducts his or her "direct examination" of these witnesses one by one. After the direct examination, the defendant's lawyer has an opportunity to "cross-examine."

What exactly is cross-examination?

Cross-examination occurs when a witness for one party is questioned by the lawyer for the other party. The cross-examiner will always attempt to test the truth or reliability of the witness's direct testimony and will also try to develop additional facts supporting his or her client's position. After the defendant finishes cross-examination, the plaintiff may wish to engage in redirect examination.

What happens after all the plaintiff's witnesses have testified and been cross-examined?

The defendant's lawyer calls the defense witnesses. One by one he or she questions them, and one by one the plaintiff's lawyer cross-examines them.

How does material other than in-court testimony come into evidence?

Each party's lawyer can request that items such as letters, memos, photos, weapons, bills, and results of scientific tests also be considered. The judge rules on the admissibility of each item as it is offered into evidence.

Can a young person testify?

Anyone who can remember significant events or evidence, express them clearly, and understand the duty to tell the truth is "competent" to testify. Minors are often placed on the stand.

In some states, if a minor is ten years old (twelve in other states) or younger, his or her ability to testify isn't taken for granted. If a party to a case believes a minor won't be able to offer reliable testimony, the judge will talk to the minor in private to determine whether he or she can understand questions, respond in court, remember important events, and comprehend the difference between true and false.

When determining a minor's competency to testify, age is often less significant than maturity. Judges have permitted children as young as three years old to testify in open court.

What is an "objection"? Why would a lawyer raise an objection in court?

A lawyer will object when an item of evidence, a question asked by the opposing party's lawyer, or a certain court procedure appears inappropriate. If a lawyer makes an objection, he or she must be ready to explain to the judge why the question, evidence, or procedure is out of line. If the judge agrees, he or she will "sustain" the objection. If the judge disagrees, it will be "overruled."

What happens after all the witnesses testify?

The lawyers present their "closing arguments." Each summarizes his or her client's case and tells the jury why it should decide the case in that party's favor.

What does a jury do?

The jury listens to the testimony of the witnesses, reviews the evidence, considers the applicable laws and earlier court cases dealing with similar legal issues, and then decides the outcome. In essence, it decides what really happened in the parties' case. The jury is often called the "trier of fact" or the "fact finder."

The jury's decision is its "verdict." When the jury brings in its verdict, one party wins and the other loses. The winner receives a judgment.

Is a case always argued before a jury?

No. The parties can agree to argue their case just before the judge. When this happens—and it often does in complex business cases—the judge decides what actually happened and renders a decision on his or her own. This type of case is called a "bench trial."

How does a jury know what legal principles to apply to a case?

After the closing arguments the judge gives the jury its "instructions," which advise the jury what laws and earlier cases to apply to the dispute between the parties.

What is a "hung jury"?

A jury is "hung" when it tries to reach a decision but can't. Since the jury is hung, no judgment is awarded, and the case must either be reargued before another jury or dropped.

Is a jury's verdict always final?

No. The losing party can ask the court—can "motion" the court—to grant a new trial. However, a judge will only grant a new trial if he or she believes that no reasonable jury could have reached the verdict that the jury returned.

DAMAGES

If the plaintiff wins, who decides how much the defendant will have to pay?

If the case is tried before a jury, the jury decides. Otherwise the judge decides. There aren't any hard and fast rules for deciding how much a plaintiff's injuries or other damages are "worth," and juries have considerable leeway in setting damage amounts, particularly in tort cases.

To calculate damages for a personal injury tort, a jury would consider evidence presented by the plaintiff's attorney regarding his or her client's medical expenses and loss of income. It might place a dollar value on both the plaintiff's pain and suffering and future employment opportunities lost due to the injury. If the damage was to property such as a car, the jury would consider the cost to repair the damage or replace the property altogether.

To determine damages in a breach of contract case, the jury would calculate the financial loss resulting from the defendant's failure to fulfill his or her side of the agreement.

APPEALING A COURT DECISION

What is an appeal? Who can appeal?

An appeal is a court review of certain issues previously decided at trial. The review is conducted by a higher court, usually called a court of appeals or appellate court. In an appeal, the losing party—the "appellant"—claims that a mistake was made by the judge or jury during the trial, causing the appellant to lose. The party who does not appeal is called the "appellee."

Sometimes, instead of using the terms "appellant" and "appellee," appellate courts use the terms "petitioner" and "respondent." For example, when a case is appealed to the US Supreme Court, the party seeking review is called the "petitioner," and the party responding is called the "respondent."

What are the main differences between trial courts and appellate courts?

The main difference is that at the trial court level, there usually is only one judge and a jury of twelve persons (though in some states a jury can consist of less than twelve), but at the appellate court level, there are three or more judges and no jury. Trial courts deal more with issues of fact and appellate courts are more focused on issues of law.

Parties and witnesses get to testify during a trial court proceeding. No parties or witnesses testify at an appellate court. Instead, attorneys on each side present argument—often 20–30 minutes each. This process is called "oral argument."

Is an appeal just a repeat of the trial?

No. Courts of appeal don't take testimony or accept additional evidence; they only review the matters brought up for review. An appeals court considers the arguments of both parties on these issues, reviews the written summaries or "briefs" of their arguments, examines the applicable law, then decides to "affirm" or "reverse" the trial court's decision.

If a party loses an appeal, can he or she take the case to a still higher court?

In some cases, yes. The federal court system and most state court systems provide two levels of appeal. In federal court, the first level is the Federal Court of Appeals, and next is the US Supreme Court. In the federal system, there are thirteen federal courts of appeal and one Supreme Court. In state courts, the first level is the state court of appeals, and the second is the state supreme court. A state supreme court may refuse to hear a party's appeal, except in states (such as Wyoming) in which there is no appeals court sandwiched between its trial courts and supreme court. Also, note that some state high courts are not called "supreme courts." For example, in New York the high court is called the New York Court of Appeals and the supreme court is actually a trial court.

The US Supreme Court has what is called "discretionary jurisdiction," meaning it has the discretion to pick and choose which cases it hears. Many state high courts also have discretionary jurisdiction. The US Supreme Court only hears select appeals, usually from the federal courts. In limited circumstances it will hear the appeal of a party who loses in a state supreme court. In Supreme Court cases the issue on appeal will involve a constitutional right or other important issue under federal law that earlier cases haven't clarified. Often the US Supreme Court will take a case when there is a split among the lower courts. This is often called a "circuit split."

FOR FURTHER READING

In General

Bergman, Paul and Sara Berman-Barrett. *Represent Yourself in Court: How to Prepare and Try a Winning Case*. 9th ed. Berkeley, CA: Nolo Press, 2016.
Hayes, J. Michael. *Help Your Lawyer Win Your Case*. Clearwater, FL: Sphinx Publishing, 1996.
Hudson, David L., Jr. *The Handy Supreme Court Answer Book: The History and Issues Explained*. 2nd ed. Canton, MI: Visible Ink Press, 2023.
Lovenheim, Peter. *How to Mediate Your Dispute*. Berkeley, CA: Nolo Press, 1996.
Schwartz, Bernard. *A History of the Supreme Court*. New York: Oxford University Press, 1995.
Van Dervort, Thomas R. and David L. Hudson Jr. *Law and the Legal System: An Introduction to Law and Legal Studies in the United States*. 3rd ed. New York: Wolters Kluwer, 2012.
Warda, Mark. *Simple Ways to Protect Yourself from Lawsuits*. Clearwater, FL: Sphinx Publishing, 1996.
Warner, Ralph. *Everybody's Guide to Small Claims Court*. 15th ed. Berkeley, CA: Nolo Press, 2014.
Woodward, Bob and Scott Armstrong. *The Brethren: Inside the Supreme Court*. New York: Avon Books, 1996.

The Jury System

Adler, Stephen J. *The Jury: Disorder in the Court*. New York: Doubleday Books, 1994.
Edah, Omatseyin Mark. *Juror: An Opportunity to Serve: An Immigrant Juror's Insight into the US Jurisprudence*. Los Angeles: Milligan Books, 1998.
Lerner, Renee Letow. *The Jury: A Very Short Introduction*. New York: Oxford University Press, 2023.

Lawyers

Allison, John. *Choosing Your Lawyer: An Insider's Practical Guide to Making a Really Good Choice*. San Rafael, CA: The Coach for Lawyers, LLC, 2013.
Azrieli, Avi. *Your Lawyer on a Short Leash*. Irvington-on-Hudson, NY: Bridge Street Books, 1997.
Ehrhardt, Audrey. *How to Hire a Lawyer: The Client's Essential Guide to Finding the Right Advocate*. Pennsauken, NY: BookBaby, 2017.
Repa, Barbara Kate. *The American Lawyer: When and How to Use One*. Chicago: American Bar Association, 1993.
Starnes, Tanya, et al. *Mad at Your Lawyer?* Berkeley, CA: Nolo Press, 1996.

OTHER INFORMATION SOURCES

Organization

Teen Court TV, 600 Third Avenue, New York, NY 10016. Home page: www.courttv.com/teens.

Online Source

American Bar Association's Lawyer Referral Directory: http://apps.americanbar.org/legalservices/lris/directory/

CHAPTER 18

How to Find the Law

How would a young person go about finding the law for a given situation?

First of all, you have to determine whether a legal situation is governed mainly by federal law, state law, or local law. There are some areas of law that are primarily federal law. For example, immigration law—discussed in Chapter 19—is largely federal law. But, family law, discussed earlier, is primarily state law. But, some issues are local law.

Fortunately, it is relatively easy to find much federal and state law online. Copies of federal statutes and state statutes are available online. Young people can go to FindLaw at http://statelaws.findlaw.com/ or to Justia at http://law.justia.com/codes/ and find links to both the US Code, which is the compilation of federal laws, and the individual state codes. Laws, or statutes, are found in sets of books called codes. Often these codes are placed into what are called annotated codes, which not only contain the text of statutes but also helpful descriptions and comments. It is relatively easy to find federal and state laws online, but finding local laws, or ordinances, is more difficult. Try accessing your city or county Web site. It may have a link to the ordinances.

To find a hard copy of your annotated code, you can go to either your public library, which should have a copy of your state code, or a law library. In addition, there are very powerful computerized databases of information run by groups like Westlaw and Lexis. However, you need to have a subscription and password to access Westlaw and Lexis (and that costs money). Talk to your librarian to see if your library has a subscription, or if another library in your area might. But before you try to find the law for a given situation, you need to ask whether it is a situation that would be governed by federal law, state law, or local law.

What is the difference between primary authority and secondary authority?

Primary authority refers to the law itself, while secondary authority refers to sources that explain or commentate about the law. Thus, a statute from the legislature is primary law, a decision from a court is primary law, and an administrative regulation from an agency is primary law. Again, primary law is the law itself.

Secondary authority refers to most other sources that explain or identify the law, but they are not the law itself.

How does one use a hard copy of an annotated code?

Annotated codes, which contain the texts of statutes, aren't hard to use. Each set has a complete topic index or a general index. Usually, the index consists of several volumes, such as A–G, H–M, and N–Z. You can look in the index using key terms to see if you can find what is called a citation to a statute. For example, if you were searching for a Tennessee law about age discrimination, you might look in the index for "age discrimination" or "discrimination." You would see § 4-21-407. The number 4 is the title number, the number 21 is the chapter number, and the number 407 is the section number.

The hard-copy volumes of the statutes list the title numbers on the spine. So you would look for the volume that contained Title 4 and then flip through until you saw 4-21-407.

Legal research in the books takes patience and the ability to read an index. If you have trouble, ask a reference librarian. Hopefully, he or she can point you in the right direction. Many legal issues are complex, and you very well may need the assistance of an attorney.

How are annotated codes organized?

Most annotated codes are organized topically into different titles. For example, there often is a title for criminal laws, a title for family law, a title for consumer protection law, a title for farming, a title for employment law, and the list goes on.

The annotated codes are "annotated" which means that after the text of the statute or law, there is mention of cases that cite or mention that statute. Thus, many legal researchers recommend that when you initially start looking for law, you start with an annotated code. Because, if you find a statute or law on point, you often can then find cases that interpret or apply that statute.

Aren't laws practically impossible to read?

No, although sometimes they can be difficult. The best way to understand what a law says is to read it over a number of times. Once usually isn't enough—any lawyer will tell you that. It's wise to photocopy the statute or ordinance once you have located it, then take the copy home and read it a few more times, carefully. Often, to understand the law you need to read not just the statute, or law, but also several court decisions that have applied or interpreted the law you are reading.

Isn't there an easier way to learn about the law?

Yes. Libraries have books on various legal topics, called secondary sources, that can help. Some of these are written for young people. First, try the reference section of your library.

You may have noticed that each chapter of this book has a section entitled "For Further Reading," which lists recently published books on legal topics for both young people and adults. These books are recommended. In addition, the organizations listed under "Other Information Sources" at the end of each chapter can be of enormous help.

How do you find out what a court case says?

Many appellate court cases are accessible for free online. For example, all US Supreme Court decisions can be found through FindLaw (http://www.findlaw.com). The easiest way to find a Supreme Court case is to simply go to Google or a similar search engine and type in the name of the case. For example, Chapter 17 discussed the important US Supreme Court decision in *Gideon v. Wainwright* (1963). That was the decision that provided that if a state court defendant was charged with a felony, he was entitled to a lawyer free of charge. You can find a copy of that decision at http://caselaw.lp.findlaw.com/cgi-bin/get-case.pl?court=us&vol=372&invol=335. You can read the decision itself and also find all sorts of commentary about that decision on the Internet.

You can also find copies of court decisions on the Web sites of different courts. For example, if you want a copy of a recent US Supreme Court decision, visit the Supreme Court's Web site at http://www.supremecourtus.gov and click on the "opinions" link on the top left corner of the Web site. If you click on "Opinions" you will then have a menu of choices that include:

Opinions of the Court
Opinions related to orders
In-chambers opinions
US Reports
Online sources cited in opinions
Media sources
Case citation finder

Most of the time you can find the opinions you need with the "Opinions of the Court" function.

What are the different types of opinions in cases?

There are several different types of opinions in cases, particularly in US Supreme Court decisions where there are nine justices with distinct judicial philosophies. If there is only one opinion, that is a unanimous opinion. But, oftentimes the court is divided. An opinion that a majority of the court (usually five justices) signs on to is called a majority opinion. That is the opinion that becomes the law of the land.

But, sometimes justices or judges disagree with the majority opinion. If an opinion disagrees with the result of a majority opinion, it is called a dissenting opinion. If an opinion agrees with the result of the majority or main opinion, but not necessarily the reasoning, that is a concurring opinion. And if an opinion is the main opinion but fails to garner a majority of the court, we call that a plurality opinion.

Why do we care about dissenting opinions?

Dissenting and concurring opinions are still important even if they are not the law at the current time. Sometimes a dissenting opinion later will become the law of the land. For example, back in 1896, the US Supreme Court made a very bad decision in *Plessy v. Ferguson*. In that decision, the court upheld a Louisiana law that required for separate railway accommodations on the basis of race. In other words, African American patrons were not allowed to ride with Caucasian patrons. The court upheld this law by an 8–1 vote.

But, Justice John Marshall Harlan wrote a solitary dissenting opinion. He famously wrote:

> But in view of the Constitution, in the eye of the law, there is in this country no superior, dominant, ruling class of citizens. There is no caste here. Our Constitution is color-blind, and neither knows nor tolerates classes among citizens. In respect of civil rights, all citizens are equal before the law. The humblest is the peer of the most powerful.

Justice Harlan is known as "the Great Dissenter" largely because of this dissenting opinion, though he had some other famous dissenting opinions too. It took the US Supreme Court fifty-eight years but the court finally overruled *Plessy v. Ferguson* (1896) in its historic decision *Brown v. Board of Education* (1954). The court recognized that segregation was unconstitutional and wrong. Justice Harlan's decision became the law of the land many years after his death.

But, that is not the only reason why we care about dissenting opinions—that they sometimes later become the law of the land. A dissenting opinion can simply look at a legal issue in a different or unique way. Many legal cases, especially those that reach the US Supreme Court, are difficult, and there is not one way to view or understand the law.

Why would we care about concurring opinions?

Sometimes, a concurring opinion will explain the law in a very effective way that later court decisions adopt as the primary vision. A good example comes from Justice John Marshall Harlan II's (he was the grandson of the Justice Harlan who dissented in *Plessy v. Ferguson*) concurring opinion in *Katz v. United States* (1967). The court dealt with whether it was constitutional for federal government agents to bug a public pay phone and listen to phone conversations without a warrant.

In his concurring opinion, Justice Harlan developed a concept he called the "reasonable expectation of privacy." He said that to determine whether an expectation of privacy is reasonable is a two-part test. First, the subject must exhibit a subjective expectation of privacy. Second, society must objectively regard that expectation of privacy as reasonable. This "reasonable expectation of privacy" test became a dominant way to analyze many search and seizure Fourth Amendment cases in the future.

With regard to court decisions, what is the importance of mandatory authority?

Mandatory authority refers to authority that is controlling for a particular jurisdiction. For example, a US Supreme Court decision is mandatory authority for lower courts. A Tennessee Supreme Court decision is mandatory authority for lower courts in Tennessee. Likewise, a California Supreme Court decision is mandatory authority for lower courts in California.

Mandatory authority is distinguishable from persuasive authority. Persuasive authority refers to law that a court may follow. Let's take an example. The Tennessee Court of Appeals may consider an opinion from the Kentucky Supreme Court. That Kentucky Supreme Court decision is persuasive authority for the appeals court in Tennessee. But, a Tennessee Supreme Court decision would be mandatory authority for the Tennessee Court of Appeals.

This distinction is very important, because the primary goal of a legal researcher is to find mandatory, primary authority bearing on our legal problem. If I am interested in finding out the constitutionality of locker searches in a public school in Tennessee, I would hope to find a pertinent US Supreme Court or Tennessee Supreme Court decision. Those decisions would be mandatory, primary authority for me in Tennessee. A decision from the Tenth US Circuit Court of Appeals or the Colorado Supreme Court, on the other hand, would be only persuasive authority.

Why would I ever care about persuasive authority if it is non-mandatory?

Good question. Sometimes, there is no mandatory authority in your jurisdiction. If your state appeals courts have never addressed a particular legal question, then you look to other jurisdictions to see if those courts have. Those court decisions might be persuasive to a court in your state.

What is a case citation?

A case citation refers to where the case is actually located in sets of books known as reporters, which contain copies of published decisions. For example, the citation for *Gideon v. Wainwright* is *Gideon v. Wainwright*, 372 US 335 (1963). 372 refers to the volume number of the reporter; US is the abbreviation for the reporter, the *United States Reports*; 335 is the beginning page of the decision; and 1963 is the year in which the case was decided. So if you went to the *United States Reports*, pulled volume 372, and turned to page 335, you would find the decision *Gideon v. Wainwright*.

It sounds complicated, but once you do it a few times, it becomes much easier.

How do you find the US Constitution?

The US Constitution is available online in many different locations. The US Senate's Web page contains a link to the US Constitution. See https://www.senate.gov/civics/constitution_item/constitution.htm.

Where do you find out about bills being considered by Congress?

The best place to go online is the congressional site at http://congress.gov/. It contains a wealth of information about both houses of Congress, the US House of Representatives, and the US Senate. You can search the current and past sessions of Congress for various bills that were introduced. You can even access committee and subcommittee hearings and testimony. In addition, each member of Congress has an individual Web page that you can access from THOMAS, a Web site operated by the Library of Congress. It is one of the most useful tools for someone who wants to learn more about the legal system at the federal legislative level.

Congress.gov replaced an earlier online site called the Thomas site at http://thomas.loc.gov, but you can still access THOMAS at http://thomas.loc.gov/home/thomas.php.

Who else can help a young person find the law?

Organizations such as those listed at the end of this chapter. Most of these organizations have a great deal of helpful information on their Web sites. If you contact the organization, it will send you information about its special areas of concern.

In addition, state and county bar associations usually have easy-to-read information on a variety of legal subjects. (A bar association is a professional association of lawyers.) Also, many bar associations have recorded telephone information on dozens of legal topics and good Web sites. Phone numbers of state and county bar associations are in the telephone book.

Bar associations often sponsor special programs to educate young people about the law, and often the lawyers who participate in them speak to student groups. The programs are very informative and are easy to follow, so watch for them.

Can't a young person simply call up a lawyer and inquire about a particular area of the law?

That shouldn't be your initial line of attack. Lawyers have a very hard time cutting away from work for phone calls from persons other than established clients. Furthermore, they are usually paid by the hour for their work, and their charges include time spent on the telephone.

FOR FURTHER READING

Davis, Judy K. and Carole Levitt. *Internet Legal Research on a Budget: Free and Low-Cost Resources for Lawyers*. 2nd ed. Chicago: ABA Book Publishing, 2020.

Delaney, Stephanie. *Electronic Legal Research: An Integrated Approach*. 2nd ed. Clifton Park, NY: Cengage Learning, 2008.

Elias, Stephen and Susan Levinkind, eds. *Legal Research: How to Find and Understand the Law*. 16th ed. Berkeley, CA: Nolo Press, 2013.
McLeod, Don. *The Internet Guide for the Legal Researcher*. 2nd ed. Teaneck, NJ: Infosources Publishing, 1997.
Murray, Jason. *The Legal List: Research on the Internet*. Lawyers Cooperative Publishing, Rochester, NY: 2022.
Van Dervort, Thomas R. and David L. Hudson Jr. *Law and the Legal System: An Introduction to Law and Legal Studies in the United States*. 3rd ed. New York: Wolters Kluwer, 2012.

OTHER INFORMATION SOURCES

Organizations

American Bar Association Center on Children and the Law, 1800 M Street NW, Ste. 200, Washington, DC 20005. (202) 331-2250.
American Civil Liberties Union Children's Rights Project, 125 Broad Street, 18th Floor, New York, NY 10004. (212) 549-2500. E-mail: aclu@aclu.org. Home page: www.aclu.org.
Juvenile Law Center, 801 Arch Street, Ste. 610, Philadelphia, PA 19107. (215) 625-0551. E-mail: HN2403@handsnet.org. Home page: www.usakids.org.
National Center for Youth Law, 114 Sansome Street, Ste. 900, San Francisco, CA 94104. (415) 543-3307. E-mail: info@youthlaw.org. Home page: www.youthlaw.org.

Online Sources

All Law: www.alllaw.com
Ask Auntie Nolo: www.nolo.com/auntie
Congress.gov: http://beta.congress.gov/
FindLaw: www.findlaw.com
Law for Kids: http://www.lawforkids.org/
Legal Information Institute (LII): www.law.cornell.edu
Public Access to Court Electronic Records: http://www.pacer.gov
THOMAS: http://thomas.loc.gov/home/thomas.php

CHAPTER 19

Immigration Law

IMMIGRATION

What does undocumented mean in the immigration field?

An undocumented person is a person who is living in the United States without proper documentation or authorization. An undocumented person either entered the United States without inspection or authorization, or they overstayed their temporary visa. Undocumented immigrants are called "undocumented" because they do not possess a valid visa or other immigration documents that allow them to stay lawfully in the United States. Another term for an undocumented person, though it has a more pejorative ring to it, is illegal alien.

What is a green card?

A green card, also known as the permanent resident card, allows an immigrant to live and work permanently in the United States with authorization. A person that holds a valid green card is called a lawful permanent resident.

How does one obtain a green card?

There are different ways a person can be eligible for a green card. An immigrant may be able to obtain a green card through their family. For example, if you are the immediate relative of a US citizen, you can apply for a green card. This would apply if your spouse is a US citizen, if you are an unmarried child under the age of twenty-one of a US citizen, or the parent of a child who is over twenty-one years of age and a citizen of the United States.

You also can obtain a green card through employment. There are certain immigrants who are considered so-called first preference immigrant workers. These include immigrants with demonstrated extraordinary ability in the arts, science, education, business, or athletics. Second preference immigrant workers include those who are a member of a profession that requires an advanced degree, have excellent ability in the arts or sciences, or seeking a national interest waiver. Third preference immigrant workers are those who are skilled workers, professionals, or unskilled workers. Employment is a major way that many immigrants obtain a green card in the United States.

There are other categories of individuals eligible for a green card. One of these is the so-called special immigrant category. These are immigrants who are religious workers, special immigrant juveniles (more on this later in a separate question), an Afghanistan or Iraqi national who worked for the US government, or an international broadcaster.

Another category of individuals eligible for a green card are those who are the victims of significant domestic abuse (battery or extreme cruelty). The abused spouse of a US citizen or lawful permanent resident is eligible to apply for a green card. An abused child (as long as they are unmarried and under twenty-one years of age) of a US citizen or lawful permanent resident also can apply for a green card. The abused parent of a US citizen also can apply.

What is special immigrant juvenile status (SIJS)?

SIJS is a method to remain in the United States for a noncitizen juvenile. A noncitizen juvenile can apply for this status if they are under eighteen or twenty-one (depending on the state they live in); unmarried; and have been abandoned, abused, or neglected by a parent. If a minor obtains SJIS status, they have permission to remain in the United States, are eligible to obtain a work permit, and are eligible to apply for a green card.

Generally, to obtain SJIS status, the minor's attorney must be able to establish that they have been abused, abandoned, or neglected by one of their parents. To do so, an adult person, usually a parent or relative, must request a court to be the juvenile's guardian. The court must determine that the abuse, abandonment, or neglect took place. The court also must determine that it would not be in the best interests of the minor to be returned to their home country.

What are other ways that noncitizen juveniles might be able to immigrate to the United States and lawfully stay there?

Noncitizen juveniles may be able to apply for a U visa, apply for protection under a federal law known as the Violence Against Women Act, and to apply for asylum.

What is asylum?

Asylum is a discretionary process that immigration authorities have the power to grant to foreign nationals living in the United States or to those immigrants who cross the border and are deemed to be refugees. Refugees are individuals who flee their country and cannot return safely because they have a well-founded fear of persecution based on their race, religion, nationality, membership in a particular social group, or political opinion.

An asylee is a person who has been granted asylum. Asylees can stay and work in the United States, can apply for a Social Security card, and can even petition to have some of their family members join them in the United States. After one year, an asylee can apply for lawful permanent resident status. Colloquially, this means that the asylee can obtain a green card.

How does a person apply for asylum?

There are different ways to apply for asylum. One way is through what is called affirmative asylum. This is where the immigrant, who is not facing possible deportation proceedings (called "removal" proceedings), applies for asylum through the US Citizenship and Immigration Services (USCIS). If the asylum officer with the USCIS refuses to grant the person asylum and the person is in the United States without authorization, the applicant is referred to an immigration court for removal proceedings. This is the process by which US immigration officials petition the court to have a person removed from the United States.

However, if removal proceedings are brought against an immigrant, that person can renew their petition for asylum. This type of asylum application is called defensive asylum. In other words, the immigrant is facing potential future deportation during the removal process and defensively responds to this action by applying for asylum.

Are there time limits on applying for asylum?

Yes, the general rule is that a person must apply for asylum within one year of entry into the United States. However, there are a few narrow exceptions. For example, if there are extraordinary circumstances that may explain why there is a delay or if new circumstances in the person's country of origin cause the person to fear persecution upon return to their home country.

What is DACA?

DACA is the acronym for the Deferred Action for Childhood Arrivals. It applies to young people who arrived in the United States when they were under sixteen years of age but never achieved lawful permanent status. The idea is that these young people should have an opportunity to remain in the United States and not live under the constant fear of possible deportation.

To be eligible for DACA you had to come to the United States before your sixteenth birthday, had no lawful status, are currently in school or completed schooling in the United States, and have no serious criminal history. Only those who arrived in the United States by June 15, 2007, were included in DACA.

What is a U visa?

A U visa is a humanitarian form of immigration relief granted to those noncitizens—including teens—who have been the victims of crime and who help law enforcement fight that crime. The applicant must submit a form to the USCIS in which indicate that they are a victim of crime. They must also obtain a certificate from a law enforcement agency that attests or affirms that the applicant assisted law enforcement in battling the crime. Without the certification from a law enforcement agency, an immigrant cannot obtain a U visa.

Some states have passed laws that assist immigrants in obtaining law enforcement certifications necessary to obtain a U visa. According to the Immigration Law Resource Coalition, the following states have such laws: Arkansas, California, Connecticut, Delaware, Illinois, Louisiana, Maryland, Montana, Nevada, North Dakota, Rhode Island, Vermont, Washington, and Wyoming. However, some of these laws only apply if the underlying crime is sex trafficking.

What is a t-visa?

A t-visa is a special form of immigration relief that can be granted to minors or adults who were victims of "severe" human trafficking or labor and who would suffer an "extreme hardship" if they were returned to their home country.

If a child is born in the United States but both of her parents are noncitizens, is that child a US citizen?

Yes, the US Constitution provides that any person born in the United States is a US citizen. Section 1 of the Fourteenth Amendment of the US Constitution provides: "All persons born or naturalized in the United States, and subject to the jurisdiction thereof, are citizens of the United States and of the State wherein they reside."

What if a juvenile immigrant commits a crime?

Most juveniles who commit a crime are not charged as adults in regular criminal court. Instead, they have what are known as delinquency adjudications in juvenile court. And a juvenile adjudication is not nearly the same thing as a criminal conviction for an adult offender. The general rule is that a juvenile delinquency does not count as a criminal conviction for immigration law purposes.

However, there are two caveats to this general proposition. The first is that most states have juvenile transfer laws in which prosecutors can try a juvenile as an adult if they commit certain very serious crimes. For example, if a juvenile shoots and kills someone, the juvenile may well be tried as an adult. A related issue is that some states have so-called youthful offender statutes. These are a hybrid between the adult and juvenile criminal legal systems.

The second caveat is that some juvenile adjudications can have an impact on immigration status. For example, immigration authorities in considering admission decisions of juveniles and adults do not simply look at whether a person has a criminal record; they also look at conduct-based actions. For example, if a minor has been involved in drug trafficking or gang activity that could have extremely negative consequences for future immigration matters even if there is not a clear conviction.

Can an undocumented or DACA student receive federal financial aid for college?

No, an undocumented or DACA student cannot receive federal financial aid for college. However, in many states, undocumented students can receive state or local financial aid. They may also be eligible for private scholarships.

Can an undocumented or DACA student receive in-state tuition?

This depends upon individual state law. In some states, undocumented or DACA students are not eligible for in-state tuition, but in other states they are.

FOR FURTHER READING

Das, Alina. *No Justice in the Shadows: How America Criminalizes Immigrants.* New York: Bold Type Books, 2020.
Kamhi, Allison and Sarah Lakhani. "A Guide to State Laws on U Visas and T Certifications." *IRCA*, April 2020. u_visa_and_t_visa_pa-04.2020.pdf (ilrc.org).
Ledesma, Alberto. *Diary of a Reluctant Dreamer: Undocumented Vignettes from a Pre-American Life.* Columbus, OH: Mad Creek Books, 2017.

ONLINE SOURCES

American Immigration Lawyer Association https://www.aila.org/
Executive Office for Immigration Review https://www.justice.gov/eoir
Find an Immigration Court https://www.justice.gov/eoir/find-immigration-court-and-access-internet-based-hearings
ILRC's one-pager on "Special Immigrant Juvenile Status" at https://www.ilrc.org/sites/default/files/resources/sijs_one-pager_jan_2022.pdf

CHAPTER 20

Issues Facing Trans Youth

TRANS YOUTH ISSUES

What is nonbinary?

Nonbinary refers to a person who falls outside the gender binary system of identifying as either boy/man or girl/woman. Instead, a nonbinary person has elements or often identifies with both genders. Nonbinary individuals, who are often trans, often prefer the pronoun "they" instead of "she" or "he."

How does a trans youth change his gender identity on documents?

To change one's gender identity or gender marker on official identification, such as a drivers' license or birth certificate, generally requires a court order from a judge in your respective state. To obtain a court order, you generally have to file a petition to the court asking for the relief that you seek. Your state may have some of these forms online for you to use. If the court grants the petition, it will sign an order that officially changes your gender identity. You can then use the language from this court order to show to officials at different state agencies.

These state agencies will have to abide by a judicial order in that respective state. Other states may require a letter from a licensed therapist that explains you are receiving gender-affirming care. Again, state laws can differ quite significantly so you will need to research the law in your individual state.

Will a court grant such a petition without a hearing?

Generally, not. If the petitioner is a teen under the age of eighteen, the court will hold a hearing to hear the petition. In fact, generally, if a person is under the age of eighteen, their parent or legal guardian will need to file the petition on their behalf. The judge may ask questions as to why the individual wants to change the gender marker. The judge also will want to determine that the individual resides in the area of the court's jurisdiction or power. This ensures that the judge has the authority to issue the requested order.

What if a trans minor's parents disagree about the change in gender?

Most courts will apply a version of a familiar standard in family law called "the best interests of the child" or the "best interests of the minor." The court will hear testimony from the minor and both parents to determine what is the best course of action for the young person. The parent or guardian who is supporting the minor's change in gender identity generally will need to provide some evidence as to why such is a good idea or positive development for the minor.

Are there different standards in different states for those seeking a change in gender identity?

Yes, state laws differ in this area quite significantly. For example, California only requires an individual to present a court order affirming the change in the individual's gender identity. No medical documentation is needed.

However, other states require medical documentation of some sort. For example, in several states—including Louisiana and Tennessee—an individual has to provide a healthcare provider's letter stating that the individuals' gender transition is permanent, completed, or successful.

Are there some states that do not allow a change in gender on a birth certificate?

Yes, there are a few states that simply do not allow a trans youth, or anyone else, to change the gender on a birth certificate. These states are Kansas, Ohio, and Tennessee.

Do any states recognize nonbinary gender identities?

A few states do recognize nonbinary gender identities. An individual who identifies as nonbinary does not identify as either male or female. Nonbinary refers to individuals who have elements of both genders and do not recognize these binary categories. The *Trans Youth Handbook* provides:

> In Arkansas, California, Colorado, Indiana, Maine, Maryland, Minnesota, Nevada, New York City, Oregon, and Washington D.C., you can get a nonbinary gender marker on your state ID and/or driver's license. In California, Colorado, Nevada, New Jersey,

New Mexico, and New York City, you can get a nonbinary gender marker on your birth certificate.

Can a transgender individual who files a petition to change the name to conform to their gender preference ask for the court documents to be sealed?

Yes, a transgender individual who can show that they would face discrimination and harassment can request a court to seal the records of the attempts to change the name. Generally, under most states laws, an individual can apply to seal records in a case if they can show by a preponderance of the evidence good cause supported by specific examples of the need for the sealing.

Recently, a New Jersey appeals court reversed a trial court's denial of a transgender individual's request to seal name-change records. The trial judge had ruled that discrimination comes in many forms and fashions and there was nothing unusual or specific to this case. However, the appeals court found that the individuals showed a likelihood of clear injury or harassment if the records were open to the public. The appeals court also focused on the privacy rights of the individual requesting the sealing of records.

What is transition-related care?

Transition-related care, also known as gender-affirming care, refers to medical procedures in which a trans person undergoes medical procedures that comport with their affirmed gender. Examples of transition-related care may include puberty blockers, gender-confirming surgeries, hormone treatment, and social transition.

Have there been many bills introduced in state legislatures against transgender individuals?

Yes. According to the American Civil Liberties Union (ACLU), there have been more than hundred bills introduced in state legislatures that are considered "anti-trans" measures. Some of the measures deny gender-affirming health care to trans youth. Other measures limit trans kids' ability to participate in sports with their preferred gender.

Do some states have laws banning transgender youth from obtaining medical care?

Some states have passed restrictive laws that prohibit trans youth from obtaining gender-affirming medical care. Some of these measures prohibit healthcare professionals from providing or even referring transgender young people for medically necessary health care. The law would also bar any state funds or insurance coverage for gender-affirming health care for transgender people under eighteen, and it would allow private insurers to refuse to cover gender-affirming care for people of any age. Many of these laws are facing court challenges currently, so make sure to stay up to date on this vastly changing legal arena.

What should a trans youth do if facing bullying or harassment at school?

The trans student immediately should report the bullying or harassment at school to the appropriate authorities—often a principal or assistant principal. One reason for this of course is the person in authority often has the ability to address the situation and take immediate corrective action by punishing the bullies or harassers. There is another reason why it is important to report the conduct to authorities—so that they are on notice that it is occurring. A school system or school officials are not liable for third-party conduct that they really don't know or should know about. Thus, reporting the harassing conduct puts school officials on notice that they must take some action to address the problem.

Do trans youth have a right to be called by the pronoun or pronouns of their choice?

Yes, school officials should address a trans youth by the pronoun of the individual's choice. There may not be an official state law that requires such, but that is the prevailing trend in school systems across the country is a general recognition that officials should use the pronoun choice of the student.

Can a trans youth use the restroom or locker room of their preferred gender identity?

Yes, according to a 2021 policy letter issued by the US Department of Education on transgender students. The policy applies to every school, preschool, college, and university that receives federal funding. One result of this policy implementation has been a marked increase in the number of schools offering single stall, gender-neutral bathrooms.

The DOE policy letter also directs schools and universities to use the preferred names and pronunciations of transgender students and let them dress according to their gender identification.

However, a few Republican-led states have passed laws that mandate anti-transgender policies in schools. The most visible example is Florida, where one bill (H.B. 1069) asserted that "it shall be the policy of every public K-12 educational institution" that "a person's sex is an immutable biological trait and that it is false to ascribe to a person a pronoun that does not correspond to such person's sex." Under the law, which applies to students and teachers alike, transgender individuals may no longer use preferred pronouns, titles, or names if they don't match their "biological sex," nor can they use bathrooms that align with their gender identity. These rules, first introduced for the 2023–24 academic year, are expected to be challenged in court as unconstitutional and discriminatory.

Can transgender athletes participate in sports teams of their preferred gender identity?

It depends on the individual state. Some states allow transgender youth to participate on either boys or girls teams based on the transgender youth's choice. However, other states have specific bans in place. These laws are being challenged in court.

Does a trans youth need parental consent for a sex-change medical procedure?

A trans teen may need parental consent before being able to undergo a medical procedure that will assist in transition-related medical care. You need to check your individual state law, as state laws vary with how they handle parental consent. In some states, older minors do not need parental consent. But, in many states, parental consent is still required.

Can an employer fire an employee simply because the employee is transgender?

No, the US Supreme Court ruled in *Bostock v. Clayton County* (2020) that an employer violates Title VII of the Civil Rights Act of 1964 if the employer fires an employee for being transgender. The court reasoned that firing someone for being transgender is, in essence, firing them because of their sex. And Title VII clearly prohibits sex discrimination. Justice Neil Gorsuch explained in his majority opinion:

> At bottom, these cases involve no more than the straightforward application of legal terms with plain and settled meanings. For an employer to discriminate against employees for being homosexual or transgender, the employer must intentionally discriminate against individual men and women in part because of sex. That has always been prohibited by Title VII's plain terms—and that "should be the end of the analysis."
>
> . . .
>
> In Title VII, Congress adopted broad language making it illegal for an employer to rely on an employee's sex when deciding to fire that employee. We do not hesitate to recognize today a necessary consequence of that legislative choice: An employer who fires an individual merely for being gay or transgender defies the law.

FOR FURTHER READING

In General

Chen, Alexander and Assaf Orr, trans. *Youth Handbook.* https://assets.turtl.co/pdfs/tenant=harvard/trans-youth-handbook.pdf.
Fisher, Fox and Owl Fisher, trans. *Teen Survival Guide.* London: Jessica Kingsley Publishing, 2018.
Gilbert, Jen and Julia Sinclair-Palm, eds. *Trans Youth in Education.* London: Routledge, 2019.
Krieger, Irwin. *Counseling Transgender and Non-Binary Youth.* London: Jessica Kingsley Publishing, 2017.

Online Sources

ACLU on Transgender Rights: https://www.aclu.org/issues/lgbtq-rights/transgender-rights
Human Rights Campaign: https:/www.hrc.org
Lambda Legal: https://www.lambdalegal.org/issues/teens
Transgender Law Center: https://transgenderlawcenter.org/

CHAPTER 21

Teens in a Virtual World

SEXTING

What is sexting?

Sexting refers to the distribution of sexually explicit digital material by juveniles. Its name comes from a combination of the words "sex" and "texting." Texting is a most common form of communication using cell phones. Instead of texting messages to each other, some teens send sexually explicit pictures of their private parts or overall nude body to others. For example, if a teenage boy or girl sends a picture of his or her private parts to another teenager, that is sexting. If a teenager sends pictures of himself or herself in lewd positions, that could be considered sexting.

Some teens will then upload the cell phone pictures to the Internet. A 2008 survey by the National Campaign to Prevent Teen and Unplanned Pregnancy and Cosmogirl.com revealed that nearly 20 percent of teens have participated in sexting. The same survey revealed that 38 percent of teens acknowledged that they or their friends had posted nude or seminude pictures on the Internet. There have been numerous incidents of teens caught sexting at school. Sometimes these acts have led not only to school suspensions but also to criminal charges.

The problem became widespread enough that state legislatures have begun to pass laws prohibiting such behavior. For example, Arkansas law provides:

> A juvenile commits the offense of possession of sexually explicit digital material if the juvenile purposely creates, produces, distributes, presents, transmits, posts, exchanges, disseminates, or possesses through a computer, wireless communication device, or digital media, any sexually explicit digital material.

The Arkansas law provides that this crime of sexting is a misdemeanor. First-offender juveniles will have to perform 8 hours of community service.

Florida's law defines the offense of sexting as follows:

A minor commits the offense of sexting if he or she knowingly:

> Uses a computer, or any other device capable of electronic data transmission or distribution, to transmit or distribute to another minor any photograph or video of any person which depicts nudity . . . and is harmful to minors
>
> Possesses a photograph or video of any person that was transmitted or distributed by another minor which depicts nudity . . . and is harmful to minors.

Note that under the Florida law, it can be a crime to merely possess the sexually explicit images in digital format. However, Florida's law also provides that a minor does not commit the offense of sexting if he or she did not solicit or request the material.

Louisiana's law on sexting is a little different. It provides:

> No person under the age of seventeen years shall knowingly and voluntarily use a computer or telecommunication device to transmit an indecent visual depiction of himself to another person.
>
> No person under the age of seventeen years shall knowingly possess or transmit an indecent visual depiction that was transmitted by another under the age of seventeen years.

These examples from Arkansas, Florida, and Louisiana show that state legislatures have defined sexting differently. One question to ask is whether there are different penalties based on the age of the offender. For example, in the state of Utah, if an adult person engages in sexting, he or she will be charged with a felony. However, if a minor engages in sexting, he or she will be charged only with a misdemeanor.

If an adult engages in sexting, the adult could face child pornography charges. There have been cases in which young adults engaged in sexting to minors and were charged under child pornography statutes. If convicted, the person has to register as a sex offender—often for the rest of his or her life.

Is there a possibility for diversion if a minor is caught sexting?

It depends on the individual state law, which may give discretion to the juvenile court judge and the prosecuting attorney for diversion, an option in which juveniles are not placed in a penal setting but in a different program more focused on rehabilitation. (For an explanation of diversion programs, see Chapter 12, "Teens and Crime"). For example, West Virginia's law gives judges and prosecutors the discretion to place a minor in a sexting educational diversion program. The law provides that any sexting educational diversion program must address the following issues:

1. The legal consequences of and penalties for sharing sexually suggestive or explicit materials, including applicable federal and state statutes;
2. The nonlegal consequences of sharing sexually suggestive or explicit materials including, but not limited to, the effect on relationships, loss of educational and employment opportunities, and being barred or removed from school programs and extracurricular activities;
3. How the unique characteristics of cyberspace and the Internet, including searchability, replicability, and an infinite audience, can produce long-term and unforeseen consequences for sharing sexually suggestive or explicit materials; and
4. The connection between bullying and cyberbullying and minors sharing sexually suggestive or explicit materials.

New York has a similar law, which provides the possibility that young persons twenty years of age or younger who commit sexting or cyberbullying may be sent to an "education reform program," as long as the alleged victim is not more than five years younger than the offender. This option may not be available in many states.

Isn't it a violation of a teen's right to privacy to prosecute him or her for sending nude pictures to a boyfriend or girlfriend?

It is questionable whether a court would accept this argument. A sixteen-year-old female in Florida advanced this argument in a case in which she and her seventeen-year-old boyfriend recorded themselves having sex and then sent the images from one computer to another. They didn't send the material to a third person. The teen argued that prosecuting her for the act violated her state constitutional right to privacy. A Florida appeals court rejected that argument in *A.H. v. State* (2007): "First, the decision to take photographs and to keep a record that may be shown to people in the future weighs against a reasonable expectation of privacy. . . . Second . . . neither [of the minors] had a reasonable expectation that the other would not show the photos to a third party." The court also explained that the Florida legislature had a compelling, or very strong, interest in ensuring that no videotape, picture, or film of minors engaged in sexual conduct was disseminated.

What happens if a teen gets caught sexting at school?

He or she likely will be suspended from school. Many school districts have developed policies specifically related to sexting. This behavior also could lead to criminal charges if school officials report the matter to local law enforcement and law enforcement officials decide to charge the teen criminally.

Sadly, many teenagers probably feel as if they all have done is engage in harmless flirting. Nothing could be further from the truth. The "harmless flirting" may result in serious felony charges and convictions.

If a state doesn't have a law specific to sexting, is there no penalty?

Not necessarily. A prosecutor may decide that the act of sexting falls under an existing state harassment, indecency, or harmful-to-minors law. Do not assume that just because your state doesn't have a sexting law, you have a free pass to engage in this conduct. There have been instances in which some older minors have been charged with, or have been threatened with being charged with, child pornography for sexting.

For example, a Pennsylvania teenager faced child pornography charges after she posted on Facebook a video of two other minors engaged in sexual conduct. A Pennsylvania court later dismissed the charges, but the teen still had to go through the turmoil of the criminal justice system. An eighteen-year-old teenager in Iowa was less fortunate after he texted a picture of his erect genitalia to a fourteen-year-old classmate with the message "I love you." The girl's father saw the text message, or sexting, and contacted the police. The eighteen-year-old was charged with and convicted of distributing obscene material to a minor.

If a teenager is convicted of a sexual offense, what are the consequences?

There are severe consequences if a teenager is convicted of or declared delinquent for committing a sexual offense. Depending on individual state law, the teenager may have to register as a sex offender. This is a stigma that follows the convicted teen and may impact his or her future negatively with regard to educational and employment opportunities, not to mention social ostracism. For example, in Iowa—where the eighteen-year-old was convicted of sexting a picture of his erect genitalia—registration for a sexual offense lasts for at least ten years and can last up to life.

CYBERBULLYING

What is cyberbullying?

Cyberbullying is electronic communication designed to harass, threaten, bully, intimidate, or abuse another person. It is online bullying, a type of conduct that has led some teens to commit suicide or at least have serious self-esteem problems. Many states now criminalize cyberbullying, and school districts have adopted policies prohibiting such conduct.

Cyberbullying is a specific type of online harassment that occurs between teens. Note that some states have broader online harassment laws that criminalize the conduct for both adults and minors. Another type of online harassment—usually applied to adults—is called cyberstalking.

See Chapter 2, "At School," for discussions of cyberbullying in school.

What are some examples of cyberbullying?

There is no specific laundry list for what constitutes cyberbullying, as harassment and bullying can take many forms. Cyberbullying can involve direct attacks on another person, indirect forms of harassment, or the posting of pictures or images of another person.

But keep in mind that the conduct generally must be intentional and must be repeated. One incident may not be enough, unless it is really egregious—because cyberbullying usually involves a pattern of conduct. Some examples of cyberbullying are repeated name-calling and mocking of another's race, religion, appearance, sexual orientation, or family. It may be a series of threats to physically or mentally torture another teen. It could be teens posting embarrassing or humiliating pictures of another teen in digital format.

Certainly teens should read their school policy on cyberbullying and refrain from conduct that harasses or demeans other teens.

Are cyberbullying laws confined to online harassment at school?

No. Cyberbullying can take place at school, but often it does not. Some state laws that address cyberbullying do not confine it to the school context. Cyberbullying is the act of transmitting, sending, or posting communications by electronic means with the purpose of threatening or harassing another person.

Electronic communication can refer to textual, visual, written, or oral communication of any kind made through the use of a computer online service, Internet service, telephone, or any other means of electronic communication to a local bulletin board service, an Internet chat room, electronic mail, a social networking site, or an online messaging service.

Other states may not use the term "cyberbullying," instead using terms such as "online harassment" or "computer harassment."

What happens if a teen creates a false profile of another teen?

Creating a false profile of another teen can have both criminal and civil law consequences. California's educational law specifically lists creating a false profile of another student online as an offense for which a student may be suspended and/or expelled. Creating a false profile could fall within a state's cyberbullying law and trigger criminal law consequences. It also could lead to defamation or invasion of privacy civil law claims, which are discussed in the next section.

ONLINE DEFAMATION, INVASION OF PRIVACY, AND THREATS

What is defamation?

Defamation refers to published false statements of fact that harm another's reputation. It includes both written and oral statements. Written defamation is libel, while oral defamation is slander. Some types of statements are defamatory per se. For example, falsely accusing someone of having a communicable sexual disease is presumed defamatory.

What is Internet libel?

Internet libel, or online defamation, is a type of defamation in which the speaker or poster makes a false statement of fact online that harms another's reputation. Sometimes young people mistakenly think that the Internet is a legal-free liability zone. Nothing could be further from the truth. If a teenager posts a false statement of fact about another on Facebook, that could be defamation.

The basic rules for print defamation apply online. Just as a newspaper article can contain defamatory material, so can material posted on a social networking site. For example, let's say a teenage student takes a dislike to one of her teachers and then posts online a false statement: "Teacher X is a pervert and a convicted sex offender." The teacher could sue the student for defamation. Don't assume that an Internet post has no legal ramifications. More and more libel cases are arising from statements that originated as posts on the Internet.

What is the significance of a public official or public figure in defamation law?

Public officials or public figures have a higher burden of proof in defamation lawsuits than private persons. A public official is a government official, such as a governor, mayor, city council member, or other politician. A public figure is someone who is famous or well-known, such as a movie star, a professional sports star, or entertainer.

A public official or public figure who sues for defamation has to show that the defendant made a false statement of fact with actual malice, which means that the defendant knew the statement was false or the defendant acted with reckless disregard as to the truth or falsity of the statement. Furthermore, the public official or public figure plaintiff has to show actual malice by clear and convincing evidence.

On the other hand, a private person suing for defamation generally only has to show that the defendant was negligent or at fault.

What is the best defense to a defamation lawsuit?

Truth is often the best defense, because true statements are not defamatory or libelous. In other words, a required element of a defamation claim is that the defendant communicated a false statement of fact. Thus, if a statement is true it cannot be defamatory.

If someone sues you for defamation, you can defend yourself by showing the truthfulness of your statement.

What if a statement is substantially true, can it be defamation?

No, under the substantial truth doctrine, if the gist of a statement is true, then it is not defamatory. Thus, if a statement is substantially true, then the defendant is protected and the plaintiff's libel claim fails.

Have school officials ever sued students for defamation?

Yes. The cases are relatively rare, but some teachers and school officials have resorted to the civil justice system for relief after their school districts do not punish students. A school district may be reluctant to punish a student for outrageous online comments that are made by the student off-campus. The school district may determine that it does not have jurisdiction over the matter. Thus, the teachers or other school officials who have been the target of false online posts may feel they have no choice but to file a lawsuit. In 1999, three teachers in Indiana sued a student for defamation after the student falsely posted on the Internet the statement that the teachers were devil worshippers.

What is invasion of privacy?

Invasion of privacy is another civil cause of action, which arises when a person unreasonably interferes with another person's right to be let alone. Several categories of invasion of privacy have developed over time: (1) appropriation, (2) public disclosure of private facts, (3) false light, and (4) intrusion on physical solitude. Appropriation refers to taking someone's name or likeness for commercial purposes without his or her permission. Public disclosure of private facts occurs when a defendant publishes private truths about a person in which the public has no legitimate concern and that cause the person shame or humiliation. False light refers to making statements about someone that places him or her in a false light in a way that would be highly offensive to a reasonable person. Intrusion refers to invasive conduct that would be highly offensive to a reasonable person.

Can these types of invasion of privacy take place in a virtual world?

Yes, they can. If a teenager posts highly sensitive information about another person on a social networking site, that could be invasion of privacy as the public disclosure of private facts. This tort, or civil cause of action, allows someone to sue even if the underlying information is true. The harm is not in the falsity of the statement, but that the information was supposed to remain private. The disclosure of medical information, such as the contracting of a sexual disease, could give rise to such a lawsuit.

What happens if a teen posts a threat about someone online?

There could be serious consequences for making threatening statements. There is no free speech right to utter true threats. Every state has a law or a series of laws that prohibits threats. There are different definitions of a true threat, but generally it is a communication that a reasonable recipient would regard as a serious expression of the intent to commit harm. Note that a communication can be a true threat even if the speaker does not actually intend to carry out the threat. True threat laws are designed to protect the recipient from the fear and disruption caused by threatening statements.

These laws by and large have survived constitutional challenges. Threats are unlawful anywhere—whether uttered to a fellow student, teacher, principal, or anyone else. If a threat is made against another student or teacher, the offending student likely will face a long-term suspension or even an expulsion. The same conduct, however, could also lead to criminal charges.

Consider the case *In re Joshua L.* (2012) in California. A high school student named Joshua L. posted a threat on his Facebook profile ranting and talking about possibly putting a bullet in the heads of two classmates. One of those classmates scrolled down Joshua L.'s Facebook page and saw the threatening language. He reported it to the school's security guard, who reported the incident to the deputy sheriff. Law enforcement interviewed the classmate and Joshua L., who said that he was just ranting and venting—that he did not really intend to make a threat.

However, the court found Joshua L. delinquent for violating a state antithreat law, which provided that

> [a]ny person who willfully threatens to commit a crime which will result in death or great bodily injury to another person, with the specific intent that the statement, made verbally, in writing, or by means of an electronic communication device, is to be taken as a threat, even if there is no intent of actually carrying it out, which, on its face and under the circumstances in which it is made, is so unequivocal, unconditional, immediate, and specific as to convey to the person threatened, a gravity of purpose and an immediate prospect of execution of the threat, and thereby causes that person reasonably to be in sustained fear for his or her own safety.

Note that this California law provides that a person can make an unlawful threat even if he or she doesn't actually intend to carry out the threat. Joshua L. argued that his posting was private and that he used Facebook as a diary of sorts. The problem with that argument was that it was posted so that other people—including the two classmates he wrote about—could read the posting.

There is a clear lesson from this case for teenagers. If you get really mad at a classmate or someone else, do not threaten by ranting or venting on Facebook. Those rants and vents may actually lead to criminal charges.

Can a teen face criminal charges for simply posting about violence but not targeting a specific person?

Yes, a teen could face charges, as it really depends on the context. There have been instances in which teens have faced criminal charges for writing comments about recent school shootings. Consider the Ohio case *In re P.T.* (2013). P.T. was a fifteen-year-old high school sophomore who posted comments on Facebook right after the terrifying school shooting at Sandy Hook Elementary School in Newtown, Connecticut. P.T. wrote:

> Kids were shot. Who cares? Dead kids are dead kids. Murder is a good thing. This is a serious status. I really think murder is a good thing. . . . I have been saying for years now that there needs to be another mass murder, I have said this too [*sic*]

> many people. . . . I'd have done this job myself if I could have. All forms of life are insignificant. . . . They are going to die. I might as well help them out.

Several parents of other students in P.T.'s school contacted the police, who placed P.T. under arrest for the criminal charges of "inducing a panic" and "aggravated menacing." He was placed in a secure facility and then later sent home with electronic monitoring. A juvenile judge declared P.T. delinquent for inducing a panic and the lesser offense of menacing. The judge placed P.T. on probation and ordered him to serve fifty-five days on electronic monitoring. The teen also had to participate in family counseling, complete 70 hours of community service, and pay court costs.

On appeal, P.T. contended that he was not delinquent for the criminal offenses because he did not threaten or target a particular person, but just spoke about violence in general. The Ohio appeals court upheld the juvenile judge, finding that "it is sufficient if P.T. was aware that his conduct would 'probably' cause another to fear physical harm." The appeals court emphasized that P.T.'s conduct "must be viewed within the context of a highly emotional, fearful, and hyper-vigilant climate existing in the immediate aftermath of the Sandy Hook shooting." The appeals court concluded that P.T. was aware that his menacing Facebook posts would cause others to panic.

IDENTITY THEFT

What is identity theft?

Identity theft is a crime in which someone uses another's personally identifiable information for fraudulent or other criminal purposes. Identity theft can occur in many ways, but teens need to be aware of the specific dangers of online identity theft. Individuals may seek out your Social Security, credit card, and banking account numbers online. They can use this information to make fraudulent purchases, empty your bank account, file false insurance claims, and apply for driver's licenses. The US Department of Justice warns that "in recent years, the Internet has become an appealing place for criminals to obtain identifying data, such as passwords or even banking information."

What are phishing and pharming?

Phishing is the sending of false e-mail pretending to be a legitimate business. The e-mail claims to need your updated personal information and seeks to obtain your bank account number or credit card number. It then provides a fraudulent link asking for the information. Be wary of any unsolicited e-mail message that requires you to click a link and then provide personal information. Common examples of phishing include an e-mail that purposes to be from a bank, asking for updated account information, or an e-mail from your credit card company that claims to be doing a security check or an update on your account.

The reality is that phishing is a real problem. Do not give out your personally identifiable information or your financial information when you receive one of these e-mails. There are other types of similar scams. One of these is pharming, in which a hacker installs malicious software on a personal computer that will redirect your clicked information on a site to a fraudulent site, which then records all your key information.

FOR FURTHER READING

Bochi, Goali Saeda. *The Social Media Workbook for Teens*. Oakland, CA: Instant Help, 2019.

Boucek, Sara G. "Dealing with the Nightmare of Sexting." *School Administrator*, August 2009. https://www.aasa.org/SchoolAdministratorArticle.aspx?id=4386.

Bowker, Art and Michael Sullivan. "Sexting: Risky Actions and Overreactions." *FBI Law Enforcement Bulletin*, July 2010. http://www.fbi.gov/stats-services/publications/law-enforcement-bulletin/july-2010/sexting.

Hanks, James C. *School Bullying: How Long Is the Arm of the Law?* Chicago: American Bar Association (ABA) Publishing, 2012.

Heitner, Devorah. *Screenwise: Helping Kids Survive (and Thrive) in Their Digital World*. New York: Routledge, 2016.

Hinduia, Sameer and Justin Pratcher. *School Climate 2.0: Preventing Cyberbullying and Sexting One Classroom at a Time*. Thousand Oaks, CA: Corwin, 2012.

Mitchell, Kimberly J., David Finkelhor, Lisa M. Jones, and Janis Wolak. "Prevalence and Characteristics of Youth Sexting: A National Study." *Pediatrics*, December 2011. http://pediatrics.aappublications.org/content/early/2011/11/30/peds.2011-1730.abstract?rss=1.

Willard, Nancy E. *Positive Relations @ School (& Elsewhere): Legal Parameters and Positive Strategies to Address Bullying & Harassment*. Eugene, OR: Embrace Civility in the Digital Age, 2014.

OTHER INFORMATION SOURCES

Organizations

American Association of School Administrators. 1615 Duke Street, Alexandria, VA, 22314. (703) 528-0700. E-mail: info@aasa.org Home page: https://www.aasa.org/.

National Center for Missing and Exploited Children, 699 Prince Street, Alexandria, VA, 22314-3175. (703) 224-2150. E-mail: http://www.missingkids.com/. Contact. Home page: http://www.ncmec.org/.

National Conference of State Legislators. 7700 East First Place, Denver, CO, 80230. (303) 334-7700. E-mail: http://www.ncsl.org/aboutus/ncslservice/ncsl-contact.aspx. Home page: http://www.ncsl.org.

Online Sources

American Academy of Pediatrics, "Talking to Kids and Teens about Social Media and Texting" (June 2009): http://www.aap.org/en-us/about-the-aap/aap-press-room/news-features-and-safety-tips/pages/Talking-to-Kids-and-Teens-About-Social-Media-and-Sexting.aspx

High Technology Crime Investigation Association Internet Safety for Children Campaign: http://www.htcia.org/isfc/.

"How Does Cyberbullying Work," by Perry Aftab: http://www.aftab.com/index.php?page=how-does-cyberbullying-work

Justice Department on identity theft: http://www.justice.gov/criminal/fraud/websites/idtheft.html
National Conference of State Legislatures on sexting legislation in 2013: http://www.ncsl.org/research/telecommunications-and-information-technology/2013-sexting-legislation.aspx
PhishTank: https://www.phishtank.com/what_is_phishing.php
Report on the dangers of phishing: http://www.justice.gov/opa/report_on_phishing.pdf
"Sex and Tech: Results from a Survey of Teens and Young Adults": http://thenati onalcampaign.org/resource/sex-and-tech
US Department of Justice, Project Safe Childhood: http://www.projectsafechildhood.gov/.
US government antibullying site: http://www.stopbullying.gov

GLOSSARY

abandonment. The act of totally ignoring one's parental duties. Abandonment usually is established by actions of a parent showing an intent to both abandon a minor child and forfeit parental rights.

abuse. Physical or emotional mistreatment of a person.

accomplice. A person who voluntarily helps another commit or attempt to commit a crime.

actual malice. This is a standard in defamation law for public officials and public figures. They have to show that the defendant made a defamatory statement knowing it was false or acted in reckless disregard as to whether the statement was true or false.

ADA. Americans with Disabilities Act of 1990, a federal law that prohibits discrimination against workers with disabilities.

ADEA. Age Discrimination in Employment Act of 1967, a federal law that prohibits discriminating against workers forty years of age or older.

adoption. A process under state law by which a family court terminates a minor's legal rights and duties toward his or her natural parents and establishes similar rights and duties with respect to the minor's adoptive parents.

advisory hearing. A procedure in juvenile court at which a minor is formally charged with a delinquent act.

AFDC. Aid to Families with Dependent Children. A federal program providing financial benefits to poor persons. This program was replaced by the Personal Responsibility and Work Opportunity Reconciliation Act of 1996.

affirm. To uphold the decision of a trial court, done by an appeals court.

affirmative action. A government or company policy intended to increase opportunities for women and minorities, especially with respect to employment.

age of majority. The age at which a young person is legally entitled to manage his or her personal affairs and enjoy the rights associated with adulthood. The age of majority is eighteen in most states.

aggravated assault. An intentional or willful injury to another, using a weapon or other instrument.

appeals court. A panel of judges with the power to review and change a judgment, verdict, or other order of a trial court. Appeals courts are also called "appellate courts."

appellant. A party seeking a review by an appeals court of a lower court's decision.

appellee. A party opposing the review of a lower court's decision. This party will have prevailed in the lower court.

arbitrary. Not based on sound judgment. Sometimes applied to a decision made by a court or jury. *The appeals court set aside the jury's decision because the appellate judges believed it was arbitrary.*

armed forces. Military, naval, and air forces, especially of a nation.
arrest. A police action that takes away a person's freedom, usually when the person is believed to have broken the law.
Asylum. Asylum is a discretionary process that immigration authorities have the power to grant to foreign nationals living in the United States or to those immigrants who cross the border and are deemed to be refugees.
attorney. A person authorized in a particular state to perform legal services for clients. An attorney's services may include giving legal advice, drafting legal documents, and representing clients in court. Attorneys are also referred to as "lawyers."
automobile exception. An exception to the Fourth Amendment's warrant requirement based on the principle that automobiles are inherently mobile and it would be impractical to require officers to obtain a search warrant before searching a vehicle.
BAC. Blood alcohol concentration, the amount of alcohol in a person's blood.
battered child syndrome. The complex of injuries that show in medical exams that a minor has been physically abused, but no obvious connection exists between the caregiver's actions and the injury. Courts often conclude that the caregiver must be the guilty party. "Sexually abused child syndrome" and "maternal deprivation syndrome" are identified in much the same manner.
battery. Any intentional and harmful application of force to another person. Examples of battery are injuring a person and giving a person medical treatment without legal permission in a nonemergency.
beyond a reasonable doubt. The level of proof needed to convict a defendant in a criminal case. When this level of proof is required, the jury must be firmly convinced that the defendant is guilty of the offense as charged.
birth parents. A person's natural parents.
blocking. The action of preventing someone, often a child, from accessing certain material online on a computer (done by using "filtering software").
breach of contract. The failure of a contracting party to fulfill the terms of a contract.
burden of proof. The duty of a plaintiff (or the duty of the state in a criminal case) to prove a point or establish facts supporting his or her case. In most tort actions, the plaintiff's burden of proof is to establish the case by a "preponderance of the evidence." In criminal cases, the state's burden of proof is to prove its case "beyond a reasonable doubt."
busing. Transferring schoolchildren to a public school that they wouldn't normally attend in order to remedy a racial imbalance in the schools.
capital punishment. The death penalty.
cause of action. Specific facts giving rise to a case against a defendant.
charter school. A quasi-independent public school that receives public money to operate.
child labor law. A state or federal law limiting the type of work a minor may legally perform and establishing the number of hours a minor may legally work per week.
child pornography. Material that depicts minors in sexually explicit activity. Child pornography is illegal to produce or possess.
child protection proceeding. A legal action, usually in state family court, in which a child protective agency requests court permission to protect a minor from neglect or abuse.
child protective agency. A government entity possessing the legal power to protect a minor from neglect or abuse, including sexual abuse.
Children's Internet Protection Act of 2001. A federal law that requires public libraries and public schools to install blocking technology on computers in order to receive federal funding for Internet hookups.
circuit courts of appeals These are the intermediate appellate courts in the federal court system. There are thirteen federal circuit courts of appeals.
civil action (also **civil proceeding**). A court case brought by a plaintiff to enforce a private legal right. Generally, civil actions include all actions that are not criminal actions. A tort action is a type of civil action.

civil rights. Rights of personal liberty, especially those established by certain constitutional amendments and certain acts of Congress.

clear and convincing evidence. A standard or burden of proof that lies between the lower "preponderance of the evidence" and the higher "beyond a reasonable doubt." This standard requires a litigant to show that something is substantially more likely than not.

compensation. Money that a civil court orders a defendant to pay a plaintiff for an injury or other loss.

complaint. A plaintiff's document, filed with a trial court, explaining the specific reason for bringing a court action.

concurring opinion An opinion in which a judge writes separately, agreeing with the result of the majority opinion but not necessarily the reasoning.

conflict of interest. In a legal matter, a clash between a lawyer's interest as a servant of the court and his or her private monetary interest. When a conflict of interest arises, the lawyer usually withdraws from the case.

conscientious objector. A person who is religiously or morally opposed to war.

conservator. *See* property guardian.

Constitution. A written instrument from which a governing body derives its authority and that also describes the limits on its powers. In the United States, the federal government is subject to the federal Constitution. State and local governments and laws are subject to both the federal Constitution and their respective state constitutions.

contempt of court. Willful disobedience of a court order, which has serious consequences. *Because Jane failed to produce certain important documents for the judge, he held her in contempt of court, ordering her to sit in jail until he received them.*

contraband. A substance that is illegal to possess, produce, or sell.

contraceptive. Any device or substance (e.g., birth control pills or condoms) that prevents a woman from becoming pregnant.

contract. An agreement between two or more persons creating a legal duty to perform a certain act. For example, a contract to purchase a car is an agreement in which one person agrees to turn over a car to another in return for the second person's promise to pay for it. Once the parties have fulfilled the duties promised under the contract, it is said to be "executed."

controlled substance. Any illegal drug or beverage.

corporal punishment. Any type of punishment inflicted on a person's body.

creation science. A belief that the creation of the world occurred as described in the Old Testament, as opposed to finding the explanation in scientific theories of evolution.

crime. An act committed by a person in violation of a federal, state, or local law.

criminal act. *See* crime.

criminal action (also **criminal proceeding**). A court case in which an adult charged with a crime is brought to trial.

cross-examination. In-court questioning of a witness by a party other than the party producing the witness. The purpose of cross-examination is to test the reliability of the witness's original or "direct" testimony.

cruel and unusual punishment. Punishment that is so severe, given the seriousness of the crime, that it shocks the moral sense of the community. The Eighth Amendment of the US Constitution prohibits this type of punishment.

curfew. A law forbidding persons (usually minors) from being on the streets at night.

custodial parent. The parent in charge of the care of a minor child after a divorce.

custodian. A person who is in charge of either another person or another person's assets.

custody. Responsibility for another person.

cyberbullying. The use of online or other technological means to bully, harass, or demean another person. Cyberbullying usually applies in the school context, and many school districts now have policies explicitly prohibiting cyberbullying.

damages. Money awarded by a court to a person who has sustained a loss or injury as the result of a breach of contract or a tort.

date rape. Forced sexual intercourse in a casual dating situation.
debauchery. Extreme sexual immorality in light of community standards.
decedent. A dead person.
decedent's estate. What a person owns at death.
deductible. The amount an insured pays for vehicle repairs out-of-pocket. After the deductible is satisfied, the insurance company then pays, but only up to its policy limits.
defamation. A tort in which a person makes a false statement of fact about another person that harms that person's reputation. Defamation includes both libel (written defamation) and slander (oral defamation).
defamatory statement. Spoken or written words that injure another's reputation and are untrue.
default judgment. A civil decision rendered by a court to a party because the opposing party failed to appear or participate after being served with notice.
defendant. A person against whom damages are sought in a civil action or against whom a conviction is sought in a criminal action.
defense attorney. A lawyer who represents a civil or criminal defendant.
delinquent. A minor who has broken a criminal law or engaged in indecent or immoral conduct. Such a person is also called a "juvenile delinquent."
delinquent act. An action by a minor that would have been a crime under federal, state, or local law if committed by an adult.
desegregation order. A court order forbidding minority status to be the basis for limiting an individual's right to hold a certain job or attend the school of his or her choice.
designated driver. A person who abstains from using alcohol or drugs in order to drive others who don't plan to abstain.
detention hearing. A juvenile court procedure to determine whether a minor should be confined to a shelter or placed in foster care until a formal hearing in juvenile court takes place.
disability. A physical or mental condition that limits a person's ability to perform at the same level as persons who do not have the condition.
disaffirm. To back out of a contract.
discriminate. To give rights or privileges to certain persons while denying them to others. Laws limiting the right of minors to purchase alcoholic beverages legally discriminate, but laws that discriminate in school or at work on the basis of gender, race, nationality, religion, age (over forty), or disability violate the federal Constitution.
disparate impact. An adverse effect on a particular class of individuals of a facially neutral employment practice.
disparate treatment. The treating of an employee differently (worse) than others. It is a term of art in employment discrimination law.
disposition hearing. A procedure in juvenile court at which the judge orders a delinquent minor into treatment or disposes of the case in some other way.
dissenting opinion An opinion in which a judge or judges disagree with the result of the majority of the court.
diversion. A juvenile court program keeping a delinquent minor out of court provided he or she agrees to perform certain tasks or duties.
due process hearing. A legal procedure at which a person has a chance to present his or her side in a dispute involving personal or property rights. *See also* due process of law.
due process of law. A course of action, usually in a legal proceeding, in which a person receives proper notice and has a chance to present his or her side in a dispute regarding legal rights. Due process of law means that no person may legally be deprived of life, liberty, or property unless the matter is reviewed in a legal proceeding.
DUI (driving under the influence). An offense committed by a person who operates a vehicle while under the influence of alcoholic beverages. In many jurisdictions, if a person's blood alcohol level is at 0.08 percent or greater, the person is presumed to be DUI.

Eighth Amendment. The amendment in the US Bill of Rights that prohibits excessive fines, excessive bail, and cruel and unusual punishment.

emancipation. A procedure that results in parents losing their authority over a minor child. An emancipation may be ordered by a court or be implied from conduct of either the minor or the parents.

employee-at-will. A person who works without an employment contract specifying why he or she may be fired or laid off.

employment-at-will doctrine. The principle that an employer may terminate an employee for a good reason, a bad reason, or no reason at all. Much of modern employment law determines whether there are certain exceptions to the employment-at-will doctrine.

employment certificate. A document issued by a school district or school superintendent giving permission to a student to hold a part-time job.

endorsement test. A means used in establishment clause cases by which a court determines whether a reasonable observer, familiar with the history and context of the governmental law or policy, would believe that the government is endorsing or promoting religion

Equal Access Act of 1984. A federal law that prohibits public high schools from discriminating against student clubs based on their philosophical or religious viewpoints.

ESL (English as a Second Language). A class or course of study taken by an immigrant to learn English.

establishment clause. The clause in the First Amendment of the federal Constitution providing for separation between church and state. The Establishment Clause prohibits government officials from aiding religion, giving a preference to a particular religion, or enforcing a religious belief.

estate. Everything a person owns.

exclusionary rule. A rule of criminal law making evidence obtained in violation of the federal Constitution inadmissible against a criminal defendant in court. For example, evidence obtained in an unreasonable search is legally inadmissible and must be suppressed.

exploit. To use selfishly or to take advantage of, as in the crime of "child exploitation."

Fair Labor Standards Act of 1938. Federal legislation setting the minimum wage and establishing other laws relating to the workplace.

family court. A state-level institution with the power to decide child abuse and neglect cases, determine paternity with respect to children born out of wedlock, and terminate parental rights.

federal court. A US-level (as opposed to state-level) institution that handles cases relating to federal law and cases between persons of different states.

federal district courts These are the trial courts in the federal court system. There are ninety-four different federal judicial districts in the United States.

federal system. The division of power between the US government and the governments of the fifty states. States have their own legal powers, such as the power to create a public school system. The federal government has separate powers, such as control over foreign trade. Both have powers in the areas of taxation and public health.

felony. A crime that is more serious than a misdemeanor. Under federal law and in most states, a felony is any offense punishable by imprisonment for more than one year or by death.

fetus. An unborn child. Usually this term is used to describe an unborn child whose major body parts have begun to form.

Fifth Amendment. A constitutional amendment providing that persons subject to the Constitution aren't required to testify against their own interests.

financial responsibility. A requirement that a driver must be able to arrange to pay for auto-related injuries to another person or damages to another person's car.

First Amendment. An amendment in the US Bill of Rights that protects individuals from governmental interference with the rights to freedom of religion, speech, press, assembly, and petition.

FMLA (Family and Medical Leave Act of 1993). A federal law that permits individuals to take paternity or maternity leave without risking job loss, under certain conditions.
food stamps. Coupons issued by a government body to poor persons to obtain food products at grocery stores.
formal hearing. A juvenile court trial.
foster home. A private residence where a minor child lives after being removed from his or her parents' home by court order.
foster parent. An adult person who takes a minor child into his or her home, either temporarily or permanently, after the child has been removed from the custody of his or her parents by court order.
Fourteenth Amendment. A constitutional amendment stating that no state may enforce a law depriving US citizens of life, liberty, or property without due process, and that all persons (including ethnic and racial minorities) have a right to the equal protection of the laws.
Fourth Amendment. The amendment in the US Bill of Rights that protects individuals from "unreasonable searches and seizures" by the government.
freedom of expression. A right set forth in the First Amendment of the federal Constitution guaranteeing that individuals may speak freely and openly.
free exercise clause. The provision in the First Amendment of the federal Constitution prohibiting the federal government or any state government from outlawing or substantially controlling the practice of religion.
fringe benefit. A job-related benefit other than a wage, such as employer-provided medical insurance.
GED (graduate equivalency degree). An education-related degree awarded to a person who didn't complete high school; the GED substitutes for a high school graduation degree.
gender bias. A preference in the workplace or elsewhere based solely on an individual's sex.
green card. A document issued by the US Immigration and Naturalization Service to immigrants, enabling them to legally live and work in the United States.
guardian. A person with the legal power to care for another or manage another's legal and financial affairs. Usually a guardian is appointed if a person is too young, too old, or otherwise unable to make important personal and financial decisions.
guardianship. A relationship existing between a guardian and the person under the guardian's legal protection. In such a relationship the protected person is sometimes called the "ward."
harassment. Excessively bothersome and inappropriate behavior toward another person. *Jane explained to the court how her supervisor had subjected her to sexual harassment at the office.*
health insurance. A written agreement in which an insurance company promises to pay expenses associated with an individual's injuries, sickness, or death.
heckler's veto. A First Amendment concept signifying that a speaker is punished because of the disruptive acts of audience members or recipients of the speaker's expression rather than any disruption personally caused by the speaker.
homeschooling. Teaching and learning grade school subjects at home, subject to state guidelines, as an alternative to traditional public or private schooling.
homicide. An act in which a person takes the life of another, either deliberately or accidentally.
human resources department. A business's department that deals with personnel issues.
IEP (individualized education program). A detailed plan of action that the school must implement in order to provide specific educational services to a child with a disability.
impound. To seize and retain custody of the property of another. *Jo's car and its contents were impounded by the police after she was caught transporting stolen property.*
inadmissible evidence. Evidence that cannot be legally introduced in court to prove a party's case because it is false or unreliable, or was improperly obtained.
indeterminate sentence. A sentence for a period of time determined by the agency supervising the sentenced person and not fixed by the trial court.
Individuals with Disabilities Education Act (IDEA) of 1975. A federal law requiring public schools to provide for students who, because of disabilities, can't learn their lessons through regular teaching methods.

initial appearance. A person's first contact with a judge after being arrested. *Lou pled "not guilty" to violating the local curfew law at his initial appearance.*
injury. Damage to another's person, property, individual rights, or reputation.
insurance. A written agreement in which one party agrees to pay the other for a type of loss or damage specifically described in the agreement. The party who is insured against loss or damage is the "insured," and the party who must pay in the event of loss or damage is the "insurer."
intake. The initial processing of a case in juvenile court.
intestacy. The state of dying without a will.
joint custody. A type of custody awarded by a divorce court in which the responsibility for the care and control of a minor child is awarded to both parents.
judgment proof. Not having the money to pay a court judgment. This makes the judgment virtually worthless to the plaintiff.
judicial bypass. A court action in which a judge orders that parental permission for a teen to obtain an abortion isn't legally required; the judge gives permission instead.
jury. A group of persons selected from the community who decide the facts of a case and determine the truth of a matter at trial.
juvenile court. A state court with the legal authority to decide cases involving delinquent, abused, or neglected minors.
juvenile delinquent. *See* delinquent.
larceny. The legal term for theft.
lawyer. *See* attorney.
legal guardian. *See* guardian.
Lemon test. The leading means of evaluating whether a governmental law, policy, or regulation violates the establishment clause of the First Amendment, developed by the US Supreme Court in *Lemon v. Kurtzman* (1971). Under the Lemon test, a law must have a secular purpose, a primary effect that does not advance or inhibit religion, and must not excessively entangle church and state. However, the US Supreme Court overruled the Lemon test in *Kennedy v. Bremerton School District* (2022).
liability. A legal obligation or responsibility to do something or pay a specified amount of money. A debt is a type of liability.
liability insurance. Insurance that covers the cost of damage caused by the insured person to another person or another's property.
libel. Written statements that are untrue and injure the personal or business reputation of another person. Libel includes statements on television or radio that have a written transcript.
life without the possibility of parole (LWOP). A sentence for criminal defendants who commit serious violent felonies, including murder. In states that do not allow the death penalty, life without the possibility of parole is the most severe sentence. The US Supreme Court has recognized that there are constitutional limitations to LWOP with respect to juveniles. Several states have eliminated LWOP sentences for all juvenile offenders no matter how serious the crime.
majority. *See* age of majority.
Mandatory authority Mandatory authority refers to legal authority that a court must follow. For example, a Tennessee Supreme Court decision is mandatory authority for a trial court in Tennessee. But, a Kentucky Supreme Court decision would only be persuasive authority.
mandatory reporter. A person, such as a nurse, who is legally required to report a known or suspected case of physical or sexual abuse.
material and substantial disruption. A level of disruption that, in the opinion of a reasonable person, interferes with daily activities to the point that an individual cannot proceed at a standard pace.
maternal preference. A tendency in the law to favor the mother over the father, particularly in child custody matters. The maternal preference may be applied when parents divorce or in cases involving children born outside marriage.

MCT (minimum competency test). A test required by a state education system to ascertain how much knowledge a student has absorbed; passing an MCT might be a prerequisite to graduating from high school or passing to the next grade level.

Medicaid. A welfare program sponsored jointly by the federal and state governments providing medical care for low-income persons.

minor. A person under the age of legal majority, which is eighteen in most states.

***Miranda* warnings.** A constitutional rule requiring that before questioning a person who is in police custody, the police must warn (a) that the person has a right to remain silent; (b) that any statement the person makes may be used against him or her; (c) that the person has a right to a lawyer; and (d) that if the person can't afford a lawyer, one will be appointed to assist him or her. The US Supreme Court articulated these warnings in *Miranda v. Arizona* (1966).

misdemeanant. A person who commits a misdemeanor, a less serious type of crime.

misdemeanor. A less serious offense than a felony, usually punishable by less than one year in prison. In most states misdemeanors are grouped according to their seriousness (such as Class A and Class B misdemeanors).

necessaries/necessities. Food, drink, clothing, medical attention, and a suitable place to live.

neglect. Negligent failure to provide care and nourishment to someone, usually to a child but also to an elderly or disabled adult.

negligence. Failing to perform an act that a reasonable person would do or performing an act that a reasonable person would not do. Suing for negligence is designed to compensate individuals harmed by the socially unreasonable conduct of others.

No Child Left Behind (NCLB) Act of 2001. A federal law that requires states to establish testing of pupils to determine what percentage of students are making "adequate yearly progress" in academic performance.

no-fault insurance. A type of automobile insurance in which each party looks to his or her own insurer for payment, regardless of who caused the accident.

nonbinary Nonbinary refers to a person who falls outside the gender binary system of identifying as either boy/man or girl/woman. Instead, a nonbinary person has elements or often identifies with both genders. Nonbinary individuals, who are often trans, often prefer the pronoun "they" instead of "she" or "he."

noncustodial parent. One of two parents who, after a divorce, is not responsible for the day-to-day upbringing of their minor child.

obscenity. The quality of being abhorrent to community morality. Hard-core pornography, which appeals to a prurient or shameful interest in sexual matters; describes or depicts sexual materials in a patently offensive way; and has no serious literary, artistic, political, or scientific value, is considered obscene. The US Supreme Court established these guidelines for obscenity in *Miller v. California* (1973). Not all pornography is illegal, but obscenity is illegal.

opinion. A written statement of a judge or appeals court setting forth the reasons for reaching a decision in a given case.

oral argument The process by which attorneys argue cases before an appellate court. The attorneys argue in front of a panel of judges.

ordinance. A law of a city government, such as a traffic or parking regulation.

OSHA (Occupational Safety and Health Administration). The federal agency charged with regulating workplace conditions and assuring workplace safety.

pain and suffering. A type of damage in a civil tort action that compensates a plaintiff for pain and suffering endured or that will be endured as the result of the tort.

paternity suit. A civil court action to prove that a certain person is the father of a particular child. If proof of paternity is established, the court will require the father to support the child financially.

pension plan. A type of fringe benefit in which the employer sets aside money for an employee to live on after retiring. Sometimes the employee is permitted to match the employer's contributions, either totally or partially.

persuasive authority Persuasive authority refers to law or legal precedent that a court may follow but does not necessarily have to follow. Persuasive authority does not bind a lower court, as does mandatory authority.

petition. A complaint filed in juvenile court that begins a case against a minor suspected of committing a delinquent act. Often a juvenile court petition is called a "formal petition."

plaintiff. A person who brings a civil action against a defendant.

plain view exception (*also* plain view doctrine). An important exception to the constitutional warrant requirement for searches and seizures, which permits a police officer to seize evidence of illegal activity without a search warrant if the evidence is clearly visible and the officer is already on the premises legally.

premium. A payment made to an insurance company to obtain insurance coverage.

preponderance of the evidence. The level of proof needed in a civil action to obtain a judgment against a defendant. When this level is required, the evidence presented by the plaintiff at trial must have greater weight than that offered by the defendant.

prior restraint. A law or rule preventing a statement or other First Amendment expression from ever being made.

privileged communication. Something spoken or written by one person to another that a legal system considers highly confidential, and therefore deems it beyond the reach of court questioning.

probable cause. Facts strongly suggesting that a certain person committed a crime. When probable cause exists, a police officer has a right to arrest and search the person.

probate. A system under state law providing for the orderly distribution of a person's property after death.

probation. A system of allowing a juvenile delinquent to avoid treatment in an institution after a juvenile court conviction.

probation officer. A person who works with and supervises the activities of a minor on probation.

procedural due process. The constitutional requirement that the government provide fair procedures, usually notice and a hearing, before depriving an individual of his or her life, liberty, or property interests. For example, public school students have procedural due process rights when they face a long-term suspension or an expulsion.

property guardian. A person appointed by a family court to manage the property of an individual who is incapable of managing his or her property because of minority, old age, or a physical or mental disability.

prosecuting attorney. An attorney who conducts criminal prosecutions against persons charged with breaking federal, state, or local laws.

protected class. A category of persons, such as women, racial and ethnic minorities, or disabled persons, that federal law protects from discrimination in certain circumstances.

public figure This is a famous or well-known person who sues for defamation, such as a professional sports star, an entertainer, or an actor/actress. Public figures can only recover for defamation if they show that the defendants made a defamatory statement with actual malice.

public law. A law passed by Congress, a state legislature, or other governmental body.

public policy. A moral position broadly held by a nation or community to promote its overall health, safety, and security.

punitive damages. Money awarded to a plaintiff in a civil action over and above the actual damages suffered. An award of punitive damages is designed to punish the person causing the damages.

rape. Forced sexual relations.

reasonable doubt. The level of doubt justifying the dismissal of a criminal case or juvenile court action. To convict a person, his or her guilt must be established in both adult and juvenile court "beyond a reasonable doubt."

reasonable person. A person who exercises ordinary or reasonable prudence.

reasonable suspicion (of criminal activity). The level of suspicion needed to arrest a minor. Reasonable suspicion is less suspicion than probable cause; it is also the amount of suspicion needed by a police officer to "stop-and-frisk" a person on the street. "Reasonable suspicion" and "reasonable cause" are synonymous.

recidivist. A repeat offender.

recklessness. Paying no attention to the fact that an act could seriously endanger the safety or life of another.

refugees. Refugees are individuals who flee their country and cannot return safely because they have a well-founded fear of persecution based on their race, religion, nationality, membership in a particular social group, or political opinion.

remand. A court order returning an appealed case to the trial court for further action.

reverse (a court decision). To revoke the decision of a trial court. This is an action of an appeals court. *The appeals court reversed the trial court's decision to convict a man of intentional homicide after deciding that the trial court refused to admit evidence regarding the man's lack of intent.*

reverse discrimination. Unfair discrimination against a nonprotected class.

revocation hearing. A juvenile court hearing held to decide whether a juvenile delinquent's probation should be set aside.

school-sponsored speech. Speech by public school students that is endorsed, controlled, or more tightly regulated by school officials. Examples of school-sponsored speech include school plays, curricular materials, school band performances, and both the names and expressive conduct of school mascots.

school vouchers. A state educational program giving parents the equivalent of tuition payments for a child's education in either a public or private school.

search and seizure. A body of law surrounding when law enforcement officers may conduct searches of individuals and their property or take persons into custody or put them under arrest. Search and seizure law is governed by the Fourth Amendment of the US Constitution.

search incident to an arrest. A personal search that a police officer may legally make at the time of arrest. No search warrant is necessary to make a search incident to an arrest.

search warrant. A written order, issued by a judge or other court employee (such as a magistrate), authorizing the search of a person or place in order to secure evidence of a crime.

segregation. A policy, often applied forcibly, requiring the separation of a racial or other group from the rest of society.

Selective Service. The division of government that administers matters relating to both required and voluntary military service.

sexting. The act of sending sexually explicit photographs or messages digitally between minors. Many states now have laws criminalizing sexting.

sexually transmitted disease (STD). A type of disease passed from one person to another through sexual activity.

sibling. A brother or sister.

slander. Making false oral statements about another that result in damage to the person's reputation.

Social Security. A national program in which payments are paid to a former worker or his or her family to replace a modest portion of earnings lost by the worker as a result of retirement, death, or disability.

sole custody. A type of custody in which one parent has full legal and physical custody of a child.

Special immigrant juvenile status. A status sought by some juvenile noncitizens as a way for them to obtain a green card and remain lawfully in the United States. They generally have to show that they have been abused, abandoned, or neglected by a parent and that it is not in their best interest to be returned to their home country.

state action. Action taken by the federal, state, or local government, or any division of such government bodies.

state court. A court system established under the laws of a state to hear civil and criminal cases arising under that state's laws.
state supreme court. The highest appeals court in a state court system. However, note that in a few states the highest state court is called the court of appeals.
statutory rape. A crime that occurs when a person above a certain age has sexual relations with a minor, regardless of whether the minor may have consented.
stop-and-frisk search. A pat down of a person's clothing by a police officer to check for weapons.
subpoena. An order issued by a court commanding a particular person to appear at a certain time and place to give testimony.
subrogate. To recover money previously paid out pursuant to the terms of an insurance company's policy. *Bill's insurance company subrogated against Bob's insurer after it paid money to Bill's doctor for accident-related injuries caused by Bob.*
substantive due process. The principle that laws must not arbitrarily or unreasonably harm or diminish a person's fundamental rights. In substantive due process, a reviewing court looks at the underlying "substance" of the law, as opposed to merely considering whether fair procedures were implemented (*see* procedural due process) before someone's liberty interests are implicated.
suppression of evidence. A court order forbidding the use of certain evidence to obtain a conviction because the police obtained the evidence illegally.
symbolic speech. Unspoken expression of an idea, such as an insignia or armband.
taking. Losing a valuable personal or property right under a particular law or regulation. In the United States, such "takings" cannot occur without due process of law.
taxes. Money legally required to be paid to a government entity.
teen/teenager. A person between ages thirteen and nineteen, generally under the age of majority.
termination proceeding. A court case that seeks to break the legal bonds between parent and child.
Terry stop. An encounter by a police officer with an individual that occurs when the officer has "reasonable suspicion" but not full probable cause to believe the individual has committed a crime.
testimony. Information given by a witness in court in response to a question or judge's order.
Title VII of the Civil Rights Act of 1964. The principal federal law prohibiting employment discrimination on the basis of race, sex, color, religion, or national origin. It applies to federal, state, or local employers with fifteen or more employees.
tort. An act caused by a person's lack of care that causes emotional injury or property damage. In tort actions in civil court, plaintiffs recover "compensation" or "damages" from defendants for injuries or losses resulting from their torts.
tracking. A school policy of placing students in different classes, usually on the basis of test scores.
unconstitutional. Violating either the federal Constitution or a state constitution.
underground newspaper. A publication produced by students independently and autonomously from school control.
US Supreme Court. The highest court in the United States, sometimes called "the court of last resort"; the court to which a select few state high court cases and all federal appeals court cases may be appealed.
U visa. A type of humanitarian relief to noncitizens, including teens, who were the survivors of certain crimes and who helped law enforcement authorities to combat that crime.
vagrancy. Loitering in a public place without a means of support and with the intention of begging or committing an immoral act such as prostitution.
verdict. A decision of a jury in a trial.
viable. Able to exist or survive independently. This term is often applied to describe an unborn child that is able to live outside the mother's womb.
viewpoint discrimination. Government discrimination against a particular speaker because of his or her views. This is a term in First Amendment law.

visa. A legal document or a mark in a passport indicating that the holder may legally enter or stay in a particular country.
visitation right. The legally enforceable right of a noncustodial parent or relative to see a minor child.
void for vagueness. Too loosely drafted to be enforced fairly (applies to laws).
waiver. Intentional surrender of a legal right or legal privilege. *The man waived his right to remain silent after receiving the* Miranda *warnings and then confessed to the robbery.*
ward. A person who is being cared for by a guardian appointed by a court.
warrant. A written order issued by a judge or other court employee (such as a magistrate) authorizing an arrest or search.
welfare. Money received by a poor person from a government entity for his or her modest needs.
Welfare Reform Act (Personal Responsibility and Work Opportunity Reconciliation Act of 1996).
workers' compensation. A program under state law that pays employees or their dependents for employment-related accidents and diseases regardless of who is at fault for the accident or disease.
zero tolerance. A get-tough approach to discipline in public schools for certain offenses, usually those involving weapons or violence. Zero-tolerance policies often require mandatory punishments for certain offenses.

ABOUT THE AUTHOR

David L. Hudson Jr., JD, is an attorney, educator, and author who has authored, coauthored, or coedited more than fifty books. He is an Assistant Professor of Law at Belmont University College of Law, where he teaches classes in constitutional law, First Amendment law, and Bar Exam Workshop. He also serves as a First Amendment Fellow for the Freedom Forum. His published works include *The Rehnquist Court: Understanding Its Impact and Legacy* (2006), *Let the Students Speak! A History of the Fight for Free Expression in American Schools* (2011), and *Freedom of Speech: Documents Decoded* (2017). Hudson received his law degree from Vanderbilt University.

INDEX

www.ingramcontent.com/pod-product-compliance
Ingram Content Group UK Ltd.
Pitfield, Milton Keynes, MK11 3LW, UK
UKHW051932150926
475560UK00005B/356